TRAFFIC

Investigation and Enforcement

Third Edition

Donald O. Schultz

Derald D. Hunt

THOMSON
™
WADSWORTH

Australia • Canada • Mexico • Singapore • Spain
United Kingdom • United States

ISBN: 0-942728-65-3
Library of Congress Catalog Number: 94-69410

Wadsworth/Thomson Learning
10 Davis Drive
Belmont CA 94002-3098
USA

For information about our products, contact us:
Thomson Learning Academic Resource Center
1-800-423-0563
http://www.wadsworth.com

For permission to use material from this text or product,
submit a request online at http://www.thomsonrights.com

Any additional questions about permissions can be
submitted by email to thomsonrights@thomson.com

Printed in the United States of America
10 9 8 7 6

DEDICATION

Dedicated to the nation's patrol and traffic officers and those who are studying the challenging and rewarding field of professional traffic investigation and enforcement.

D.O.S.
D.D.H.

Since the Revolutionary War in 1776, 1.2 million Americans have died in combat. Since 1900, more than 2.5 million Americans have died in automobile accidents.
National Safety Council

TABLE OF CONTENTS

PREFACE

The purpose of this text is to serve as a guide for traffic-enforcement responsibility. It is intended not only to assist the beginning traffic and patrol officer, but also to provide a comprehensive text for use in traffic courses offered in colleges throughout our nation.

The responsibility for the enforcement of state and local traffic laws, accident prevention, and traffic collision investigation is, indeed, a challenging task. Each year tens of thousands of Americans are killed or injured on our nation's roadways. Property damage and other direct and indirect costs of traffic collisions have become one of the most personally devastating and wasteful drains on our economy.

Traffic and patrol officers play a vital role in attempting to stem the tide of unnecessary death and destruction which can be attributed to the traffic problem. As those responsible for the basic enforcement of traffic laws, officers must use every modern method and technique available to them to assure driver and pedestrian safety.

Additionally, traffic and patrol officers are also roadway experts—who often advise desk-bound traffic engineers of the need to widen or repair highways and city streets to reduce accidents caused by engineering deficiencies. Considering the critical importance of their many roles, it is the obvious that education must be a high priority for traffic enforcement officers. Both on and off duty, they must be able to inform drivers about the laws and about what is expected of roadway users.

ACKNOWLEDGEMENTS

The authors wish to acknowledge the following law enforcement and related agencies for their cooperation and vital contributions to this text.

Anaheim Police Department, California
Birmingham Police Department, Alabama
Broward County Police Academy, Florida
Buena Park Police Department, California
California Highway Patrol
Cincinnati Police Department
Costa Mesa Police Department, California
Denver Police Department, Colorado
Dothan Police Department, Alabama
Federal Bureau of Investigation
Florida Highway Patrol
Fort Lauderdale Police Department, Florida
Institute of Police Technology and Management, Florida
Long Beach Police Department, California
Los Angeles County Sheriff's Office, California
Los Angeles Police Department, California
Maryland Police Training Commission
Metropolitan Dade County, FL, Department of Public Safety
Miami Police Department, Florida
National Insurance Crime Bureau
New York Police Department, New York
Oakland Police Department, California
Olin Corporation, Signal Products
Orange County, CA Sheriff-Coroner's Office
Plantation Police Department, Florida
Pompano Beach Police Department, Florida
Portland Police Department, Maine
Topeka Police Department, Kansas
University of North Florida, Jacksonville

Chapter One

TRAFFIC LAWS AND ENFORCEMENT

A BRIEF HISTORY

The term "traffic accident," inferring an act of God or unavoidable happenstance, was coined by the press in reports of the first traffic collisions. We know, of course, that traffic accidents are not caused by fate. Traffic collisions—a more appropriate term—are caused by inattention, poor judgement, drug or alcohol use, too much speed for the conditions, and other violations of the rules and laws of safe driving. Having made this clarification, the authors bow to the traditional use of the term "accident" in this text.

Traffic control has been necessary ever since man first shouldered a burden and collided with another person or object on a narrow trail. With the taming of wild animals and their subsequent use as beasts of burden, traffic accidents have increased.

The development of the wheel added to the problem, and as transportation developed over the ages, the traffic problem grew even greater. Paralleling advances in transportation were improvements in thoroughfares: first trails, then roads. The ancient Romans spread their civilization by means of a network of hard-surfaced pavements over the then-known world. These roads were so well constructed that some of them, weathering the ravages of time, remain visible today.

Traffic Control

Traffic control soon became mandatory. Those accidents invest-igated by the Romans led to certain control measures: weight limits were imposed to prevent the breakdown of vehicles and the destruc-tion of pavements; restrictive laws were passed to regulate the movement of persons and property; encroachments upon rights-of-way by roadside businesses were restricted and roads were designed with a minimum of grades and curves to facilitate travel. In fact, it was here that man first discovered the three "E's": Engineering, Education, and Enforcement. Today, these remain the basic principles of traffic control.

The methods of supervising traffic developed during the days of the Roman Empire, and were so comprehensive and practical that they were used by many succeeding generations. Because there were no appreciable improvements in the means of travel, there was no necessity to improve or alter that early program, and it was not until the twentieth century that the need arose for any major change. Private and public transportation was accelerated tremendously by the advent of the motor vehicle, accompanied by a huge upsurge of traffic problems. New regulations and adjust-ments in traffic laws became mandatory.

Prior to the development of the automobile, persons were accustomed to vehicles drawn by animals. Maximum speeds were about 6 miles an hour, or 9 feet a second. By comparison, 100 miles per hour equals roughly 150 feet per second. Animals instinctively shied from contact with other animals drawing vehicles. From about 1900 until the present, highway speeds have obviously increased dramatically and the animal, with its instinct for self-preservation, has been removed from the front of the vehicle. The increased speed resulting from automation and the congestion arising from the increase in vehicular traffic have made death, injury, and property damage all-too-common occurrences.

NEW METHODS

Present-day traffic supervision is an attempt to lessen these occurrences by applying more advanced techniques to improve the three "Es" of the Roman days, so that the rapid transportation of persons and property may be accomplished on our highways with a minimum amount of conflict. The best traffic control techniques are learned primarily from information obtained from accident investigation.

To achieve minimum conflict, traffic supervision must be planned; if planning is to be accurate, it must be based on facts, not guesswork. The application of new methods of control lags behind the demand for them because of the enormous increase in motor vehicle use. When traffic supervision can keep pace with technological progress and the increasing number of motor vehicles, we will be at the threshold of controlling the rising death rate on the highways. Without adequate accident investigation and complete reporting, this objective can never be attained.

VEHICLE CODES

Shortly after the invention of the motor-driven vehicle it became apparent that rules and regulations governing the drivers of this new invention had to be established, and that strict enforcement of the rules of the road would soon be necessary. Thus we have the setting for the modern-day state vehicle codes and for determining the responsibilities of the city, county, and state police in enforcing the provisions of these codes.

A quick reading of any of our fifty state vehicle codes will demonstrate the fact that just about any driving situation that could occur on our roadways has been covered by some traffic law. To enforce all traffic laws would be an impossibility; therefore, individual patrol and traffic officers must use a common sense approach and enforce those laws which, when violated, create the greatest probability of an accident. This procedure is sometimes termed *priority or selective enforcement.*

MOVING TRAFFIC VIOLATIONS

Besides driving under the influence of alcohol and/or drugs, which will be discussed fully in Chapter 4, the National Safety Council has listed eight other driving offenses as principal accident-causing violations. These violations include:

1. Excessive speed
2. Failure to yield right of way
3. Following another vehicle too closely
4. Improper turning movements
5. Driving on center lines

6. Failure to heed stop signs
7. Improper passing
8. Disregarding signals

Excessive Speed

Accidents resulting from excessive speeds may cause a great deal of property damage, serious injuries, or even death. All states have established a maximum speed limit to fit the conditions of the geographical area. In the more congested areas, freeways are posted 55 miles per hour. A maximum speed of 65 miles per hour is usually allowed in more open, rural areas. These maximum speeds are usually intended for wider, more modern freeways, turnpikes, and improved state highways. Other roadways are governed by either a basic speed law or a *prima facie* (referring to laws that are always applicable, unless otherwise specified) speed limit.

Figure 1.1 Excessive speed invariably leads to more severe vehicle damage and increases the injury and death rate in any accident. *(Courtesy of the Fort Lauderdale, Florida, Police Department)*

Although excessive speed causes greater damage, more serious injuries and greater likelihood of death, few collisions are the result of speeding, alone. Most law enforcement agencies respect the need for a certain amount of enforcement tolerance and judgement on the officer's part. For example, a citation for 48 miles per hour in a posted 45 mph zone, or 60 mph in a 55 mph zone, may not be the most productive use of an officer's time.

Note: To travel one mile at 20 miles per hour requires three minutes; at 40 mph, one and one-half minutes; and at 60 mph, one minute. To save two minutes, you increase your stopping distance 227 feet and greatly increase the likelihood of disaster.

Basic Speed Law

In jurisdictions using the "Basic Speed Law," the wording of such a section usually reads as follows:

No person shall drive a vehicle upon a highway at a speed greater than is reasonable or prudent having due regard for weather, visibility, the traffic on, and the surface and width of, the highway, and in no event at a speed which endangers the safety of persons and property.

This type of law not only allows a driver to exceed posted speed limits, if it is safe to do so, but assumes that the posted limit could also be too high under certain conditions.

Prima Facie Speed Limit

To be in violation of a *prima facie* speed limit is to drive in excess of a permitted or posted speed limit. No other factor is required to be considered. The "burden of proof" that driving in excess of a posted speed limit is safe is on the driver.

Failure to Yield Right-of-Way

A great percentage of the accidents that occur on our roadways are the direct result of a driver failing to yield the right-of-way. A basic definition of *right-of-way* is "the privilege or legal right to the immediate use of the roadway." This type of violation involves not yielding in the following circumstances:

1. At uncontrolled intersections
2. When entering a through highway
3. When a yield sign is posted
4. When authorized emergency vehicles signal to pass
5. At flashing red or yellow lights
6. At red, green, or yellow directional arrows
7. When turning at intersections
8. When pedestrians have right-of-way
9. When entering roadway from a private drive

This type of violation is difficult to prove because often the parties involved will offer firm opinions on their "right" to initiate the maneuver. With the large amount of arrow-type signal designs, mixed with standard three-phase (Tri-phase) signals, there often exists confusion by drivers not familiar with different geographical areas.

Some older, out of state, or foreign country motorists can easily be confused with yielding requirements. This is especially true when speed could be an associated factor of the collision. It is difficult for the average driver to estimate the speed of other vehicles which might possibly cause a conflict. Educating drivers in right-of-way violations would be very time consuming. The final convincing factor might rest with the courts.

Following Too Closely

The majority of rear-end accidents can be attributed to following too closely. The basic elements of following too closely involve:

1. The distance of the vehicle to the preceding vehicle
2. The speed of the vehicles involved
3. The traffic on, and the condition of the road

Figure 1.2 Right-of-way violations account for a great percentage of traffic accidents. *(Courtesy of the California Highway Patrol)*

When deciding whether to issue a citation for this violation, an officer must attempt to collect enough evidence to prove or substantiate the violation of "following too closely." The officer should obtain statements from all witnesses who can testify:

1. to the distance between the vehicles involved,
2. speed of the vehicles just prior to the collision, and
3. any intended movements of passing, lane changes, etc., prior to the impact.

Figure 1.3 While accidents where following too closely is the primary reason for the impact, most often "unsafe speed for the conditions" is the official charge against the violator. Although air bags are helping, this type of collision still causes thousands of injuries and millions of dollars in property damage, annually. *(Courtesy of the Costa Mesa, California Police Department)*

Total Stopping Distance

Total stopping distance is how far it takes to brake to a stop from the time the driver first perceives the danger until the car is brought to a complete stop. These three elements are involved:

1. Perception Distance—Driver sees something to stop for
2. Reaction Distance—Driver reacts by applying brakes
3. Braking Distance—Driver slows to a stop by braking

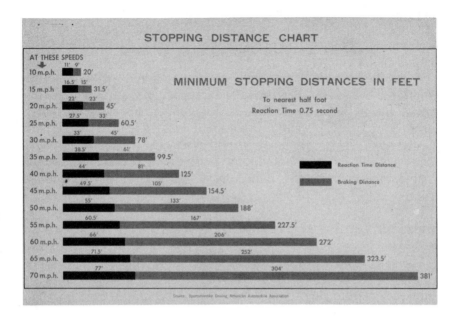

Figure 1.4 Minimum automobile stopping distances in feet. This chart shows how far a car travels, at various speeds, from the instant a driver realizes he must stop, until the car actually stops. Chart shows distance traveled *after* danger becomes apparent and while driver is *thinking*, "hit the brakes!" This average "reaction time" is three-fourths of a second. Chart also shows distance traveled *after* brakes have been applied and total stopping distance. Based on tests made by the Bureau of Public Roads. *(Courtesy of the Automobile Club of Southern California)*

The Three-second Rule for Stopping Distance Safety

According to the Public Safety Department of the Automobile Club of Southern California, the best rule to determine a safe following distance is the "Three-second Rule." Here is how it applies. When the vehicle in front of you passes a point you have chosen on the road ahead, count how long it takes you to reach that point. If you are three seconds behind the other vehicle, you should be able to count "one thousand and one, one thousand and two, one thousand and three." In order to see, decide and react to a vehicle slowing ahead, you need a *minimum* of three seconds: time to recognize what's happening, time to react, and time to stop.

Using this rule should provide sufficient following distance to avoid a collision in most situations, However, a tired, inattentive or impaired driver takes longer to perceive, decide and react.

Vehicles pulling extra weight or with poor brakes stop more slowly. Braking distances are greater on slippery or gravel roads or uneven surfaces. Under these latter conditions, the driver should use a four-second or longer rule.

A number of authorities feel that there should be one vehicle length for every 10 miles per hour that a vehicle is traveling. This would mean that a car or truck going 60 miles per hour on a turnpike or freeway should be 6 vehicle lengths behind the vehicle preceding it. This rule is often not practical on heavily traveled roadways, but no car should ever be so close to another as to be unable to stop suddenly, if necessary, without hitting the car in front.

Improper Turning Movements

The principal type of improper turning movements, which causes a number of accidents, involves making a right or left turn at an intersection from the wrong lane.

Figure 1.5 Example of the results of an improper turning movement.

This type of violation occurs quite frequently in tourist areas where drivers are often not familiar with the street locations or fail to observe roadway markings. Turning without giving the proper signal is another frequent cause of accidents.

Driving Over Center Lines

Naturally the main factor in this violation is driving along the center of the roadway. This type of violation may occur when the vehicle is going up or down a curved incline or because of driver inattention. The possible result is obvious.

Failure to Heed Stop Signs

The driver of a vehicle is required to make a full stop at the limit line of a "posted" intersection. A "posted" intersection is one with a stop sign in place. If a pedestrian is crossing the roadway within a marked crosswalk or within any unmarked crosswalk at an intersection, even if no stop sign is posted at a crosswalk, the driver must come to a complete stop before the crosswalk and yield the right-of-way to any pedestrians crossing the roadway. The driver must bring the vehicle to "0" mph with the car wheels no longer moving to achieve a legal stop. Rolling through the limit lines or into the intersection is technically illegal. The front portion of the vehicle must stop prior to the first roadway marked limit line to successfully complete this requirement. Violators will fall into three different categories:

1.   Those who drive through the intersection at a speed which indicates that they did not observe the posted stop sign or simply did not consider that other vehicles might be at the intersection.
2.   Those who do not make a full stop. The speed may be from 5 to 10 miles per hour at the violation point.
3.   Those who stop behind the limit line (usually behind a vehicle making a legal stop) and then just drive through without observing the other cars. Often accidents at four-way stop intersections can be traced to this type of activity.

Improper Passing

The improper-passing violation can take on many forms, although generally it entails:

1. Passing on the left when it is not safe
2. Passing on the right when state regulations prohibit such movement, or doing so unsafely
3. Passing at an intersection
4. Passing at a railroad crossing
5. Passing on a curve
6. Passing in a prohibited passing area
7. Passing a school bus when lights are flashing
8. Unsafe vehicle conditions

Disregarding Signals

This violation would apply whenever a driver fails to comply with traffic signals or traffic-control devices. Rolling "stops" cause many accidents. A car is not stopped as long as there is any forward motion, i.e., if the wheels are still turning, even slightly. It is a violation to stop at a stop sign behind another car, and then when the car in front moves, to proceed past the stop sign without stopping your car a "second time" before proceeding through an intersection.

EQUIPMENT VIOLATIONS

Although equipment violations may not appear to be as important as the moving offenses previously discussed, many accidents are the direct result of faulty vehicular equipment. Usually patrol officers are not expected to issue citations for equipment violations. Traffic officers, however, because of their total commitment to the traffic problem, do have the time and training to concentrate on such violations. Faulty vehicular equipment most likely to cause an accident are:

1. Faulty brakes—the number-one equipment violation found by most traffic officers

2. Faulty lighting devices—headlights, taillights, signal lights, and brake lights
3. Damaged windshields
4. Non-functioning windshield wipers
5. Worn tires and suspension system
6. Faulty exhaust system—a great many accidents are the result of carbon monoxide leakage in the vehicle
7. Defective horn—without a properly working horn, the driver cannot warn another of a possible danger
8. Faulty steering

Figure 1.6 Results of poorly maintained brakes often include innocent victims. Note child's crushed bicycle under the car.

CITATIONS VERSUS WARNINGS

The great majority of patrol and traffic officers throughout our country would rather warn an offender than issue a citation.

Usually, however, the rule of thumb is to warn a driver causing a minor infraction of the traffic law and to cite those who cause violations that would most likely cause an accident. A police agency cannot effectively set a policy of when or where to issue or not issue a citation. This is a decision that only the officer observing the offense is qualified to make.

Most traffic officers will average about 50 percent warning and 50 percent citations issued. Some departments have found great success at issuing written "warning" tickets to educate violators. This has proven to be a valuable tool in an effort to reduce traffic accidents. The violation is described on the document along with the basic information to identify the violator. Computer programs can be established to monitor habitual offenders.

THE QUOTA SYSTEM

For a police agency to establish a written or unwritten policy prescribing the number of citations that an officer should write is to set a quota system. There are many reasons *against* the establishment of such a system. Among them are:

1. The officer may write inferior (borderline) citations in order to meet a quota.
2. Officers may feel that they are writing citations just to make money for the city, county, or state instead of performing a traffic enforcement function.
3. A well-worded warning, as opposed to a citation, may result in a more careful driver and reap many future benefits for the law enforcement agency
4. Forcing quotas infringes on an officer's "discretionary decision making"
5. Forcing quotas to improve an officer's performance might encourage poor quality enforcement
6. In order to meet a quota, officers may be tempted to write "easy to catch" violations as opposed to the type of violations which cause the most accidents

Luckily, quotas are no longer employed in our modern police agencies. Police administrators realize that an alert traffic officer has no problem in spotting significant violations and that common sense will be the guide in deciding whether to issue a verbal or written warning or to cite the offending driver.

THE DEPARTMENT OF MOTOR VEHICLES

To be able to drive a vehicle is a privilege and not a right. The state departments of motor vehicles can therefore refuse to issue a license or learner's permit to an individual who fails to pass a written test, or driving-skill test, or both. Under certain conditions a driver may also have his or her driving privileges suspended. Thus the Department of Motor Vehicles can play a major role in preventing accidents by not allowing unqualified drivers to be licensed. Although the penalty for driving without a driver's license is often quite lenient, stiff fines are sometimes imposed when the judge feels the driver needs to be taught a lesson.

There are many other duties performed by state departments of motor vehicles, some of which are direct aids to the police traffic function. Among these are:

1. Registration of motor vehicles (complete information includes the owner's name and address, the description of the vehicle, the identification number of the vehicle, and the license number)
2. Assistance in providing driver education
3. Compilation of accident records
4. Retesting drivers when requested to do so by police personnel, or due to a driver's age or health
5. Compilation of violation records

THE POINT SYSTEM

The point system is a logical method of removing bad-risk drivers from the roadway. In essence, points are added or removed from the driver's record for each moving violation. There are two ways in which this system could operate:

1. Starting from zero and adding points until a number is reached within a specified time, indicating that the driver is a bad risk, e.g., a driver may be allowed four points in a twelve-month period, six in twenty-four months, or eight in thirty-six months.
2. Starting with a set number and deducting points for each moving violation, driving-while-intoxicated, or being the cause of an accident.

Naturally, the point system can only be effective when the state department of motor vehicles is able to maintain current data. It is also effective only when judges are aware of the traffic problem and levy strict fines for driving with a suspended driver's license. With an alert department of motor vehicles records section, an aggressive police traffic-enforcement unit, and informed judges, the point system can be an effective tool for keeping the nation's roadways safe. (See Appendix A: State of Maine Point System.)

TICKET-FIXING

What constitutes ticket-fixing? Many citizens, law enforcement students, and active police personnel have heard the term but do not quite understand what it means.

Naturally, patrolmen and traffic officers spend a portion of their work shifts stopping traffic violators. Those drivers who have committed minor traffic offenses which call for oral or written warnings are shortly released by the officer with no official punitive action resulting. Drivers who have committed violations of the traffic code serious enough (in the judgement of the officer observing the violation) to deserve a citation are issued one. The traffic violator should have three choices following receipt of a citation:

1. To plead guilty and pay the fine imposed by the court system
2. To plead not guilty and have the case tried by a judge, referee or jury
3. To post bail, in person or by mail, and forfeit same by not appearing and contesting the case in court—where allowed by law

TRAFFIC CITATION AJUDICATION

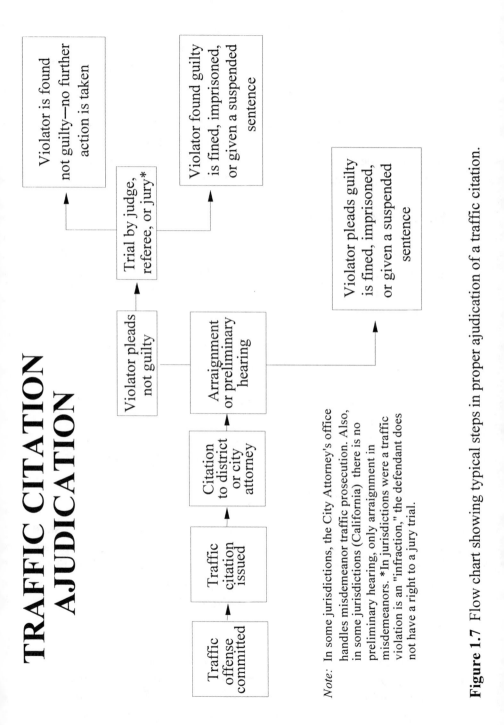

Traffic offense committed → Traffic citation issued → Citation to district or city attorney → Arraignment or preliminary hearing

Arraignment or preliminary hearing → Violator pleads not guilty → Trial by judge, referee, or jury*

Trial by judge, referee, or jury* → Violator is found not guilty—no further action is taken

Trial by judge, referee, or jury* → Violator found guilty is fined, imprisoned, or given a suspended sentence

Arraignment or preliminary hearing → Violator pleads guilty is fined, imprisoned, or given a suspended sentence

Note: In some jurisdictions, the City Attorney's office handles misdemeanor traffic prosecution. Also, in some jurisdictions (California) there is no preliminary hearing, only arraignment in misdemeanors. *In jurisdictions were a traffic violation is an "infraction," the defendant does not have a right to a jury trial.

Figure 1.7 Flow chart showing typical steps in proper ajudication of a traffic citation.

In some rare cases, in jurisdictions still open to the spoils system, there is a fourth alternative: to call the officer's chief or other high-ranking official and have the citation altered to a lesser infraction or removed completely from police files by "voiding" it. This fourth choice places the violator in a position of being "above the law."

Ticket-fixing, then, is the act of removing from the police files a traffic citation which was written in good faith by a police officer prior to its being delivered to the prosecutor's office or the courts. Is it a moral violation? Yes. Is it a criminal offense? Yes!

Ethical Considerations

The removal of a traffic citation from the due process of law is a clear violation of the national *Law Enforcement Code of Ethics,* which is the basic ethical guideline for the police service. In part it states:

> *I will never act officiously or permit personal feelings, prejudices, animosities or friendships to influence my decisions. With no compromise for crime and with the relentless prosecution of criminals, I will enforce the law courteously and appropriately, without fear or favor.*

> **Peace Officer Code of Ethics**

Legal Considerations

Ticket-fixing is always considered a criminal act, as state legislators have realized the seriousness of this type of police misconduct. It may be a misdemeanor in some jurisdictions; however, others view it as a felony. An example of this would be Section 6200 of the Government Code of the State of California which states:

> 6200. *Every officer having the custody of any record, map, or book, of any paper or proceeding of any court, filed or deposited in any public office, or placed in his hands for any purpose, who is guilty of stealing, wilfully destroying,*

mutilating, defacing, removing or secreting the whole or any part of such record, map, book, paper, or proceeding, or who permits any other person to do so, is punishable by imprisonment in the State prison not less than one nor more than 14 years.

Section 6201 of the Government Code states that:

6201. *Every person not an officer referred to in Section 6200, who is guilty of any of the acts specified in that section, is punishable by imprisonment in the State prison not exceeding five years, or in a county jail not exceeding one year, or by a fine, not exceeding one hundred dollars ($100.00), or by both such fine and imprisonment.*

To help avoid these traps, many states have enacted laws to punish the unprofessional practice of voiding citations (For example: California Penal Code Section 853.6 and California Vehicle Code Section 40500d).

Departmental Morale

Naturally, police agencies employing ticket-fixing tactics will often have a severe morale problem. Certain individuals who are able to live above the traffic laws may boast of their abilities to friends, neighbors, and often to the citing officer. When the statement, "I'll just have this citation taken care of," is heard, the working street police officer should become suspicious. The great majority of police personnel believe in fair and honest practices for every citizen. If a bank president, secretary to the mayor, councilman's sister, or a police administrator's neighbor can have a traffic citation pulled from the files, then everyone cited should also have this service.

After a period of time, if ticket-fixing continues, the working police officers will feel that writing citations as a means of traffic enforcement has become useless and may issue fewer citations. Surely a police officer would feel that he or she was being unfair to issue a citation to a person without great wealth or political influence, knowing that this individual would have to pay a fine, lose points against his or her driver's license, or have his or her insurance rates increased, while the influential person goes free.

A Method of Protecting Police Integrity

Having read Section 6200 of the Government Code of the State of California, one might feel reasonably secure in thinking that things like ticket-fixing are not practiced in that state. Quite recently, as a matter of fact, a complaint was issued against a medium-size police agency in Southern California for widespread ticket fixing. As a result, the city manager retired, along with the chief of police, the assistant chief of police, and other top police administrators. One might wonder: Couldn't this happen anywhere? Another question might be: Why retirements and resignations instead of grand jury indictments?

In some states, legislative officials now consider that the best way to eliminate temptation on the part of a weak police administrator is perhaps to issue state-supplied, numbered citation forms. This procedure makes it mandatory for *all* citations issued to be returned to a central accounting center controlled by the state. Computer processing of these specially numbered citations also insures an accurate accounting. In these states local politicians and other persons who might have been able to sway a police administrator's sense of duty will have to learn to obey the law or suffer the consequences in the same way ordinary citizens would.

Investigating Complaints of Ticket-Fixing

Of course, complaints of ticket-fixing should be investigated immediately to prove or disprove the allegation. The credibility of the police agency and its personnel rests on the ability of the agency to keep its own house clean. Often the charge is not supported by facts, and the investigation will clear the agency. Should the charge be supported by facts, then it is the responsibility of all police personnel who have knowledge of this criminal activity to demand that there be an immediate halt to the illegal procedure. Traffic citation integrity is the duty of all sworn police personnel, regardless of rank, or length of time on the job.

Chapter Two

VEHICLE STOPS

GENERAL CONSIDERATIONS

All too often stopping a vehicle is commonly considered a "routine" task, even though each year scores of police officers are injured or killed while performing this police function. The victims range from inexperienced rookies to overconfident or careless veteran street police officers. Of course, the great majority of traffic stops result in no peril or jeopardy for the officer. Unfortunately there are usually no obvious indications that a violator will become hostile or attempt to injure or kill an officer. Because of this, all patrol and traffic personnel must regard each and every vehicle stop as a potential risk or deadly confrontation. Only after the violator has returned to the roadway should you relax your defenses.

Prior to Vehicle Stop

There are certain specific rules that you, as an officer, should observe each time a vehicle is stopped. First, approach and position the police unit close enough to discourage flight and to read the license tag accurately. However, don't park so close that the person stopped can easily back into and disable you or your vehicle. Second, inform your radio dispatcher of your location and license number of vehicle to be stopped.

Assessing Risk

What is the nature of the offense? Consider what you *suspect* about the offense in addition to what you see or have been advised. How many occupants are readily visible? Numbers, size, sex, age, attitude, behavior and chemical condition are all factors that may require additional backup.

Vehicle Stop

Activate your emergency lights and tap the horn as a signal to the driver to pull to the right of the roadway. If the driver fails to heed horn signals, the siren and high-beam lights may be used for extra effect. Look ahead and plan the stop location. Direct the driver to pull off the road, e.g., into a parking lot or similar place, whenever possible. At night make the stop in a lighted area, whenever possible.

Position of Police Unit

The position of the unit should be off-set 2 to 3 feet to the left of the violator's vehicle and approximately 8 to 10 feet to the rear of the vehicle. The width of the roadway and roadway shoulder are factors to be considered. Passing traffic must be considered as a genuine hazard. Think safety! Many officers have been killed and injured by fast-moving vehicles passing the stop site.

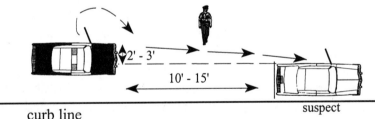

2' - 3'

10' - 15'

curb line   suspect

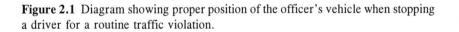

Figure 2.1 Diagram showing proper position of the officer's vehicle when stopping a driver for a routine traffic violation.

Officer's Approach to Vehicle

Walk close to the left side of the violator's vehicle to a point even with the center door post, observing the rear seat area through the rear side windows. Request the violator's license from this point.

At all times during the stop, approach to the vehicle, and violator contact, be constantly alert for suspicious or hostile actions by the violator.

Problem Vehicles

Vans present special problems because of their four points of entry and exit, i.e., two front, sliding side and back doors. Park farther back and at night turn your headlights on high beam. You can order the driver to turn on interior lights over your public address system. Consider walking around your unit to approach a van from the right rear. Stop at the right rear corner and place your palm on the rear door to detect movement in the van. Listen for movement and conversation. Vehicles with heavily tinted windows should be tactically handled similarly to vans. Almost without exception, heavily tinted windows—generally after-market—are illegal and a violation of your state's vehicle code.

Officer-Violator Contact

Having obtained the operator's license, explain in a polite but confident manner the reason for the traffic stop. Have the operator remain seated in the vehicle (during routine stops only—not for driving-while-intoxicated situations or other involvements). Then proceed to the right-hand curb or the right of the vehicle; for added safety never stand between the vehicles.

After completing the citation, present it for the offender's signature. At the same time, explain that the signature constitutes only a promise to appear and in no way indicates an admission of guilt. During this final period of contact, remain polite and, by maintaining composure, retain control of the conversation; refuse to enter into any debates or arguments with the operator.

Assist the offender back into the traffic flow prior to reentering the patrol vehicle.

DO'S AND DON'TS OF TRAFFIC STOPS

- *Do* stop your vehicle out of the traffic lane, behind the violator's car.
- *Do*, before leaving your vehicle, record the violator's license number and give communications the proper signal and license number.
- *Do* decide what you are going to do and say.
- *Do* make a direct and positive statement regarding the alleged violation.
- *Do* compare information on driver's license and establish identity.
- *Do* write a citation as rapidly as possible and explain fully.
- *Do* retain driver's license until the citation is completed and signed.
- *Do* assist violator to reenter traffic safely.

. . . .

- *Do not* consider the traffic violation a personal affront.
- *Do not* argue with, berate, or threaten the violator.
- *Do not* expose yourself to personal hazards—be alert.
- *Do not* open the conversation in a sarcastic or derogatory manner.
- *Do not* accept anything the violator offers you except the document requested.
- *Do not* detain the violator any longer than is absolutely necessary to accomplish your purpose.
- *Do not* follow violator's vehicle immediately after termination of enforcement action. (Exception: when the violator shows hostility or commits a violation upon leaving. Such a violator often commits another violation—sometimes a major one—because of anger).
- *Do not* quote fines. Often fines vary depending on different judges. Courts do not appreciate officers quoting punishments. Quoting a fine which turns out to be considerably different than imposed may lead to complaints against the officer.

TRAFFIC STOPS BY LOCATION

Downtown Area—Large Cities

Different traffic stop procedures are used depending on the location of the stop. Evaluate the necessity for the stop. Due to the congested nature of the area and the lack of room in which to pull a vehicle over, some nonhazardous violations can be overlooked.

Activate all emergency lighting on your police unit and check to make sure that vehicles around you are aware that you are going to initiate some action. From directly behind the car to be stopped, signal the driver to pull to the right, at the same time make sure it is safe for him to do so. Move to the right with the vehicle to be stopped.

As soon as the violator stops, move to his or her car in the prescribed manner, obtain his or her license, and give directions to an off-street location if one is immediately available. A suitable location might be a parking lot, an open driveway (such as a service station), or an alley. Issue the citation as expeditiously as possible to avoid further congestion.

Suburban Area

Attempt to create minimum traffic hazard by avoiding intersections, bus stops, and business driveways. If the stop is made after dark, choose a location which is well lighted, if possible.

Rural Area

Do not activate emergency lights or give an indication that you wish the violator to stop until you are within a short distance from the violator. This will deter possible flight on an open, high-speed road.

Direct the violator to pull completely off the roadway to the right. Avoid stopping on the roadway, on hills, at curves, and at points narrowed by guard rails, etc. Because of the higher speeds used on rural roads, be constantly alert to other traffic when making the initial stop and during foot approach to the violator's car. Due to the speed factor of other traffic, if at all possible, the violator should remain in his or her car during the stop.

Expressways, Turnpikes, or Freeways

For both the officer and the violator, the expressway stop is by far the most hazardous of the routine vehicle stops. This is because of the number of traffic lanes available, the congested or heavy traffic present, and the relatively high speed limits on expressways. Use extreme caution at all times and give drivers of all vehicles in the immediate area of the police unit a clear indication of your intentions prior to making an attempt at enforcement action or apprehension.

When making an expressway stop, activate all emergency lighting equipment on your vehicle. Gain the violator's attention and direct him to the *right* side of the road. Move to the right lane directly behind the violator, give directions and make sure all traffic present is aware of the lane changes. Be alert for sudden reactions by the violator during the initial indication to stop and the change of lanes to the right.

Approach the violator and conduct the entire enforcement transaction on the side of the roadway away from the flow of traffic. When practical, make the initial approach to the driver from the right (passenger) side of the vehicle. This will avoid conflicts with high speed traffic on the left of both vehicles. Avoid median stops if possible.

FELONY STOPS

In making a felony stop the officer or officers involved have prior knowledge of, or reasonable cause to believe that, a serious offense has been committed and that their personal safety may be jeopardized. The felony stop should be made in a manner conforming to a standard routine and must not be done in a hurried manner. Above all, each move by the officer must be planned thoroughly prior to execution.

Officers Killed Statistics

It is indeed sobering to realize that seven percent of officers fatally injured on vehicle stops were killed in a moving vehicle and were shot through the windshield, open window or body of their car. Twenty-eight percent were killed *after* the stop, but *before* getting out of their cruiser. Twenty-two percent died while approaching the violator, and forty-three percent were killed while talking to the violator.

Felony Stop Procedure

Upon initial observation of the suspect vehicle, notify the radio dispatcher of the description, direction of travel, and location of the vehicle, requesting that all units in the area be advised and a backup unit dispatched. Attempt to follow the suspect vehicle until your backup unit(s) arrive and are positioned close to the rear of the initial police unit making the stop.

Select a stop site which is as free as possible from congestion and pedestrian traffic and notify the radio dispatcher of the location. From a safe distance activate the emergency lights and siren on the police unit, indicating that the vehicle should pull to the curb. Do not, under any circumstances, pull the police unit alongside the suspect vehicle.

There are two commonly practiced procedures for felony car stops that offer optimum protection to arresting officers. They are: (1) The multiple-unit, side-by-side method and the more conventional (2) two-unit staggered-to-the-rear method. Both of these procedures are described and pictured in more detail, below.

1. **Multiple-unit, side-by-side: ("Riverside" Stop)** This consists of two or three police units side-by-side, directly behind and at a safe distance from the suspect's vehicle. Usually three abreast—with officers positioned outside of the driver's position—to offer coverage on both sides and to the rear of the suspect's vehicle. The Riverside Stop was developed by the Riverside, California Police Department and is now practiced nation-wide. This procedure allows for best:

- Visual coverage
- Communications between officers
- Arrest and control techniques on multiple suspects

2. **Two-unit, staggered:** The two-car conventional method is similar to the above, except that the police units are lined up to the rear of one another, and the officers approach the suspect's vehicle in a slightly different manner as pictured. Either the two unit staggered or side-by-side procedure is selected generally depending on department policy, the stop situation, type of roadway, or the topography of the stop site.

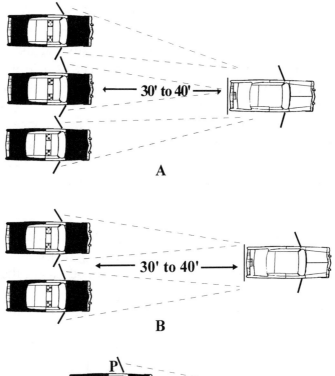

A

B

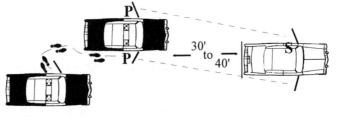

curb line

C

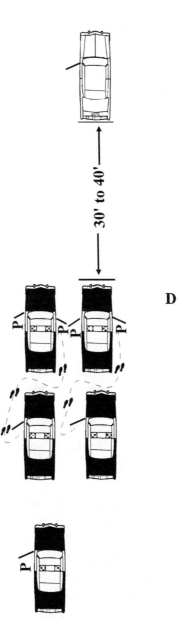

Figure 2.2 Alternative felony car stop procedures. Diagram A, depicts a 3-unit, side-by-side stop. Diagram B, pictures a 2-unit, side-by-side stop. Diagram C, shows the conventional 2-unit, staggered-to-the-rear method. Diagram D, illustrates use of multiple units—the 5th unit is typically the arrest and control team.

Once the stop is initiated, immediately draw your weapon while exiting the police unit, and take cover behind the unit's open door. Always leave your passenger door unlocked prior to the stop for access by support officers responding to your unit for protection. Depending on the background and scene location, the passenger back-up officer might choose to use the shotgun as his or her primary weapon.

After exiting, command, in loud and clear tones (the public address system on the police unit may be used), all persons in the vehicle to take the following actions:

Driver: Shut off engine and place hands, palms out, flat against windshield.

Front-seat Passenger(s): Place hands, palms out, flat against the windshield.

Rear-seat Passenger(s): Place hands on top of heads and in plain view.

The phrase "hands up" should always be avoided, as weapons and disposable contraband are often hidden in hat liners and behind sun visors.

At this point, the occupants of the vehicle should be removed in the following manner, with the officer constantly alert for attempts to obtain weapons or dispose of contraband:

Driver: Instruct the driver to use his or her right hand, only, to carefully remove the ignition key and toss it out the open driver's-side window. Next, order the suspect driver to put both hands and arms out the open driver's-side window. Once in plain sight, have the suspect open the driver's-side door from the *outside*. With the opening of the door, the subject should be told to exit and stand away from the open door.

If the suspect is wearing a loose shirt, blouse or a jacket, have the subject pull out and lift this loose clothing to expose the waistband area. Have the suspect turn slowly around while in a standing position, so that officers can view all sides of his or her body for possible weapons. The suspect can then be put into a prone position or ordered to walk backwards to a designated team of arresting officers.

Front-seat Passenger(s): Order passenger(s) to slide across the seat and exit via the driver's door with hands palms up and in plain sight. After giving similar instructions as were given to the driver, eventually order the passenger(s) to a prone position away from any other suspect(s).

Rear-seat Passenger(s)—Two-door vehicles: Order passenger(s) to crawl over the back of the front seat and exit via the driver's door. Position him or her in the same manner as the other passengers.

Rear-seat Passenger(s)—Four-door vehicles: Any passenger(s) in the left rear seat, should open the rear door with his or her *right* hand from the *outside* and leave the vehicle. Any other rear-seat passenger(s) should slide out and exit from the same door with their hands always in plain view above their head.

Multiple suspects should be ordered out one at a time and placed into a prone position, hands in plain view, face to one side, looking away from all officers, and legs spread far enough apart so that officers can clearly watch every body movement. Suspects can then be searched individually by a designated search and arrest team.

If there is sufficient evidence to charge the suspects with a crime, they should be searched, handcuffed and transported to the jail facility for booking.

Night Felony Stop

The procedure for nighttime felony stops is the same as for daytime stops, only great consideration must be given to the fact that darkness can mask the actions of the suspects. In making the stop, high-beam headlights should be used to illuminate the interior of the suspect vehicle. If the police unit is equipped with a spotlight, it should be directed at the rearview mirror of the suspect's car in such a manner that it will reflect and illuminate the entire interior.

The night felony stop is a much more hazardous undertaking than a daytime stop and the advisability of using a backup unit cannot be overemphasized.

**Felony
Night Stop**

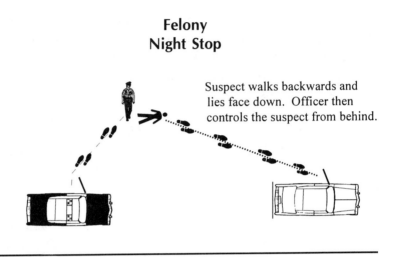

Suspect walks backwards and lies face down. Officer then controls the suspect from behind.

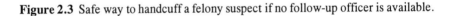

curb line

Figure 2.3 Safe way to handcuff a felony suspect if no follow-up officer is available.

DO'S AND DON'TS OF FELONY STOPS

- *Do* alert communications.
- *Do* make sure of your location.
- *Do* wait for your backup, if possible.
- *Do* draw your weapon as you alight.
- *Do* remain behind the unit door until all occupants of suspect car are clear.
- *Do* remain alert for attack or flight by suspects.
- *Do* illuminate the area as much as possible at night.

....

- *Do not* pull alongside the suspect vehicle.
- *Do not* expose yourself to possible danger.

- *Do not* approach the vehicle.
- *Do not* use the phrase "hands up."
- *Do not* relax your vigilance at any time.

OTHER OFFENSES

The traffic officer while primarily concerned with the apprehension of persons committing hazardous moving violations, should always remain alert to the possibility of the commission of other criminal offenses involving motor vehicles. In the United States today, an overwhelming majority of the crimes committed involve the use of a motor vehicle at some stage of the commission, flight, or disposal of illegally obtained goods.

In view of this, the traffic officer should learn to be alert to all indications of criminal activity and should be aware of all such occurrences within his or her area of responsibility.

Some of the most common arrests resulting from routine traffic stops are in the following areas.

Driver's Licenses

The fact that a person must have a driver's license to operate a motor vehicle is obvious and when the driver is not in possession of one, an arrest may be made. In some jurisdictions, a citation, only, may be issued for the infraction of non-possession of a license.   When a violator is found to be driving with a suspended or revoked license, you may choose to issue a citation or book the offender into custody. In some states, the vehicle may be impounded until proof of ownership can be obtained by the driver or owner, who can then legally take possession of the vehicle. However, there follows a number of less obvious license violations that should not be overlooked by the officer.

Driving with Another's License or a Stolen License

This offense is most likely uncovered by comparing the information on the license with the physical characteristics of the driver and by questioning the operator about a middle name, date of birth, and other information on the license.

Forged or Fraudulently Altered Driver's Licenses

The officer who has thoroughly schooled himself in the form, numbering system, and manner of issuance of his or her state's licenses will find that a high percentage of the arrests can be made for violations in this area.

Vehicle Registrations

In making the traffic stop, all tag numbers should be checked, and the officer should be alert to the fact that a negative tag check does not rule out a violation. Common vehicle registration violations include a stolen or improper tag. Some indications of this type of violation are:

- Dirty tags on a clean car or the reverse
- One tag on vehicle in states that require two
- Tags attached with wire, magnets, etc.
- Type of tag not proper for vehicle to which it is affixed (i.e., wrong weight class tag, commercial tag on passenger car, local inspection sticker with out-of-state tag or vice versa)
- Partially torn or multiple tabs on license plate

AUTO THEFT

Auto theft is the costliest crime that confronts law enforcement officials and the American public. The average property loss resulting from auto thefts is greater than the combined losses of all other crimes for personal gain. For this reason, auto theft concerns not only specialized auto-theft investigators, but all police officers as well. Traffic officers must be thoroughly acquainted with the basic problems generated from auto thefts and must also know what they should do to help combat the growing rate of auto theft. For the officer to be successful in detecting stolen vehicles, he must be able to locate and identify them.

Detection of Stolen Vehicles

There are many ways in which the alert officer can sharpen his or her powers of observation. The spotting of stolen cars is a knack that all traffic officers should develop.

DRIVER ACTIONS AND VEHICLE CONDITIONS TO OBSERVE

- Do occupants seem unsuited to the car?
- Is a juvenile driving a new or expensive car?
- Is the driver of a new car shabbily dressed?
- Is a juvenile driving a vehicle bearing an out-of-state or a distant county's license plate?
- Does the driver "overdrive" the car after noting that he is being observed? Does he drive slowly or become overcautious?
- When approaching from the rear, does he suddenly slow down and refuse to pass?
- Are there exaggerated hand and other signals?
- Is the driver obviously concerned about being stopped?
- At the first opportunity, does the driver change course of travel?
- Is the driver unfamiliar with the vehicle? (Are there jerky stops, gnashing gears, etc.?)

Vehicles Without Lights

The thief may have accidentally disconnected some of the wiring.

Vehicles Parked in Dark or Deserted Areas at Night

A vehicle parked a with door or doors open may indicate that the driver is not the legal owner and has left the door open for easy flight.

Vehicle Conditions Pointing to Auto Theft

An officer should look for answers to the following questions when observing a license plate:

- Is it current?
- Is it attached unusually (wire, string, rubber bands, new bolts, etc.)?
- Is it bent or repaired?
- Is it battered?
- Is it a cut plate? (a plate made by cutting two plates in half and then placing the opposite halves of each together)
- Is there a clean plate on a dirty car, or vice versa?
- Do the front and rear plates match?
- Is there one plate in a state requiring two?
- Is there a missing tag or sticker needed to validate licenses?
- Were the plates issued before the vehicle was manufactured?
- Were plates previously attached by bottom holes now attached by top holes, or vice versa?
- If the vehicle bears a license plate from another state, is there luggage in the car?
- Does the vehicle bear an inspection or registration renewal sticker?
- Is the rear license plate covered with bugs? (indicating it was once a front plate)

If the car is damaged or does it show signs of unlawful entry such as:

- Broken vent or window glass?
- Ignition punched out or damaged?
- Steering column or steering wheel damaged?
- Broken door handles?
- Trunk lock punched out or lid pried open?
- Car being operated in damaged condition? (occurs often in joy-riding offenses)
- Are any of these items missing, indicating that the car has been stripped?
- Hub caps

- Radio, tape deck, CD player
- Spare tire
- Accessory lights, etc.

Inspection of Car Interior

See whether the car is littered with trash, food, maps, or newspapers. Does it have the appearance of having been slept in? Is the ignition in place? Has the ignition been jumped or wired around?

Ask operator to turn ignition on and off. Observe whether the driver places his or her foot on the brake and releases the clutch. Does the driver disconnect wires to kill the engine? Check to see if the key operates the switch. Is there any evidence of glass or vents being scarred by prying?

Roadside Interrogations

Interrogation of the suspect should take place on the roadside where the car was stopped. Ask the driver for his or her license and question the driver to verify that the license presented is really his. Request ownership papers, or vehicle registration and ask where, when, and from whom he purchased the car, whether it is financed and, if so, by whom?

Types of Auto Thefts

Automobile thefts may be divided into four categories, each defined according to the reason for which the car was stolen.

Joy-Riding

This category of automobile theft accounts for the majority of stolen automobiles reported. One large police department reported that 80 to 85 percent of the car thefts investigated were cars taken for joy rides. This classification is dominated by youthful offenders who steal an automobile for transportation, racing, or thrill-seeking. The greatest contributing factor to this type of theft is the car owner's failure to lock the car door or the ignition, or to remove the key from the car.

Use in Crime

Criminals steal automobiles to provide transportation to the scene of other crimes and to reduce the possibility of identification. Opportunity and type of automobile required determine the methods employed by the criminal to start the engine.

To further reduce the element of identification, the "criminal" auto thief may alter the license plates. The numerals may be repainted or covered with mud. Criminals have been known to cover the license plates with a heavy grease to which dirt adheres, or merely to bend the plate to hide the identifying numbers. Quite often a criminal will actually switch license plates.

The interior dome light and the license plate light may also be broken to prevent recognition. The rear seat cushions may be removed to allow room for the proceeds of the crime, and the trunk lock may also be broken.

Stripping

This type of theft is committed to remove parts and accessories for personal use or for resale. Motors, floor shift (manual) transmissions, bucket seats, wheels (especially those made of magnesium alloy—mags), blowout-proof tires, four-barrel carburetors (quads), chrome trim, batteries, radios, alternators, etc., find a ready market with the youthful car enthusiast or the unscrupulous auto-parts dealer. These parts are usually sold or exchanged at unofficial "dragstrips" or drive-ins.

Professional Theft Ring

Over the past few years the recovery rate of stolen automobiles has been gradually decreasing. Experts attribute this condition to the increasing activity of organized theft rings. These criminals camouflage a car by altering its appearance—exchanging parts, repainting, replacing serial numbers, and forging state certificates of title and certificates of origin, etc. Many of these automobiles are transported to other localities and sold. Sometimes the dissembled body parts are sold to automobile body shops who use these parts to rebuild wrecks.

Methods of Stealing Cars

Owner carelessness is the greatest single factor contributing to automobile theft. The ignition system which does not require locking to turn off the motor has helped to perpetuate the car owner's negligence. Fortunately, all newer cars now require that the engine is turned off and the ignition locked, before the key can be removed. Over one-half of the automobiles reported stolen in the United States either had the key in the ignition or the switch unlocked. A Canadian study reported similar findings.

The screwdriver has become the automobile thief's favorite tool. It is second only to the unlocked ignition as a means of starting the engine. The screwdriver is used to either force and damage the lock cylinder of the ignition switch or to remove the keeper ring, which secures the ignition lock assembly to the dashboard. In the latter practice, the ignition lock assembly is taken out and replaced with an ignition lock for which the thief has a key. Such a replacement ignition assembly, which will fit all similar makes of cars, can be purchased for about seven dollars and provides the means to steal an unlimited number of automobiles.

The wire jumper, consisting of two alligator clamps attached to a short piece of electrical wire, is employed less frequently. Car thieves realize that they no longer need to risk being observed attaching this device to the battery and coil of the automobile when the ignition system is easily accessible from inside the car. Duplicate or master keys are occasionally used to start an automobile engine. However, this technique accounts for only a very small portion of the total number of automobiles stolen.

Ask questions that the real vehicle owner should be able to answer concerning the speedometer reading, the brand of tires, the approximate mileage, when the car was last serviced and by whom. Check this information against the service sticker on the door.

Check numbers on any papers presented against vehicle identification numbers (VIN) on vehicle. Do they correspond? Do they appear to have been tampered with? Look for signs of VIN plate replacement. Be sure you are satisfied that the driver is telling the truth.

OLDER VEHICLE IDENTIFICATION NUMBER LOCATIONS

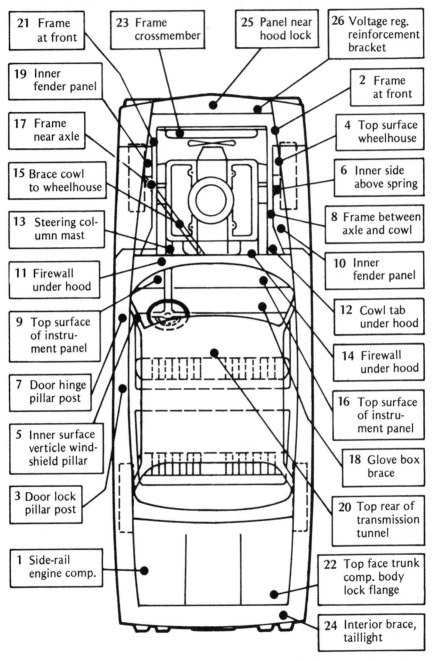

21 Frame at front

23 Frame crossmember

25 Panel near hood lock

26 Voltage reg. reinforcement bracket

19 Inner fender panel

2 Frame at front

17 Frame near axle

4 Top surface wheelhouse

15 Brace cowl to wheelhouse

6 Inner side above spring

13 Steering column mast

8 Frame between axle and cowl

11 Firewall under hood

10 Inner fender panel

9 Top surface of instrument panel

12 Cowl tab under hood

7 Door hinge pillar post

14 Firewall under hood

5 Inner surface verticle windshield pillar

16 Top surface of instrument panel

3 Door lock pillar post

18 Glove box brace

1 Side-rail engine comp.

20 Top rear of transmission tunnel

22 Top face trunk comp. body lock flange

24 Interior brace, taillight

Figure 2.4A Vin's for older cars and motorcycles. (See Appendix E for Current VIN charts)

OLDER VEHICLE IDENTIFICATION NUMBER LOCATIONS

VEHICLE IDENTIFICATION NUMBER LOCATIONS

Make					
American Motors	1973-1969.... 9	1968.... 9 and/or 4	1967-1960..... 4
Avanti	1973-1966.... 7	1964-1963...... 2	
Buick	1973-1968.... 9	1967-1962 & 1960 7	1961 ... 7, 11, 15
Riviera	1964 11	1963......... 14	1961-1960..... 7
Special	1961 15	1960.......... 7	
Cadillac	1973-1968.... 9	1967-1965...... 2	1964-1963.....23
	1962-1960.... 21		
Eldorado	1973-1968.... 9	1967.........17	
Checker	1973-1970.... 9	1969.......9, 11	1968-1960.....11
Chevrolet	1973-1968.... 9	1967-1960...... 7	
Camaro	1973-1968.... 9	1967.......... 7	
Chevelle	1973-1968.... 9	1967-1964...... 7	
El Camino	1973-1968.... 9	1967-1964...... 7	
Chevy II	1969-1968.... 9	1967-1962...... 7	
Chevy Nova	1973-1970.... 9		
Vans	1973-1967.... 7	1966-1962 3	
Corvair	1969-1968.... 9	1967-1965...... 1	1964-1960..... 3
Corvette	1973-1968.... 5	1967-1963...... 18	1962-1960... 7, 13
Greenbrier	1965........ 3	1964.......... 7	1963-1961..... 3
Vega	1973-1971.... 9		
Chrysler	1973-1968.... 9	1967-1960...... 7	
De Soto	1962-1960.... 7		
Dodge	1973-1968.... 9	1967-1960...... 7	
Edsel	1960........ 8		
Ford	1973-1969.... 9	1968.......... 16	1967-1963.....12
	1962-1960.... 8		
Fairlane	1973-1969.... 9	1968.......... 16	1967-1962.....19
Falcon	1973-1969.... 9	1968.......... 16	1967-1963.....19
	1963-1960.... 15		
Clb. W & Bus	1973-1972.... 26	1971-1968...... 13	1967.........20
	1966-1963.... 24		
Maverick	1973-1970.... 9		
Mustang	1973-1969.... 9	1968.......... 16	1967-1963.....19
Pinto	1973-1971.... 9		
T-Bird	1973-1969.... 9	1968.......... 16	1967.........12
	1966-1961.... 25	1960.......... 8	
Bronco	1973-1966.... 8		
Imperial	1973-1968.... 9	1967-1960...... 7	
Jeep & Willys	1973-1960 7, 11, 14		
Lincoln	1973-1969.... 9	1968.......... 16	1967-1966 6
	1965-1961.... 10	1960.......... 22	
Mark III	1973-1969.... 9	1968.......... 16	
Mercury	1973-1969.... 9	1968.......... 16	1967-1963 12
	1962-1960.... 8		
Meteor	1973-1969.... 9	1968.......... 16	1967-1965 12
	1963-1962.... 19		
Comet	1973-1971.... 9	1968.......... 16	1967-1963 19
	1963-1960.... 7		
Montego	1973-1969.... 9	1968.......... 16	
Oldsmobile	1973-1968.... 9	1967-1960...... 7	
Plymouth	1973-1968.... 9	1967-1960...... 7	
Pontiac	1973-1968.... 9	1967-1960...... 7	
Shelby	1970-1969.... 9	1968.......... 16	
Studebaker	1966-1960.... 7		

Figure 2.4B Older vehicle identification number locations. *Note:* Since 1968 all domestic vehicle identification numbers have been located on the left corner of the dash, visible through the windshield from the outside. Corvette vin's are located on the left side of the windshield post. (See Appendix E for current vin charts)

NARCOTICS AND OTHER CONTRABAND

With each stop the traffic officer makes, there exists the possibility that the vehicle or its operator is in possession of contraband. Current court restrictions in the area of search and seizure generally preclude searching all vehicles stopped, but the alert officer, through careful observation, may build probable cause for a legal search or may possibly see contraband items in plain view, thus allowing an immediate seizure. In the traffic stop, the officer is not prohibited from making a visual search of the vehicle and its occupants during any traffic contacts.

Types of Contraband

The most frequently found types of contraband are:

Narcotics and narcotics paraphernalia
Stolen goods
Untaxed cigarettes
Moonshine or untaxed whiskey
Gambling paraphernalia
Counterfeit currency
Burglary tools
Auto-theft implements or car-stripping tools
Extra license tags
Illegal firearms and other weapons
Explosives

Detection of Contraband

The officer should make the following observations prior to stop:

- Does the driver or passengers attempt to throw items out of vehicle?
- Are attempts made to conceal items under seats or in headliner?
- Does the back of suspect vehicle sag, possibly indicating the presence of heavy items, i.e., safes, engine blocks, transmissions, etc.

Figure 2.5 Assortment of types of weapons that have been taken from vehicles as a result of a thorough search by an alert police officer.

When approaching the vehicle after a stop the officer should:

- Be alert for actions indicating any attempt to conceal items in the vehicle.
- Observe the contents of the vehicle.
- Be alert to passengers attempting to dispose of items while officer is busy with the operator.
- Check both sides of the vehicle for items disposed of and view interior from both sides.

ARREST TECHNIQUES

A part of the responsibility of every traffic officer—no less than any other officer—is that of making arrests. The process of physical arrest is probably the most hazardous of all tasks the police officer must undertake. Therefore, a knowledge of the element of a proper arrest, detention, and transportation techniques is essential for traffic or patrol officers.

Informing the Suspect

The offender should be clearly informed that he or she is under arrest and what the exact charges are.

The arrested party should *not* be *"Mirandized"* until just prior to conducting a custodial interrogation. Any voluntary (not in response to questions) statements, comments, etc., made by the suspect can be admitted in evidence. Suspects often make voluntary and incriminating statements on their way to the police station or jail. After the suspect is in custody and prior to conducting an interrogation, the suspect should be informed of his or her *Miranda* rights, as follows:

MIRANDA WARNING

1. You have a right to remain silent. Do you understand?
2. If you do say anything, we can and will use it against you in court. Do you understand?
3. You have a right to an attorney before and during questioning. Do you understand?
4. If you cannot afford an attorney, one will be appointed for you, free of charge, before questioning. Do you understand?
5. You may stop answering questions or discussing the matter with us at any time. Do you understand? (If expressed waiver desired, ask: "Do you want to talk to me (us) about what happened?")

Rights advisement should always be read from a standard form and not given from memory to avoid error or claims by the defendant that you didn't advise on some portion of the warning.

CITY OF COSTA MESA
POLICE DEPARTMENT

DR _____

You have the absolute right to remain silent. Anything you say can and will be used as evidence against you in court. You have the right to consult with an attorney, to be represented by an attorney, and to have an attorney present before any questions are asked and during any questioning. If you cannot afford an attorney, one will be appointed, free of charge, to represent you before any questioning, if you desire.

I _____ on this _____ day of _____, 19_____,

have read my above stated rights, and fully understand them. I am writing the following statement

voluntarily, freely and of my own will and without duress or promise from Officer_____

and/or_____, who have identified themselves as police officers from the City of Costa

Mesa.

With these rights in mind:

_____
_____
_____
_____
_____
_____
_____
_____
_____
_____
_____
_____
_____
_____
_____
_____
_____
_____

WITNESS: _____

_____

CMF 0110-42 (PD 15) Revised 1/85

Figure 2.6 Standard form advising suspect of *Miranda* rights—with space for suspect's brief written statement.

Searching the Suspect

Immediately following notification of arrest, all prisoners should be searched as quickly and thoroughly as possible. You should keep in mind that a thorough search may save your life and a sloppy search may cost you your life. In searching prisoners, the margin for error is small and the price of failure great—usually death or disability for the officer.

Prior to transportation, each officer should make sure the police unit is clear of any contraband. If a prisoner attempts to discard narcotics or weapons, by hiding them in the unit, you may find the contraband in the unit later. If such is the case, the suspect may properly be charged with additional violations. All police units should be inspected prior to and after each transporting incident.

How to Frisk

The purpose of the frisk is to discover and remove obvious weapons and evidence. The method of frisking involves running the hands over a suspect's clothing and "patting down." The search however, is much more thorough.

How to Search

Follow a pattern and do not skip-search. By searching one part of the body, skipping to another, and then returning to the original part, the searcher may forget which areas were searched, and a weapon may be overlooked. Use the Grasping-hand method; do not slide or pat with your hand when searching. Only by grasping the subject firmly can you discover small objects and weapons.

Always search from the rear of the suspect. Searching from the front makes you vulnerable to a knee in the groin, slaps, eye gouges, and judo. When necessary, however, handcuffed females may be searched from the front.

Keep the suspect off balance and one hand on the suspect's back area to enable you to maintain effective control. Keep your eyes on the suspect's head and shoulders; any attempts at movement by the suspect will be evident in this area first. Always keep your gun out of the reach of the suspect.

If possible, have another officer present when you are going to search more than one suspect.

Figure 2.7 Standing search showing a common place for hiding a hand gun.

Places to Search

Along with searching obvious places, such as pockets, the following areas should also be searched:

1. Palms of the hands
2. Sleeves
3. Center of the back
4. Back of the collar

5. Hats
6. Hair
7. Mouth—for narcotics and other small objects
8. Lapels
9. Neckties
10. Watch pockets
11. Belts, waistbands, and surrounding body area
12. Crotch area
13. Shoes
14. All other objects the suspect may be carrying, such as lunch boxes, suitcases, etc.

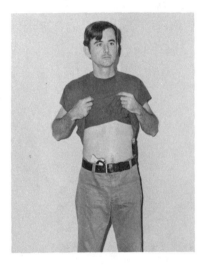 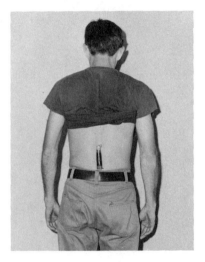

Figure 2.8 Without a proper search this suspect could be concealing a small semi-automatic (in suspect's belt, center right) or a hunting knife (suspect's left side) while in the police unit, police station or booking area.

Figure 2.9 The small of the back is an easy and common place to hide a weapon—in this photograph, a hunting knife.

Search Positions

It is possible to be attacked while searching. There can be no foolproof method. The following search positions are those most commonly used by officers, some of which you may find more effective than others. Realizing that many officers on the street develop their own style of searching, these positions are offered as basic information. While reviewing these positions, remember that a well-conducted and thorough search greatly reduces the element of danger to you and frequently leads to the discovery of evidence that might otherwise be overlooked.

Standing-position search: This position can be used to search someone for weapons or any threatening objects. You may also have the subject place both hands on the back of his or her head and tightly interlace the fingers. The feet are spread apart as far as possible without falling. The waist is arched forward which puts the subject slightly off balance.

The officer approaches from the rear and with one hand applies a firm hold on the subject's interlaced fingers. The officer pushes the back side of the subject near the waist to keep him or her off balance. While standing with one foot between the subject's feet, the officer's weapon side should be away from the subject. The officer can then start to frisk the subject while remaining in control.

Kneeling search position: Place the suspect in the hands-up or hands-on-head position. Stand at the rear of the suspect and command him to kneel and cross his ankles, toes pointing back and out. Grasp the suspect's left shoulder with your right hand. In this manner, your forearm forms a bar for protection across the suspect's shoulder, protecting you from the suspect's right arm. Do not let the suspect sit back on his heels; keep him off balance by having him lean forward. Should it become necessary, a slight shove will force the suspect to fall forward to the ground.

First, search the upper half of the suspect's left side; then grasp the suspect by his belt or waistline with your left hand. Release your right hand and replace your left hand grip with the right hand. Do not lose contact. Proceed to search the lower left side of the suspect. Reverse the procedure and search his right side.

Figure 2.10 Kneeling search method—note that suspect's arms
are handcuffed behind his back.

Prone-position search: The prone-position search is made by
ordering the suspect to lie face down with his arms and hands
stretched out to the side. Either spread the suspect's legs wide apart
or cross them to prevent leg movement. If it is necessary to turn
the suspect over, make sure he rolls away from you.

The prone-position searching technique is more commonly applied
to more serious, or felony cases. It is often used on felony vehicle
stops, and/or with multiple suspects where maximum control is
appropriate. In the prone-position search the suspect is placed:

- Face down
- Head to one side, away from officers so that suspect can't see officers' approach and control procedures
- Arms stretched out to the side, palms up
- Legs apart, inside of ankles down

Figure 2.11 Prone position search. The prone position has replaced the wall search because it offers better control of the suspect and greater officer safety.

Wall search position: This position, in which the suspect is required to lean against a wall with hands and feet spread, is no longer commonly used by law enforcement agencies and is not recommended. The wall search does not provide adequate control of the suspect and poses greater danger for the officer than the other techniques described here.

Handling Evidence Resulting from a Search

Upon finding evidence on a suspect's person, the searching officer should immediately alert the guarding officer of the discovery. This is obviously done so that the second officer can testify to the finding of the evidence. For safety reasons, it is recommended that the searching officer, who finds a weapon or contraband on the suspect, should hand it to his or her guarding back-up partner to secure.

When searching more than one suspect, make sure evidence taken from one suspect does not become mixed with that taken from others. If the suspects are wearing hats, place all evidence found on each suspect in his own hat. Make the suspects aware of the recovered evidence and record any statements they make regarding that evidence.

Searching Females

Laws governing search and seizure make no distinction between the treatment of men and women. As previously stated in searching incidental to a lawful arrest, you may search a person of either sex when warranted. However, searching a female always presents problems for male officers. The basic principle to follow when a female must be searched for evidence or weapons is to handcuff her hands behind her back and transport her to the jail to be searched by a matron.

Although male officers should avoid searching women prisoners, there will be times when such a search is mandatory. Certainly, if you observe a female with a gun, you should take it from her immediately. When more thorough searches are deemed necessary, attempt to get a disinterested woman to witness the search. Be sure to record necessary information about this witness in the report where applicable.

Remember that you can search a female if you have probable cause to believe that she has evidence related to the offense and that it is possible that she may be able to dispose of the evidence before a policewoman could administer a search. Under any circumstances, you must be certain that an immediate search is unquestionably necessary.

Recommended steps in searching females:

1. Whenever possible, male officers should avoid searching a female while you are alone.

2. Check the purse. Generally, women will carry weapons such as guns, knives, hat pins, or fingernail files in their purses.
3. Have the female remove her coat and search it thoroughly.
4. Instruct the suspect to kick off her shoes prior to further searching. This enables her to retain her balance and affords you a chance to remove evidence or weapons from the shoes. When transporting the female, do not give high heeled shoes back to the suspect; keep them in the front seat of the car with you.
5. Search the hair first. It is usually not necessary to disarrange the hair to any great degree, but a thorough search should be made since many hair styles make it possible to conceal large as well as small items.
6. Check for bandages on the arms and wrists. This is an ideal method to conceal razor blades and small articles of evidence.
7. Search the blouse lapel and be sure no weapon is hanging around her neck on a chain.
8. Check the brazier straps in the area of the back. Use the palms of your hands for this search.
9. For your protection, use the back of your hand when searching the sides of the female's body. Use your right hand for the left side of her body and vice versa.
10. When about to search the front of the suspect's body, explain to her that you intend to conduct such a search and that it will be done without offending her.
11. With the female handcuffed and facing you, check the front brassiere shoulder straps which terminate at the brassiere proper.
12. Using the outer side of your hand, check the area between the breasts. This can be done rapidly and still be effective. Any further search in the area should be done by a matron. However, if a weapon is noted concealed in the brassiere, you are well within your rights in removing it.

13. Searching the area below the waist is best conducted by using the back of the open hand. Be sure you never put yourself in a position in which you appear to be embracing the suspect. If the female is wearing a belt, check it by running your thumb around the inside.
14. If a female subject is wearing baggy clothing, sometimes your baton can be used to locate any protruding solid objects by sliding it sideways along the body.

The suspect could be wearing a dress, a skirt, shorts, or slacks. Each type of attire should be searched as follows:

Dress and Skirt: Standing behind the suspect, grasp the lower edge of the dress through the suspect's legs and draw the dress back between the legs in a twisting motion, making in essence a pair of pants. With the back of the hand, check the leg area. Any weapon will normally be visible beneath the dress once it has been tightened up. If a weapon is felt or observed, you can raise the side of the dress up like a pant leg and remove the article. In order to search the outside of the thigh and leg, once again use the back of the hand. Occasionally, female suspects have concealed weapons or evidence in the lower leg portion of a girdle. Usually, when the dress is tightened up, these articles will become apparent to the searching officer.

Shorts and Slacks: Shorts and slacks are easier to search than dresses. It is recommended that the back of the hand be used for the search. Don't overlook items stuffed into the tops of high-top shoes.

Remember, all searching of female prisoners should ideally be conducted by a female officer. The aforementioned techniques are offered as possible solutions to those cases that are exceptions to the rule.

HANDCUFFING AND RESTRAINT TECHNIQUES

Every police officer who fully senses his responsibility for his or her own personal safety as well as the safety of his fellow officers recognizes that every felon or suspected felon must be handcuffed at the time of arrest. Officers have been killed or seriously injured because they negligently underestimated the potential for violence, emotional instability, or recklessness of those they arrested. While making an arrest, an officer must remain constantly alert and exercise maximum caution.

In addition to felony and serious misdemeanor suspects, all dangerous, resisting, and violent prisoners must be handcuffed. Failure to do so is inviting an attack, which may result not only in the prisoner's escape, but in unnecessary injury, shooting, and confusion. Many departments have a policy of handcuffing all prisoners being transported.

Some considerations you must bear in mind when handcuffing are the effects it has upon the person being handcuffed, upon the family of the suspect, and upon those persons crowded about the scene of the arrest.

There have been numerous occasions where the arrested person has submitted to arrest without resistance, but then became antagonistic and violent upon being handcuffed. Many prisoners will react violently when faced with handcuffing in order to preserve their outward appearance of boldness, confidence, or dignity. This normally occurs when the suspect is being handcuffed in front of a crowd or his own family.

Relatives frequently become aroused when they observe a member of their family being handcuffed, especially if the restraining devices are applied in front of the suspect's children. Improper or hasty action on the part of police may lead to arrests for interference or battery upon a police officer which could have been avoided. Handcuffing a suspect in a crowded place, where the prisoner again risks losing "face," frequently spurs the crowd into taking physical action against the arresting officers.

Tact and consideration on the part of officers at the scene can often help prevent these problems from occurring. When handcuffing is necessary, if possible, take the suspect away from family members or the crowd. If the family should follow you to your car, convince them that the handcuffing is to prevent the prisoner from injuring himself and to keep him from accumulating additional charges, such as battery and resisting arrest.

Handcuffs are a restraining not a subduing device. The handcuffed individual may still be dangerous if the cuffs are not properly applied. The officer's first concern is to restrain the prisoner's arms behind the prisoner's back, thereby limiting his freedom of movement. Remember, a handcuffed suspect can still run!

Dangerous or Violent Prisoners

Dangerous or violent prisoners should be handcuffed prior to searching; always handcuff with the palms facing outward. As a matter of fact, many safety conscious officers handcuff every person they arrest prior to searching.

The receiving or transporting officer should place his cuffs on the prisoner's wrists prior to removing the other officer's cuffs. Never remove the first officer's handcuffs until the receiving officer's cuffs are on and double-locked. Double locking cuffs make them much more difficult to pick. This procedure also prevents the handcuffs from constricting the subject's wrists and protects the officer from lawsuits resulting from possible physical damage from too-tight cuffs. Suspects have also been known to tighten their cuffs themselves, in an attempt to get the officer to stop enroute to loosen the cuffs and, thus, provide an opportunity to escape.

Use of Hobble Restraining Devices

A hobble-type restraining device can be invaluable in controlling a suspect who may give an indication of violent resistance. Properly used, it can significantly reduce the chances of injury to officers and subjects. The hobble can be applied so as to prevent running, yet still permit walking. A hobble device is also useful for uncuffing potentially violent persons. As shown below, it can be used on ankles, knees and elbows. It allows for transportation of a subject in a vehicle in a seated position, but removes the ability to kick out windows. The hobble-type device should be used with the suspect's hands handcuffed behind his or her back. It should never be used around the neck or head.

There are several excellent hobble devices on the market. They are made of virtually unbreakable woven nylon-type material. Two of the better known are manufactured by Safariland, Monrovia, California (pictured below) and Ripp™ Restraints, Orange City, Florida.

Figure 2.12 The Safariland Hobble. Comprised of a very strong woven nylon strap with bronze end-clips, the Hobble is used for controlling violent or resisting suspects. It is effective used along or in conjunction with handcuffs.

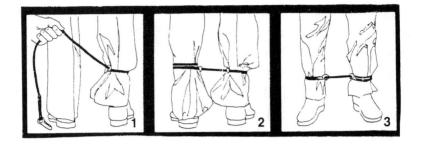

Figure 2.13A The use of hobble-type restraint devices. To keep a suspect from running but still allows for walking, the hobble is applied as shown in windows 1 through 3.

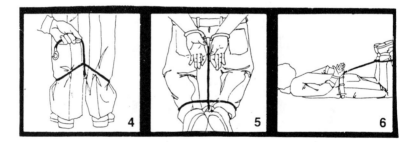

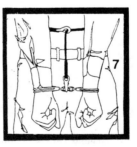

Figure 2.13B To control a violent subject from kicking, the hobble is utilized as illustrated in windows 4 through 6. A subject is prevented from "stepping through" his or her handcuffs, by using the technique shown in window 7.

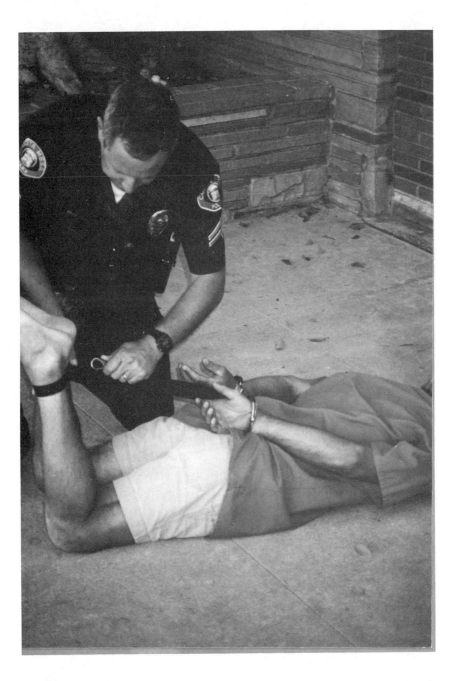

Figure 2.14 Arresting officer applies hobble device to further restrain the already handcuffed prisoner.

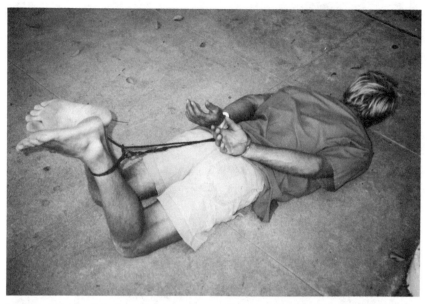

Figure 2.15 Violent suspect is well controlled with cuffs and hobble. Never, never leave a hobbled suspect on their stomach, roll to side. Note: Many departments have prohibited the hobble.

Handcuffing Two Prisoners with One Pair of Cuffs

Do not handcuff the two suspects right hand to left hand. This affords them too much movement. From a search position, two prisoners should be handcuffed right wrist to right wrist. Handcuffing two prisoners with one pair of handcuffs has its limitations. There are certain steps you can follow when you are alone and it is necessary to handcuff two prisoners.

With the right wrist of suspect #1 handcuffed, order suspect #2 to drop his right hand back toward you. Maintain firm pressure on suspect #1 and watch both suspects carefully at all times. Apply a short reverse grip on suspect #2's right hand and twist it slightly toward you. Cuff suspect #2's right wrist to suspect #1's right wrist.

In this position, both suspects may be effectively controlled by the one officer. The suspects may be turned around and will be able to walk without tripping over each other, yet their movements are restricted to the degree that running is difficult.

If two pairs of cuffs are not available, the method outlined above will serve as a temporary restraining measure. However, it is always better to call an assisting officer and handcuff with two pairs of cuffs.

Handcuffing Hands in Front of the Suspect

As a rule, never handcuff the suspect's hands in front of the body. However, if necessary for some reason (deformed arm, plaster cast, etc.), be sure that you cuff the suspect's hands so that the palms are facing outward. Remove and replace the suspect's belt backwards with the buckle in the rear. If necessary, secure the suspect's hands close to the body by slipping them under the belt and tightening it. This precaution restricts the movements of the suspect to a safe degree. However, it is still necessary to watch the suspect closely.

After placing handcuffs on a prisoner's wrist, always tug at the ratchets to ensure that they are locked securely. Next, double-lock the handcuffs so that they may not be slipped or removed.

Common Handcuff Tricks Used by Prisoners

Particular care should be given when searching suspects and prisoners for gimmicks such as the following that may be used to disengage handcuffs.

1. Carrying a handcuff key secreted somewhere on their person.
2. Using a 2-inch long strip of brass edging from a wooden ruler to "slip" the handcuff by disengaging the teeth in the ratchet. A woman's bobby pin serves a similar purpose.
3. Soldering a small tip to the ink cartridge of a ball point pen. Since the diameter of the ink cartridge is almost the same as a handcuff key, its application is very effective.

An Alternative to Handcuffing: the "Flex-cuf" Tie

Recently police across the United States started using a restraining device known as the "Flex-cuf" tie. The tie is a 22-inch-long, lightweight, flexible nylon strap.

The arrangement of a single, high-strength steel barb, mounted in the bottom of a preformed strap head, provides one-way locking action. This, together with a central groove running the entire length of the strap, locks the strap in an infinite number of adjustable positions according to limb size.

Properly used, this device provides an effective restraining aid without the need for heavy metal handcuffs. Since it is expendable (it must be cut to be removed), it eliminates the need for a key.

Place the flex-cuf around the subject's wrists or ankles, groove side against the body, thread the serrated tip through the eye. Draw up the tie. Do not apply more tightly than required to prevent escape.

Figure 2.16   Applied Flex-cuf.

The preferred manner is to bind a prisoner's wrists behind his or her back. Arms are crossed behind the prisoner and the tie is looped around the crossed wrists. For additional security it is possible to loop the tie through the prisoner's belt to prevent unnecessary movement.

If it becomes necessary for any reason to bind a prisoner's hands in front, use the cross wrist or back-to-back method. Never bind the wrists with palms together. This is dangerous since the prisoner can still use his or her hands as weapons. It is also possible to remove the tie with the teeth, especially if it is not drawn tightly enough.

The length of the tie permits binding a person's ankles when necessary. The most effective method is to cross the ankles before drawing tight. Two prisoners may be bound together by using a restraining tie looped through the ties on the wrists.

The tie is produced with a matte finish for the purpose of marking and/or identification. A nylon marking pen may be used to write information on the tie. Information such as place of arrest, time, date, and name of arresting officer can be recorded.

The flex-cuf is an easily carried, versatile device that is readily adaptable to multiple arrests. A note of caution—it has been found that heat will cause the tie to become brittle and break. Therefore, do not store in direct sunlight.

Cigarette lighters, matches, etc., may be used to heat the flex-cuf in an attempt to break it. Be sure that the tie is applied properly so that prisoners cannot use this method of escape.

Chapter Three

PURSUIT DRIVING

The purpose of this chapter is to reduce the hazards of conducting pursuits by discussing proper procedures and pointing out important precautions of which every officer should be aware. Every year hundreds of patrol and traffic officers are injured and killed during one of the most dangerous of police undertakings—the vehicle pursuit. Each vehicle chase is usually unexpected and unlike any prior pursuit. (See Appendix C, for Exemplary Pursuit Driving Policy.)

PURSUIT-OFFICER QUALIFICATIONS

There are certain basic qualifications which must be met if a law enforcement agency is to successfully apprehend violators in high-speed pursuits without experiencing a high accident-frequency rate with resultant deaths, injuries, property losses, and lawsuits.

To apprehend hazardous moving violators, as well as car thieves, fleeing armed robbers and other fleeing felons, law enforcement agencies must provide rigorous training for drivers who will engage in pursuit driving. It is essential that new and inexperienced traffic law enforcement officers be given considerable training before being permitted to do pursuit work. All law enforcement officers must constantly exercise good driving judgement and should learn from each adverse driving situation encountered so that it is not repeated.

Emotional stability is an important factor. You cannot afford to lose your temper if someone offends you on the highway. You must develop a thorough knowledge of the laws applicable to motor vehicle operation—especially safety laws and laws of physics pertaining to speed, centrifugal force and moving objects.

It is imperative that all field officers maintain a thorough and up-to-date knowledge of all roadways in their jurisdiction. If involved in a pursuit, this will aid you in your efforts to apprehend the criminal with as few conflicts as possible. As feasible, you should traverse every road in your assigned area or "beat" and learn the location of all sharp curves, blind intersections, stop signs, dangerous sections of the roadways, etc. This will help you to anticipate trouble and thus avoid unnecessary risks in future driving. For example, some streets become slippery when wet; others do not. Seasonal factors such as fallen leaves may result in slippery streets in some areas. Varying temperatures, ice, and flash floods are other potential hazards, and the officer should keep such possibilities in mind. To know the area, the officer must necessarily consider all of its peculiarities and use this knowledge advantageously for better driving.

An officer should also develop sufficient skill to be able to manipulate traffic signal control devices without having to waste time trying to remember how each functions. When you become aware of an emergency, you must respond instantly and correctly. Being able to handle emergencies effectively is an essential part of good law enforcement in general and pursuit driving in particular.

An officer involved in a pursuit must be equipped with a police vehicle that is in top shape, performs well, and is able to respond adequately to simple hazards in the roadway. Most law enforcement agencies are able to equip their police units with heavy duty suspension and special performance packages. Operating officers should know, not only their personal limitations, but also the capabilities and limitations of their assigned police units as well. Police vehicles should be equipped with all safety equipment, including an approved safety belt, driver's side air bag, and anti-lock (ABS) brakes. Such special equipment can help protect you from being killed or seriously injured.

WHEN TO PURSUE

High-speed pursuits may be justified in certain circumstances; for example, in the apprehension of a driver who is imperiling the lives of motorists or pedestrians through negligent or dangerous operation of a motor vehicle. However, in many respects, high speed pursuits are a "no win" situation for the officer. California Highway Patrol findings indicate that one in three pursuits will end in a collision—with a 10 percent chance that someone will be killed or injured. Even if your vehicle is not involved in a collision, you and your agency could be held civilly liable for other complications resulting from the pursuit.

Deciding to pursue is always a process of weighing the hazards presented by the pursuit against the hazards being created by the violator. All pursuits are hazardous because they involve moving through traffic under emergency conditions. Good driving habits and specialized pursuit driver training will help minimize the dangers involved in a normal pursuit. Good judgement will help in weighing the risks involved in starting a pursuit.

The seriousness and type of violation are important factors in deciding whether or not to pursue. Violations which present continuing danger to other road users (i.e., driving while intoxicated, or reckless driving) may require immediate pursuit. Some violations do not create a great or immediate danger to highway users (i.e., equipment or registration violations). Pursuit in these cases is not "urgent."

Other violations are of the "completed" type (i.e., the danger to other road users is over when the violation is completed). Examples of such violations include driving through stop signs or red lights, or passing illegally. Pursuit in such cases is usually much less urgent and may not be justified.

Roadway and traffic conditions at the time of detection are other important factors in making a decision to pursue. During periods of congestion, pursuit may be impossible or extremely hazardous. Weather conditions such as fog, rain, or ice also make a pursuit difficult. These factors may demand that pursuit either not be initiated, or discontinued.

The type of patrol equipment the officer is using has an important bearing on the decision to pursue. Is the car you are operating plain or marked? The officer must know the limitations of the equipment being used under various conditions of pursuit. An officer should not pursue in an unmarked car, but rather should try to stay close and radio for assistance.

What you are doing at the time of detection affects your decision to pursue. Sometimes you will be more urgently occupied, such as on the way to an injury accident call or other emergency. You must, therefore, weigh the importance of what you are doing against the need for the pursuit. Often it is much more effective to use the radio to direct other units in the area to follow-up and pursue the vehicle.

THE HIGH-SPEED CHASE

A high-speed chase may originate in a variety of ways. It often begins when the police attempt to stop a traffic violator, and the violator accelerates in an effort to evade apprehension. Also, fairly common is the case of an individual traveling at an excessive rate of speed who attracts the attention of the police and merely continues at the same reckless speed. In some instances, this violator may not even know the police are pursuing.

Another type of situation that leads to the high-speed chase is one involving the attempted apprehension of criminals who have previously committed a crime and whose whereabouts have just become known. It may involve the pursuit of the perpetrator of a freshly committed crime, such as a bank robbery or a hold-up, from which the criminal is attempting a getaway. Still another situation that gives rise to the high-speed chase involves individuals who get a perverted thrill from the dangers of highway racing. The police pursuit may be the outgrowth of a prearranged race which the officer is investigating, or the violator may deliberately invite what he deems to be a race against the pursuing officer. This type of individual, usually a male, is often boastful of his prowess in being able to outdistance and get away from police cars.

These situations, which lead to high-speed chases by the police, illustrate how varied the reasons for pursuit may be and, similarly, how the pursued drivers differ in response to pursuit. All these violators have one common denominator—their disregard for their own safety and that of other users of the highway. Any police officer who regularly patrols or works traffic in a police car will sooner or later encounter these violators and will face the necessity of making a number of urgent decisions as to the proper course of action.

The discovery that a violator is attempting to evade apprehension by outrunning the officer creates a series of problems for you. If you exert your best efforts to apprehend the fleeing driver by pursuit, you run the risk of being severely criticized by the press, and also by irate taxpayers. If newspaper accounts of the pursuit give it a certain amount of color and embellishment, criticism of the officer is likely, even though you were successful in apprehending the violator and no one was hurt in the process. If innocent people are killed or injured in the chase, either by the officer or by the violator, the wrath of the press will be leveled at the unfortunate officer—oftentimes more so than at the fleeing violator. There is always a high likelihood of a lawsuit being filed against the officer and the agency, even if the officer's actions were exemplary.

Figure 3.1 Results of a pursuit that perhaps should have been abandoned.

As discussed earlier, the officer is thus confronted with the dilemma of whether to pursue and possibly risk lives—or to let the violator go. Obviously there is no easy solution. You must exercise your best judgment in each individual case—based on the pursuit policy of your agency.

In pursuing a suspected felon, the officer may radio ahead for assistance in intercepting the vehicle. This may not be possible, however, unless the officer has been close enough to give the license number or a sufficient description of the car. Furthermore, an officer further down the highway will not necessarily be in a better position than the pursuing officer to apprehend the speeding vehicle.

Obtaining the license number of the vehicle is not always sufficient to sustain a conviction or even an arrest. Naturally, it would not be of any value if the car or license plates were stolen and the thief escaped. Also, the license number identifies the vehicle, but does not identify the driver.

To those inexperienced in pursuit driving, merely setting up a roadblock may seem to be the easy and logical solution. Unfortunately it is not that simple—a roadblock can be more dangerous than a high-speed chase. Any blocking off of highways being used by the traveling public involves the possibility of endangering innocent people and requires the utmost safeguards to avoid or reduce these dangers. What course of action, then, would be most consistent with good police practices and with sound principles?

The police should never announce to the public that they will not chase high-speed drivers. There should be no doubt in the minds of the public that anyone who attempts to evade apprehension by high-speed driving will be pursued, caught, prosecuted, and severely punished by the courts. It would be dangerous to let anyone think that immunity can be obtained by increasing the flagrance of the offense. It should be made very clear to those who might be tempted to try to outrun the police that the police take a very determined stand against such an attitude—that a speed-up will cause intensification, not slackening, of the police efforts and subsequent punishment.

Siren Limitations

Most officers rely much too heavily on the limited protection provided them by their siren. Even though you are using your emergency lights and siren, remember that most drivers can't hear your siren in time to react and move to the right if you are approaching at high speed. Tests indicate that only 26 percent of drivers could tell from which direction the sound of the siren was coming.

Also, tests prove that even under ideal conditions, the maximum distance the siren could be heard in a closed car averages only 125 feet. If you are traveling at 50 mph, this gives other drivers about six seconds warning time to react and take appropriate action. This isn't much time if you are approaching a nearly blind intersection.

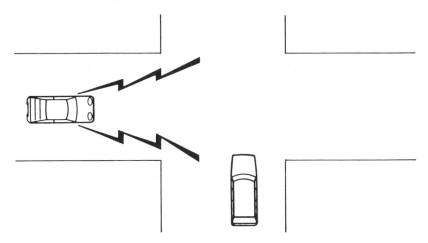

Figure 3.2 If your police unit is approaching an intersection at 50 mph, drivers of vehicles presenting a collision hazard have a maximum of only six seconds, on average, to react properly from the time they hear your siren.

The Person Pursued

In making a pursuit as effective as possible, it is wise to evaluate the person being pursued. The pursuing officer seldom knows what type of driver is being chased until the apprehension is made. At times, usually without advance notice or warning, the pursuit of felons becomes necessary. This type of driver—an armed robber, for example—may take any chance to escape, including passing on blind curves, hill crests, or in the face of oncoming traffic. Such a person has no concern for other people and their safety, and quite frequently will force a motorist off the road if the maneuver will increase the possibility of escape. At times, this type of violator may go so far as to deliberately attempt to wreck the pursuing officer's car. This type of driver may be expected to take advantage of any opportunity to help himself and hinder the officer, regardless of the after effects. Moreover, should the officer be involved in an accident, the violator obviously would not return to assist. Pursuit of such drivers requires skill, good judgement, and persistence, if apprehension is to be accomplished.

A drunken driver normally drives in an irresponsible manner, weaving along at the peril of every other motorist on the road. At times, like the felon, and under certain circumstances, the subject may drive at top speed. His or her actions and reactions differ from those of an average felon, however, in that he may "lose himself" completely in a dangerous situation and collide with another vehicle without making any apparent effort to avoid an accident. A pursuing officer cannot afford to follow too closely, because in case of an accident, it might be impossible for the officer to avoid colliding with the suspect's vehicle.

During pursuit, an overhead flashing warning light and siren should be used constantly to warn all other motorists of danger. Frequently a drunken driver will slow down upon encountering a car which is moving slowly. It is possible that the driver may be slowed to a stop at this point. If the officer continues the pursuit, he or she must properly protect other motorists and pedestrians by using warning lights and the siren. Sooner or later the pursued vehicle driver will either stop voluntarily or be involved in an accident.

Pursuit of violators who are not committing hazardous moving violations does not merit excessive and unnecessary risks to the pursuing officer. Also, pursuit of merely "suspicious vehicles" must be terminated in the interest of safety of other roadway users.

Identification of Pursued Vehicle

A list of wanted cars or a "hot sheet" may be available to the officer in the patrol car. In the pursuit of violators, one of the officer's first duties is to identify the vehicle as soon as possible. The vehicle should be identified by year, model, make, body type, color, and license number. Such identification is very significant and important, particularly if a high-speed pursuit ensues. If the violator is traveling in the opposite direction when observed, it is wise to make an identification as completely as possible for later use.

It is not always possible to get all of this information, but an effort should be made to obtain information as completely as possible. But limited information is better than none at all. Correct information will assure that the right car is stopped and not some similar one. The peculiar features of a car make positive identification possible and easy (i.e., a defective or damaged fender would assure positive identification). Accessories also make identification easier. In addition, the officer may note unusual features of the driver or passengers, such as clothing, hair, hat, glasses, etc.

The officer should advise dispatch and other units in the area of the vehicle's description while in pursuit. This is especially important when:

1. Working in an isolated area,
2. Pursuit is prolonged and fast, or
3. The vehicle being pursued is stolen or involved in some other crime.

DRIVING POSITION

While pursuing another vehicle, the police unit will probably be operating above normal limits. Since quick, precise control of the vehicle is essential, the following recommendations must be adhered to in order to ensure that the police vehicle remains within the driver's control during the pursuit.

1. The seat should be adjusted to a comfortable position so that the driver's feet reach the pedals easily and without strain. Driver's hands should be comfortably placed on the wheel.
2. The seat belt should be snugly fastened to ensure the driver's safety and comfort at all times. A secure seat belt will prevent the officer from sliding about on the seat when turning sharply.
3. The steering wheel should be held it the 10 o'clock and 2 o'clock positions (or, if you prefer, with the hands directly opposite each other, at the 9 o'clock and 3 o'clock positions). The hands should never be crossed over one another while turning a corner because this requires that one hand let go of the wheel when returning to the standard driving position.
4. When possible, all loose material lying in the front seat should be shoved to the right-front floorboard or to the rear seat. This will prevent items from becoming lodged under the brake or accelerator and impeding or blocking their function.
5. The driver should check the gas gauge to see that there is enough fuel.

PURSUIT TECHNIQUES

The violator must be kept in sight, if possible. The police officer should watch for actions that indicate that the violator may try to escape, such as sudden bursts of speed or quick turns. You must try to identify the vehicle during pursuit and allow maneuvering room to avoid being boxed in.

You must he aware of conditions that favor the violator's vehicle. The most important of these is a signal change from go to stop. You must decide whether to go through the stoplight or not.

Other factors favoring the violator's escape are the influx of traffic or heavy traffic approaching on a two lane highway. Sometimes the use of the emergency light and siren will assist an officer in overcoming these two difficulties. Certain behavior of the violator's vehicle can indicate the driver's intentions. At night, he or she may turn off the car's lights, gun the engine for a quick burst of speed, or prepare for a sudden turnoff or turnabout. It should be remembered that those who attempt to escape turn right far more often than left. This is usually to avoid turning into oncoming traffic. The officer should maneuver into a control position as soon as possible, taking sufficient safety precautions. You should not wait for additional violations. Prolonged pursuit for this purpose increases the hazard both to yourself and to other traffic.

Once the vehicle has stopped, the officer should confirm the identity of the vehicle by verifying the registration number with the Department of Motor Vehicles. If the officer failed to write down the license number earlier, try to get it at this point. Also, quickly note driver and occupants. Remember the position of the driver accurately so that you can refute any possible denial by the driver that he or she was driving the vehicle at the time of the violation. The officer should also note any suspicious behavior by occupants, such as concealing objects or tossing them out of the vehicle. You may have to return later to search for these things if the occupants prove to be criminals or wanted persons.

The Takeoff

The officer should select a location for stationary observation from which pursuit can be undertaken quickly and effectively. The spot selected should permit good visibility, and the road surface should be smooth and free from loose material. In addition to those factors, the officer should make sure that the spot selected allows space for proper maneuvering to get on the road and underway after detection of the vehicle to be pursued.

Takeoff spots located on straight stretches of highway between intersections are safest. Intersection positions permit greater observation and coverage but are more dangerous. Takeoff spots located on hills or curves increase the hazard of the maneuver.

Takeoff spots at signalized intersections are special problems. The takeoff in pursuit of a vehicle may require an officer to cross a moving stream of traffic. In selecting a takeoff spot, the officer should position the police vehicle so as to incur as few conflicts as possible. Because most enforcement work done at signalized intersections is directed at stoplight violations, proper positioning can help the officer to use the traffic signal to get under way.

Streets which are congested or those which have parking on one or both sides make the selection of a stationary takeoff spot difficult. Pursuit which requires the officer to enter a stream of traffic which is moving at high speed, usually encountered on limited-access highways, calls for extreme caution. Wherever possible, the officer should pick a location where he or she can take advantage of an acceleration lane or shoulder to bring his or her speed up to that of moving traffic before entering.

Takeoff from moving patrol normally means moving from a position in a line of traffic. The start of takeoff may be merely a continuation of the officer's observation of a potential violator. Pursuit usually starts when the officer has observed a violation. However, in the case of a speeder who has been paced for a sufficient distance to establish evidence of the violation, pursuit starts when the officer discontinues pacing and begins to overtake the violator's vehicle to make the stop. The officer should always keep a clear space ahead for maneuvering.

Proper maneuvering demands space. When patrolling, the officer should keep sufficient distance between himself or herself and other traffic, to permit quick stopping or turning. When stopped in traffic, as for a stop sign, you should keep one or two car lengths ahead of you clear, so that you may quickly turn or move into another lane of traffic without having to wait for vehicles ahead of or behind you to move.

Pursuit Maneuvers

During the pursuit, the officer should be aware of several driving techniques that will help to catch the fleeing suspect.

Depending on vehicle design, when approaching a point where it is necessary to slow down, you should lower the gear shift to the second position and, when appropriate, continue to brake. This movement has three advantages:

1. It relieves some of the stress from the brakes and moves it to the gear box, thus reducing brake fade (loss of brake power).
2. The lower gear forces the rear wheel to revolve more rapidly, giving more control and power when turning a

corner, thus preventing spinouts and allowing the officer to "power out" of a spin if it should occur.

3. It allows faster acceleration after turning a corner.

While approaching corners, the officer must be aware of excessive speed. Often the officer is lured into excessive speed maneuvers by concentrating too heavily on the other vehicle and not watching his or her own speed. All of these techniques will facilitate entering the corner slowly and exiting quickly, which is the best way around any corner.

It must also be remembered that while a corner is a good place to gain on a suspect, it is also a likely place to hit the rear of the suspect's vehicle, causing damage to the radiator of the police vehicle and thus allowing the suspect to escape. If the radiator is seriously damaged, the engine will overheat and freeze if the chase is continued.

Pursuit Turns

A pursuit officer should realize that a decision to stop a vehicle traveling in the opposite direction must be made in a split second. This is necessary because if both vehicles are traveling in opposite directions at a speed of 60 miles per hour, within fifteen seconds, one-half mile will separate the two cars. If the officer pulls off and stops, within seven and one-half seconds the other car will be one-eighth of a mile away. If one adds to this the additional distance the other car will travel while the pursuit officer is making a turn, it becomes obvious that the pursuit officer must take prompt and decisive action if pursuit is to result in the apprehension of the driver of the other vehicle. The greater the distance a motorist can gain between himself or herself and the pursuit unit, the greater the chances for escape.

The suspect may, for example, lose himself or herself in heavy traffic and turn off unobserved into a driveway or side road, or may be able to use the timing of traffic signal lights to enable the suspect to gain distance on the pursuing officer.

In order to minimize the time-lag element when beginning pursuit of a car traveling in a direction opposite from that of the pursuit car, a pursuit officer must be able to instantly size up the roadway situation and decide what type of turn can best be made in order to take up the pursuit.

There are four acceptable ways in which an automobile may be turned. These are (1) the "U" turn, (2) the right side-road turn, (3) the left side-road turn and (4) the "Y" turn. For purposes of this study, these have been designated as pursuit turns. The location at which the turn needs to be made will determine which turn should be used.

1. The U Turn: The U turn is considered to be the fastest and safest way to turn an automobile around and should be used whenever traffic conditions and turning area permit. In order to make a U turn it is necessary to have a circle area 40 feet to 42 feet in diameter. It is not necessary that this area be paved, but it should be free of obstructions or holes that might obstruct travel or cause damage to the patrol vehicle.

2. The Right Side-Road Turn: This turn may be used on two-lane roadways. It is considered to be the safest turn for this type of road, where the roadway width plus the width of roadway shoulders are not wide enough for the U turn. This type of turn requires a side road to the right. Very little backing is required on the main roadway, and only one traffic lane must be crossed. This type of turn will not usually be made where the side road carries a heavy traffic load.

3. The Left Side-Road Turn: This turn should be made where space will not permit a U turn, and no right hand side-road is available for a right side- road turn. It involves crossing traffic but very little backing up.

4. The "Police" or "Y" turn: This turn is not recommended where other kinds of pursuit turns may be used. There are times, however, when it is impossible to make one of the above described turns without traveling a considerable distance to find an available turning space. In this situation, in order to prevent the escape of a vehicle traveling in the opposite direction, this turn must be used.

    This turn is accomplished by quickly stopping the police unit, putting it in reverse, and while backing up, turning the wheels to the left so that the police unit makes a "reverse U turn" and ends up facing in the opposite direction. The vehicle is then shifted to forward to proceed in the direction of the vehicle to be pursued.

Obviously, this can be a very dangerous maneuver if other cars are close behind or approaching from in front. It should never be attempted on a curve or where a clear roadway cannot be seen for a considerable distance.

AVOIDING HAZARDS

Special techniques are necessary to avoid particularly hazardous situations.

Skid Control

Prior to invention of the Antilock Braking System (ABS), braking was one of the more common hazards encountered in pursuit driving. Antilock brakes allow you to continue to steer when the brakes are fully applied—even on slippery road conditions. This adds a considerable measure of control and safety. ABS brakes also allow shorter stops. Antilock brakes, along with electronic traction control, which reduces wheel spin on slippery roads and during hard acceleration, are both major contributions to safer pursuit driving.

Anti-lock brakes should not be pumped. They should be continuously applied with a steady and firm pressure until the car stops. This permits maximum braking without locking any one or all of the four wheels. The driver can, therefore, concentrate on trying to steer around a hazard rather than necessarily stopping short of it. However, no brakes (conventional or antilock) can stop short on ice, for example.

Power Skid

Common to the pursuit situation, the power skid is the result of too much power for the road conditions. The power skid is generally triggered by accelerating too quickly around a corner or exceeding the critical speed of a curve. Excessive power causes the driving wheels to spin, thus reducing the necessary friction to keep the auto from sliding sideways. "Fishtailing" is a characteristic of this skid. A car in a power skid acts essentially in the same manner as a car skidding with its rear wheels locked.

To control a power skid, the driver should ease up on the accelerator, let the car stabilize, and counter-steer. If the car is moving so fast that it is obvious that it cannot stay on the road, the driver should try to aim for a clear spot off the highway. Counter-steering at the right time may make the difference between hitting a tree and skidding into an open field. Remember, it is essential to reduce speed before going into a turn in order to maintain control.

Spinout

To spinout is to make a rotational skid in an automobile. This is a very difficult skid to control. The best you can hope for maybe keeping the car on the road and pointed in the right direction. Spinouts occur for several reasons:

1. Exceeding the critical speed of a curve or corner, i.e., driving so fast that the rolling tire loses its friction and slides off the roadway.
2. Running into loose material (snow, ice, gravel) on a curved roadway or on corners.

Again, this skid may be prevented by controlling the vehicle's speed while entering into and negotiating through a curve, as its principal cause is driving too fast for road conditions.

Hydroplaning

Hydroplaning, or "skidding on water," has only recently been researched. It is definitely a cause of skids and occurs on wet roadways. In a standard police vehicle, partial hydroplaning begins at about 35 miles per hour and exaggerates with speed. At about 55 miles per hour the tires can be completely floating on top of a thin layer of water and may not be in contact with the pavement. If this occurs, there can be no friction and a gust of wind, a change of road grade, or a slight turn can cause an uncontrollable skid.

Knowledge of hydroplaning is limited, but it can be controlled. If the vehicle is partially hydroplaning and a skid occurs, the driver can gain control by compensating for the specific type of skid. But, if the vehicle is totally hydroplaning, all the driver can do is to release the accelerator and ride out the skid.

Good tires with deep tread help prevent hydroplaning. Tread forces the water to escape from under the tires and tends to prevent complete hydroplaning at normal highway speeds.

Bumps and Dips

Another area of concern are the bumps and dips usually found at intersections. Aside from the obvious possibility that hitting the bump may tear a hole in the oil pan, there is also the chance that the driver will temporarily lose control of the vehicle if the suspension is fully collapsed.

It is recommended that when approaching a dip, the driver brake rapidly to a point just before the dip. You should also prepare for a jolt by firmly gripping the steering wheel. Then the accelerator should be applied to allow the front suspension to expand, thus allowing the springs and shock absorbers to handle the dip.

SAFETY DURING PURSUIT

Safety is a prime consideration when you are moving at a speed faster than the surrounding traffic. Avoid startling other traffic. When approaching a hazardous traffic situation, you should use the siren with judgment and pass with extreme caution.

An officer should try for quick apprehension. Quick apprehension lessens danger to the officer, violator, other traffic, and pedestrians. The alert officer will think about using shortcuts, even before a violation is spotted.

The greatest dangers involved in pursuit obviously come from surrounding traffic or from the violator. That is why the officer must be very conscious of the location of other vehicles, especially on high-speed roads. You should make certain that there is sufficient maneuvering room between yourself and those in front, to the side, and behind. Some drivers, either because of nervousness or fear, easily become excited and unpredictable. When the violator realizes a police car is pursuing, he or she may cause an accident by running off the road or into oncoming traffic. The violator may also endanger other traffic and the pursuing officer by trying to elude apprehension.

An officer ought not to become so intent upon the vehicle being pursued that he or she forgets other traffic. You should use your rearview mirror while in pursuit, keeping in mind the position of traffic behind you as well as in front.

Intersections are a special source of danger. You must never approach an intersection at a speed greater than that at which you can come to a stop if another car should enter from the adjoining street. Bursts of speed should come only between intersections. You should slow down as you approach each intersection until you are sure you can proceed through safely. When you determine that the intersection is clear, you should begin to accelerate and repeat the procedure as you approach the next intersection. Placing your foot lightly on the brake pedal as you approach each intersection will permit you to brake instantly if an emergency arises. You should avoid passing at intersections. A passing maneuver can be made as you leave the intersection and should be completed before you arrive at the next intersection.

Collisions in connection with pursuits, should they occur, will be handled as any other accident. The priority of police services must be given first to the prevention of further injuries, so the officer must abandon pursuit to attend to first aid, traffic control, and fire prevention. However, every effort to apprehend the violator responsible for the accident should be made.

Whether to Abandon or Continue Pursuit

The decision to terminate a pursuit takes "guts" and willpower. Nobody likes to lose, but what may be the real price of "winning?" Is serious injury or death really worth the risk? More and more, society is demanding that officers who choose to take up a pursuit, be held accountable for their conduct and the natural consequences of their decisions.

Pursuits, therefore, should be abandoned when it is clear that the hazards are too high and/or that conditions clearly indicate that further pursuit would be futile. If the pursued is a suspected or actual felon, the decision to abandon pursuit will be made under quite different circumstances than if the pursued is a minor traffic violator.

The possibility of having to abandon pursuit should impress the officer with the importance of identifying pursued vehicles and maintaining communication with headquarters (dispatch) and other units. An officer should use the radio to coordinate the efforts of assisting back-up units to apprehend the violator. Remember, a warrant can be obtained later, if the suspect driver can be identified.

Each pursuit is unique and cannot be taken lightly by pursuing participants. While all law enforcement officers are committed to "getting their man," certain obligations require serious consideration to insure preservation of life and property.

Generally, the successful pursuit ends when the officer has established a position of total control (the driver decides to surrender) and all vehicles have come to a complete stop. However, other reasons for termination can result from a collision, departmental policy, or the violator escaping.

It can often be more difficult to decide when to break off a high speed chase than it is to start it in the first place. When is it no longer worth the risk? You must be careful not to let the pursuit become a vendetta. Here are four factors which should cause you to consider abandoning pursuit:

- Speeds are reaching beyond the limits of your police unit
- You are exposing innocent people to unnecessary danger
- Weather or road conditions preclude the maximum use of your police unit
- The vehicle you are chasing shows no sign of stopping—even if and when you do catch up to it.

Pursuit by More than One Vehicle

When more than one vehicle is involved in a pursuit, there are certain basic rules which must be obeyed.

1. Passing. Do not pass another police vehicle just to improve your position. If the police vehicle in front of you is disabled, waves you by, or for some other reason cannot keep up the pursuit, then you will be obligated to pass. But to pass just to improve your position is senseless and dangerous.

2. Spacing of Vehicles During Pursuit. The distance between one police vehicle and another during pursuit will be predicated to a great degree on the condition of the roadway, type of area, speed, etc. Generally speaking, however, it is recommended that the scale of one car length be used for each 10 to 20 miles per hour of speed.

3. Number of Vehicles Involved. Nothing is more ridiculous looking or wasteful than 19 police cars in pursuit of one suspect. When conditions do not dictate to the contrary, the number of cars in the pursuit should be kept to a workable number—five seems realistic. Though it really does depend on the specific situation.

Departmental Policy

Most law enforcement agencies have a written policy on when to pursue and when to terminate a pursuit. Each officer must be given a copy of this policy, and it should be reviewed and discussed with all officers in training sessions. Note: See Appendix C for an example of a city police department pursuit driving policy. To maintain accountability, receipt of a copy of the policy must be noted in the officers files.

PURSUIT LIABILITY

As stated previously, vehicular pursuits are an inherently dangerous but necessary part of law enforcement's obligation to promote law and order in our society. Unfortunately, some accidents are unavoidable, and some pursuit-related liability is probably an inevitable consequence of this obligation. The law places a duty on all officers to operate your vehicle with due regard for the safety of others.

One slight mistake can cost literally millions of dollars. More than ever before, law enforcement agencies are held accountable for the results of any actions taken by pursuing officers. If you make the wrong decision, not only can the city suffer great financial burdens from civil suits, but you can also expect to experience the trauma associated with major injury or loss of life.

Officers involved in fatal accidents resulting from police initiated pursuit will most often require follow-up psychological treatment. No one relishes the thought of possibly sharing responsibility of the death of an innocent victim. The emotional experience can be disturbing enough to eventually end a law enforcement career.

Remember that a pursuit can become "all consuming." It is easy to become personally caught up in the heat of the chase when your adrenaline starts flowing and you have a couple of close calls. Catching the violator becomes a matter of "pride," your vision tunnels in on the violator—both literally and figuratively—to the exclusion of hazards around you. At this point, you are on the thin edge of disaster! It takes a great deal of maturity to realize that further hazard to innocent people can no longer be justified and, thus, discontinue pursuit.

Legal Liability Concepts

The legal theory underlying most pursuit-related lawsuits is that the officer was negligent in conducting the pursuit. A negligence action is based on proof of the following four elements:

1. The officer owed the injured party a duty not to engage in certain conduct.
2. The officer's actions violated that duty.
3. The officer's negligent conduct was the proximate (direct and related) cause of the accident.
4. The plaintiff (suing party) suffered actual and provable damages.

Negligence litigation focuses on the alleged failure of an officer to exercise reasonable care under the circumstances. Therefore, it is in the officer's best interest to be prepared for the potential pursuit. A "plan of action" should be thought out and considered prior to the event. Such a plan must include all department policies and procedures related to pursuit driving.

Pursuit Reporting and Documentation

Formal pursuit reporting by law enforcement agencies is a "must" for tracking and analyzing police-involved vehicle chases. Because many pursuits result in serious injuries and major property losses, some jurisdictions have designed reporting procedures and forms to encourage awareness and responsibility within the agency. In California, for example, all vehicle pursuit data must include the following critical information which is later reviewed by the California Highway Patrol:

1. Whether any person involved in a pursuit or a subsequent arrest was injured, specifying the nature of that injury.
2. The violations which caused the pursuit to be initiated.
3. The identity of all officers involved.
4. The means or methods used to stop the suspect being pursued.
5. The charges filed with the court by the prosecuting attorney.

VEHICLE MAINTENANCE

The maximal effectiveness of a given law enforcement agency hinges on its ability to efficiently utilize its personnel complement and its allotted automotive equipment. Traffic injuries sustained by police personnel, and the corresponding loss of work hours, naturally make a unit less effective. Excessive mechanical failures and accident damages not only increase the operating cost of the motorized equipment, but seriously restrict the full exercise of the department's total police capability.

If a police agency is to carry out its mission with utmost efficiency and obtain the full dollar value of its investment in personnel and motorized equipment, it must develop a well-managed vehicle maintenance program. Steps must be taken to promote personnel safety and to assure the constant and complete availability of the motorized equipment.

DEPARTMENT OF CALIFORNIA HIGHWAY PATROL

PURSUIT REPORT

CHP 187 (Rev 12-92) OPI 042

NUMBER - *For CHP Use Only*

NUMBER - *Other Agency Use Only*

IMPORTANT - READ CAREFULLY

Vehicle Code Section 14602.1 requires that "every state and local law enforcement agency, including, but not limited to, city police departments and county sheriffs' offices, shall report to the Department of the California Highway Patrol, on a form approved by that department, all vehicle pursuit data". This form has been developed to record this information.

The definition of "vehicle pursuit" and instructions for completing and submitting this form are on the reverse.

SECTION I - THIS SECTION IS MANDATORY FOR ALL CALIFORNIA LAW ENFORCEMENT AGENCIES

A. CHP AREA/AGENCY NAME	B. DATE OF PURSUIT	C. TIME PURSUIT INITIATED	D. TOTAL TIME OF PURSUIT (Minutes)	E. AGENCY NCIC

F. DID YOUR AGENCY/AREA INITIATE THE PURSUIT?   a ☐ Yes   b ☐ No

G. I.D. NUMBERS OF OFFICERS INVOLVED (*Do Not List Names*)

H. ORIGINAL VIOLATION OBSERVED BY AGENCY INITIATING THE PURSUIT
a ☐ Felony   b ☐ Misdemeanor   c ☐ Infraction   SECTION: CODE:

I. MOST SERIOUS VIOLATION SUSPECT(S) CHARGED WITH UPON TERMINATION OF THE PURSUIT
a ☐ Felony   b ☐ Misdemeanor   c ☐ Infraction   d ☐ Other: SECTION: CODE:

J. IF THE SUSPECT WAS ☐ WAS NOT ☐ APPREHENDED, WHICH OF THE FOLLOWING MOST NEARLY DESCRIBES THE EVENT TERMINATING THE PURSUIT?
a ☐ Pursued driver voluntarily stopped
b ☐ Forcible stop
c ☐ Pursued vehicle became disabled
d ☐ Pursuing vehicle became disabled
e ☐ Pursuit aborted by law enforcement agency
f ☐ Pursued vehicle and pursuing vehicle collided
g ☐ Pursued vehicle involved in collision
h ☐ Pursuing vehicle became involved in collision
i ☐ Pursuit continued by allied agency
j ☐ Pursued vehicle escaped pursuing vehicles
k ☐ Other:

K. WERE THERE ANY INJURIES INCURRED AS A RESULT OF A COLLISION? a ☐ Yes b ☐ No
If yes, indicate the number of each type of injury:

	Police Officer(s)	Suspect(s)	Other(s)
Fatal Injury	___	___	___
Severe Injury	___	___	___
Other Visible Injury	___	___	___
Complaint of Pain	___	___	___

L. WERE ANY INJURIES INCURRED AFTER THE VEHICLE PURSUIT? a ☐ Yes b ☐ No
If yes, indicate the number of each type of injury:

	Police Officer(s)	Suspect(s)	Other(s)
Fatal Injury	___	___	___
Severe Injury	___	___	___
Other Visible Injury	___	___	___
Complaint of Pain	___	___	___

SECTION II - THIS SECTION IS MANDATORY FOR CHP

M. LOCATION AND/OR ROUTE(S)

N. AGENCY INITIATING THE PURSUIT

O. CHP PARTICIPATION REQUESTED? a ☐ Yes b ☐ No c ☐ N/A

P. NAME OF REQUESTING PERSON

Q. NAME OF SUPERVISOR IN CHARGE

R. TIME NOTIFIED

S. INVOLVEMENT IN PURSUIT a ☐ In Pursuit b ☐ Via Radio c ☐ Via Telephone d ☐ None

T. HIGHEST NUMBER OF CHP UNITS IN PURSUIT AT ONE TIME
Ground ___ Air ___

U. NUMBER OF ALLIED AGENCY UNITS INVOLVED
Ground ___ Air ___

V. OTHER CHP AREAS INVOLVED (Enter 4-digit NCICs)

W. TOTAL PURSUIT LENGTH (Distance)

X. ROADWAY TYPE - MAXIMUM SPEED ATTAINED
☐ Maximum Freeway Speed ___   ☐ Maximum Surface Street Speed ___

Y. IF THE "YES" BOX WAS CHECKED FOR SECTION "K" ABOVE, COMPLETE THE FOLLOWING BOXES REGARDING THE COLLISION
a ☐ CHP involved
b ☐ Pursued vehicle involved
c ☐ Other law enforcement agency involved
d ☐ Other party involved

Z. TYPE OF FORCIBLE STOP IMPLEMENTED:
a ☐ None b ☐ Spike Strip c ☐ Roadblock d ☐ Ramming e ☐ Channelization f ☐ Other

AA. CHP GUIDELINES FOLLOWED? a ☐ Yes b ☐ No

BB. DAMAGE TO CHP EQUIPMENT? a ☐ Yes b ☐ No

CC. INJURY TO CHP PERSONNEL? a ☐ Yes b ☐ No

DD. SUSPECT NAME(S)

EE. SUSPECT STATUS a ☐ In custody b ☐ Released

FF. EVADED ARREST a ☐ In Vehicle b ☐ On Foot c ☐ Other

GG. PURSUED VEHICLE TYPE a ☐ Automobile b ☐ Motorcycle c ☐ Pickup/Van d ☐ Truck Tractor/Trailer e ☐ Other

YEAR	MAKE	MODEL	LICENSE

FORMS ATTACHED:
☐ CHP 555 ☐ CHP 202 ☐ CHP 208 ☐ CHP 270 ☐ CHP 268

COPY OF CHP 187 FORWARDED TO:
☐ Production Controls ☐ Division

SUPERVISOR'S SIGNATURE

COMMANDER'S SIGNATURE

CHP ONLY: REFER TO HPM 70.6, CHAPTER 4, FOR INSTRUCTIONS ON COMPLETING SECTION II AND THE NARRATIVE/CRITIQUE
DESTROY PREVIOUS EDITIONS

Figure 3.3 Typical Pursuit Report form required in most states following a vehicle pursuit by: "One or more officers attempting to apprehend a suspect operating a motor vehicle while the suspect is attempting to avoid arrest by using high speed driving or other evasive tactics while failing to yield to officer's signal to stop." (*Courtesy of California Highway Patrol*)

A police vehicle maintenance program is designed to create and stimulate an awareness of the principles of traffic safety, to assure the operational efficiency of the motorized equipment, and to reduce maintenance and repair costs.

Its efforts are directed toward achieving the following objectives:

1. Preventing accidents,
2. Assuring the proper performance of the motor vehicle and its related equipment,
3. Preventing premature wear and replacement of parts,
4. Maintaining operational vehicles and preventing violent fluctuations in the workload of the vehicle maintenance department, and
5. Reducing the need for major repairs.

Such a program, as a matter of course, includes the total vehicle, that is, proper operation of the unit as well as that of the accessories and emergency devices.

Identifying Equipment Failure

The officer assigned to a vehicle is most familiar with its normal operation. As such, that officer is generally the first to notice the development of a minor or major mechanical defect or failure. However, these symptoms may prove meaningless if the officer is not prepared to initiate immediate preventive measures. Supervisory personnel must, therefore, properly inform each officer of his or her role in the department's vehicle maintenance program. To further assure participation, management should make policy, prepare directives, and provide the necessary supervision.

Visible defects or apparent mechanical malfunctions may be identified by conducting a basic inspection before assuming control of the vehicle. Minor defects requiring repairs or adjustment discovered during the tour of duty should, in turn, be reported on a check list or other report form at the end of the work day. If these vehicle-status reports are to be meaningful, the servicing agency, in turn, must take action on the reported malfunctions before the vehicle is reassigned to service.

The officer's personal safety, as well as that of others, is related to the operating condition of his or her vehicle. Before starting a tour of duty you should inspect the following areas:

- Glass: All glass surfaces, including the headlights and the side and rearview mirrors, should be clean. The windshield should be free of smears.
- Steering: The front wheels must be properly aligned; this may be noted by tire wear. The steering wheel should not have excessive play.
- Windshield Wipers and Washer: Wipers and the washer must be in working order even in dry weather. Brittle or worn wiper blades should be replaced. Don't forget to check the windshield washer reservoir level.
- Horn: The horn must be checked to determine if it operates with a loud, clear signal.
- Headlights: The officer must check to see if both low and high beams are functioning. At night, the angle of the beam must be tested to determine whether the lights are properly adjusted.
- Spotlight, Taillights, and Brake Lights: A test should be run to determine whether they are in working condition. A replacement unit or bulb must be obtained before assuming normal duty.
- Turn Signals: Both left and right, front and rear flasher signals should be checked to determine whether they are functioning properly.
- Exhaust System: A check should ensure that it is tight, quiet, and free from leaks. Carbon monoxide fumes inside the car can be deadly.
- Brakes: The emergency brake should hold the car on any grade. The foot brakes should hold evenly before the pedal is one inch from the floor. A vehicle with defective brakes must be immediately serviced or not assigned to duty.
- Tires: The air pressure and the condition of the tires should be checked; they should have ample tread, be free of bulges, cuts, breaks, and uneven wear. The air pressure recommended by the manufacturer should be maintained.

- Oil: The dip stick should indicate an ample amount.
- Battery: Modern batteries rarely need the fluid level checked. However, it must be secure in its case and free from corrosion.
- Radiator: The fluid level in the reservoir must be at the proper "hot" or "cold" level line. A 50 percent solution of water and radiator anti-freeze solution should be added to the reservoir, if needed. Never open the high pressure radiator cap because of the danger of exploding scalding steam and fluid.
- Fire Extinguisher: It must show full pressure on the gauge to be ready for use.
- Radio: Two-way radios must be in good operating condition.
- Siren and Emergency Lights: They must be ready for an emergency.
- Spare Tire, Jack Tools, First Aid Equipment: Their condition should be checked to assure their ready availability.
- Car Cleanliness: The car should be clean inside and out. An emergency car wash should be requested if it is needed before the regularly scheduled period. Remove any paper accumulation from the car's interior, including the area under the seats and the litter bag.
- Maintenance Sticker on Door Frame: A check will determine when lubrication and oil changes are due.

Inspection Before Starting Engine

After completing the outside inspection of the police vehicle, the following inspections and adjustments are made before starting the engine:

- Check the Odometer: Record the mileage and note whether the vehicle is due for its periodic maintenance servicing.
- Adjust the Seat: Make sure that the seat is adjusted to proper leg length.
- Lock the Doors: In case of an accident, the impact is less likely to force the doors open. This precautionary measure also reduces the possibility of being thrown from the vehicle.

- Adjust the Mirrors: Position the inside rearview mirror to allow the driver to observe fully the traffic to the rear of the vehicle. Adjust the sideview mirror to cover the area that cannot be seen from the inside rearview mirror. This area, on the left-rear of the automobile, is known as the "blind spot," as it cannot be seen through the rearview mirror.
- Fasten Seat Belt: In case of a collision, the seat belt may protect the officer from serious injuries.
- Adjust Sun Visors: The visors can be tipped to the front or to the side to give shade from the blinding effects of the sun. Check the sun visor extensions.

Normal Operation

During the normal operation of the police vehicle, the following gauges must be closely watched:

- Speedometer: A periodic glance at the speedometer will serve as a guide to operating the vehicle within reasonable and safe speed ranges.
- Fuel Gauge: The gauge indicator should not read less than the one-quarter-full mark.
- Oil Gauge: This gauge shows the pressure of the oil as it flows through the engine. The warning light should be heeded.
- Temperature Gauge: This indicates the temperature of the water in the cooling system. Any sudden rise or drop in temperature should be investigated. Water is added only via the radiator reservoir.
- Amperage meter Gauge: This instrument shows the "charge" and "discharge" rate of the battery. Normally, a battery charges (stores) energy during daylight driving and discharges (releases) energy during night driving. When the red warning light or the indicator pointing to discharge is operating, the battery will require immediate attention or servicing.

Preventing Malfunctions

Seldom is the average motor vehicle exposed to the wear, stress, and demands placed upon the police unit. It must meet the requirements of turnpike speeds and at the same time have the mechanical endurance and capability to operate long hours at low or normal speeds. Its engine is seldom turned off and is likely to be left idling when the vehicle is not in motion. These conditions, in themselves, are severe tests of the vehicle's ability to perform with dependability and efficiency.

Consequently, if the police driver is not adequately prepared to follow preventive maintenance measures, the neglected and abused vehicle is likely to develop premature and frequent engine breakdown and equipment failure. By necessity, a police vehicle maintenance program must then stress proper vehicle operating methods in addition to instilling in its personnel an awareness of the importance of properly caring for the motorized equipment.

Idling

The officer should turn off the vehicle's engine whenever stopped for any length of time, e.g., handling a call, conducting an investigation, etc. Excessive engine idling impairs the vehicle's performance and leads to numerous malfunctions requiring repair. Unnecessary and continued idling may cause engine overheating, spark plug failure, carbon deposits in the cylinder heads, damage to automatic transmissions, damage to exhaust valves, and unnecessary use of fuel.

If the engine must be left idling for a short period of time, the shift selector should be left in park. This eliminates a "drag" on the engine and also prevents the vehicle from creeping or being propelled forward if the accelerator is accidentally depressed. The parking brake should also be set.

Preventive Maintenance While Refueling

Take advantage of the refueling stop to recheck the vehicle and to carry out basic preventive maintenance measures.

1. Whenever possible, refuel the vehicle when the fuel gauge reads one-fourth or less empty. With more fuel in the tank, there is less condensation of moisture in the tank, less chance of pumping sediment through the gas line, and less chance of running out of gas.
2. Have the oil level checked and refilled if needed.
3. Check the water level of the radiator reservoir. Use caution in removing the cap.
4. Check the fluid level of the battery. Add water, preferably soft or distilled water, if the top of the cell plates are exposed.
5. Inspect the battery terminals, connections, battery cables, and electrical circuits. The battery terminals should be covered with a light layer of grease. Do not allow corrosion deposits to remain on them.
6. Inspect the condition of the fan belt. A damaged belt may cause overheating or additional trouble in the future. Look for leaks in the cooling system, especially the hose connections.
7. Clean the windshield and other glass surfaces, including the lights.
8. Inspect the tires for cracks, cuts, and blisters. Check the air pressure to determine whether it conforms to the manufacturer's recommendations.

Periodic Maintenance Checkups

Most departments have a regular preventive maintenance schedule. Usually after a vehicle has traveled a designated number of miles, or after a certain period of time, the unit is submitted to periodic maintenance servicing. At this time, the following preventive maintenance measures are taken:

1. Lubrication of the vehicle according to the manufacturer's recommendations,
2. Oil and oil filter change;

3. Examination of the tires for cracks, blisters, rocks, or glass in treads, excessive wear, etc., replacement of tires when necessary;
4. Inspection of the differential, transmission, or transaxle, adding lubricants or fluid as needed;
5. Inspection of the exhaust system;
6. Air filter cleaning or replacement;
7. Brake inspection, adjustment, including addition of fluid if necessary;
8. Engine tune-up, including spark plug replacement; and
9. Tire rotation, alignment and balancing.

Maximum-Performance Checkup

A police vehicle operated in extreme climatic conditions or for extended periods of time at maximum performance needs to be periodically inspected during the tour of duty.

This examination is extended to include some or all of the following areas:

1. Oil and water levels;
2. Battery, to determine whether it is securely fastened to its mountings;
3. Air pressure in the tires;
4. Wheel lug nuts, as the strain of maximum performance operation may loosen them and allow a wheel to come off.

In addition, the driver must maintain a close watch of the fuel gauge to determine the need to refuel, the engine heat indicator to prevent overheating, and the oil pressure gauge to determine if the engine lubricating system is functioning properly.

Chapter Four

DRIVING UNDER THE INFLUENCE

Each year thousands of American lives are lost as a result of accidents caused by drivers who have been drinking. Many thousands more end up maimed or paralyzed for life. Driving under the influence (DUI) of alcohol or drugs, or driving while intoxicated (DWI), is a serious traffic and social problem throughout our country. Besides the tragic loss of lives, the millions of dollars spent on injuries and property damage, make this offense currently the country's number-one traffic law enforcement problem.

Note: The terms "DUI" and "DWI," mentioned above, are often used interchangeably by law enforcement and the public. For simplification, the authors will use DWI to mean either or both in this chapter.

To compound the drinking-while-driving violations, Americans have recently experienced a sharp increase in drug-related driving offenses. Today's officer must be trained to recognize not only the driver who is under the influence of alcohol but also the driver under the influence of drugs, as well as the driver who is combining both drugs and alcohol.

Officers must realize that in driving offenses, the amount of alcohol or drugs ingested need not approach that which produces the condition known as drunkenness—rather, the amount required is only that which impairs the normal faculties of the individual.

The driver operating with impaired faculties is a potential instigator of a fatal or serious-injury accident and, as such, presents a clear-cut challenge to the police officer's primary duty—the protection of life and property.

For the police officer to perform his or her duties in the field of DWI enforcement, proficiency must be attained in the following areas:

- Knowledge of how alcohol or drugs affect the body
- Methods of detection

- Field and chemical testing
- Arrest methods
- Preparing reports and documents
- Courtroom testimony

PROPERTIES OF ALCOHOL

The substance called ethyl alcohol, or ethanol, is the primary constituent of alcoholic beverages. As a pure chemical, it is clear, colorless, and odorless. It is generally harmless when consumed in moderate quantities, but when consumed in sufficiently large quantities, it can be lethal. Its effect on the body is that of a depressant and anesthetic, not a stimulant. It is produced by the fermentation of such organic substances as fruit, fruit juices, malt, cereal grain extract, vegetable pulp, molasses, etc. The maximum natural alcoholic content of fermented beverages is 10 to 13 percent by volume.

Distilled beverages such as whiskey, vodka, gin, and rum, are produced by heating fermented alcohol mixtures. Since alcohol boils at a lower temperature than water, the alcohol can be boiled off (distilled) and captured, increasing the alcoholic content of the distilled beverage.

Congeners

In addition to alcohol and water, alcoholic beverages contain numerous compounds or impurities known as congeners. Congeners typically impart a characteristic flavor and odor to the beverage and give rise to what people call the "smell of alcohol or beer" on a person's breath. However, congeners constitute a very small proportion of the total volume of an alcoholic beverage. There is no evidence that congeners contribute to the depressant effect of alcoholic beverages.

Proof System

The proof number of a beverage represents twice the percent of alcohol by volume (e.g., a 100-proof beverage contains 50 percent alcohol by volume). Most "hard liquors," such as whiskey, have a maximum of 40 to 50 percent alcohol by volume, or 80 to 100 proof. The remainder is made up of water and congeners. Most wine and champagne is about 12 percent alcohol, except for sweet (fortified) wines which are about 20 percent alcohol. Beer, ale and stout vary between 10 to 18 percent alcohol, with ale and stout containing the higher percentage of alcohol.

ALCOHOL IN THE BODY

Alcohol passes readily through all membranes in the body and is absorbed directly into the blood stream. For chemical testing purposes, the amount of alcohol in the blood is termed Blood Alcohol Concentration (BAC).

BAC is expressed in weight of alcohol per volume of blood—typically the weight of alcohol, in grams, per 100 milliliters of blood or grams of alcohol per 210 liters of breath. Thus, a BAC of .08 (8/100ths) percent is equal to 80 milligrams of alcohol per 100 milliliters of blood. BACs are expressed as fractions of 1 percent concentration of alcohol in the blood. In most states a BAC of .08% is prima facie (on its face) evidence that the driver is under the influence. In most states it is, of course, illegal to drive with a BAC of .08% or higher. Although, even a BAC below .08% does not mean that it is safe or legal to drive.

In breath testing, the officer may encounter the term BAQ, which stands for Breath Alcohol Equivalent. The term represents the alcohol concentration as measured from a breath sample. Numerically, the terms BAC and BAQ are identical. Thus when a person with a BAC of .08 percent is given a breath test, a reading of .08 percent BAQ should also be obtained.

Alcohol Absorption

Alcohol can be absorbed through the lining of the mouth. However, such absorption is normally insignificant since the fluid typically leaves the mouth rapidly. The mouth of a person who has merely rinsed with alcohol (not swallowed any alcohol) will be free of alcohol after about twenty minutes.

Stomach and Small Intestine

About 25 percent of the alcohol consumed is absorbed by the body directly into the blood stream unchanged through the stomach wall. The exact amount is variable and is influenced by the emptying time of the stomach. The remaining alcohol is absorbed by the small intestine. Very little alcohol gets past the first 8 to 10 inches of the small intestine.

Alcohol Absorption Rates

The rate of absorption varies somewhat from person to person and varies in the same person at different times. Alcohol passes into the bloodstream within one or two minutes after consumption. Most alcohol is absorbed within 15 minutes and nearly 90 percent within one hour. Nearly all alcohol is absorbed within an hour and a half; however, in some cases nearly three hours may be required for total absorption.

Absorption through the stomach wall is slow and represents only a small portion of the total intake; absorption through the small intestine—which the stomach empties into—is rapid. Food in the stomach delays absorption by holding the alcohol in the stomach longer; this applies to eating both before and during the intake of alcohol.

Elimination of Alcohol

Alcohol is eliminated from the body by a biochemical reaction and direct excretion. From 90 to 95 percent of alcohol in the body is burned up (oxidized) by being converted to carbon dioxide and water in the liver. A small amount (two to eight percent) is excreted, unchanged, through the breath, urine, tears, saliva, and perspiration.

Rate of Elimination

On average, the body metabolizes (burns and dissipates) alcohol from the body at the rate of approximately one drink per hour. For example, a person weighing 150 pounds will eliminate about one ounce of 80-proof whiskey or one 4-ounce glass of wine or one 12-ounce glass of beer per hour. The rate of elimination is not significantly affected by stimulants (drugs, coffee), or exercise (i.e., increased breathing rate, physical exercise). It is a myth that coffee will help sober-up an intoxicated person. As one wag put it, "all you end up with is a wide-awake drunk."

Note: The rates of elimination previously quoted are averages and should be used with care as a means of estimating a person's BAC at some time prior to a chemical test.

Concentration of Alcohol in the Body

In general, a heavier person must consume more alcoholic beverage—but not much more—than a lighter person to achieve the same Blood Alcohol Concentration (BAC). There is approximately the same amount of alcohol in a 12-ounce bottle of beer as there is in a 4-ounce glass of wine, and 4-ounces of 100-proof liquor (even if mixed with non-alcoholic drinks). Food in the stomach will delay absorption and result in a lower BAC than would be obtained if the stomach were empty. Food will also result in a more prolonged BAC.

Effects on the Body

The intake of alcohol affects specific areas of the body.

- Circulatory System: There is no evidence that alcohol significantly improves circulation. Following absorption into the blood, alcohol enlarges the vessels of the skin and permits an increase in skin blood flow. This accounts for the flushed face of the drinker.
- Kidneys: Alcohol stimulates the kidneys to produce urine, but moderate use of alcohol does not appear to cause any kidney damage.
- Liver: Heavy use of alcohol causes an accumulation of fat in the liver, a condition referred to as fatty liver. This may result in an inflammation of the liver, commonly called

There is no safe way to drive after drinking. These charts show that a few drinks can make you an unsafe driver. They show that drinking affects your **BLOOD ALCOHOL CONCENTRATION (BAC)**. The **BAC** zones for various numbers of drinks and time periods are printed in white, grey, and black.

HOW TO USE THESE CHARTS: First, find the chart that includes your weight. For example, if you weigh 160 lbs., use the "150 to 169" chart. Then look under "Total Drinks" at the "2" on this "150 to 169" chart. Now look below the "2" drinks, in the row for 1 hour. You'll see your **BAC** is in the grey shaded zone. This means that if you drive after 2 drinks in 1 hour, you could be arrested. In the grey zone, your chances of having an accident are 5 times higher than if you had no drinks. But, if you had 4 drinks in 1 hour, your **BAC** would be in the black shaded area...and your chances of having an accident 25 times higher. What's more, it is **ILLEGAL** to drive at this **BAC** (.10% or greater). After 3 drinks in 1 hour, the chart shows you would need 3 more hours—with no more drinks—to reach the white **BAC** zone again.

REMEMBER: "One drink" is a 12-ounce beer, or a 4-ounce glass of wine, or 1¼-ounce shot of 80-proof liquor (even if it's mixed with non-alcoholic drinks). If you have larger or stronger drinks, or drink on an empty stomach, or if you are tired, sick, upset, or have taken medicines or drugs, you can be **UNSAFE WITH FEWER DRINKS**.

TECHNICAL NOTE: These charts are intended to be guides and are not legal evidence of the actual blood alcohol concentration. Although it is possible for anyone to exceed the designated limits, the charts have been constructed so that fewer than 5 persons in 100 will exceed these limits when drinking the stated amounts on an empty stomach. Actual values can vary by bodytype, sex, health status, and other factors.

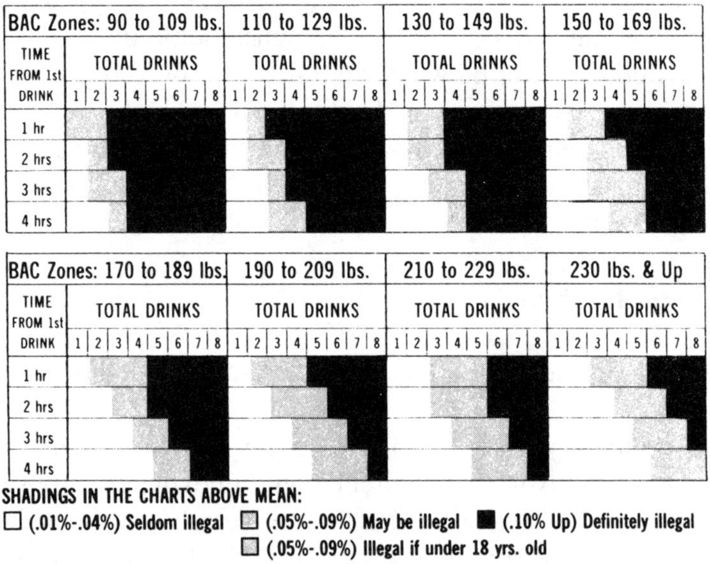

BAC Zones: 90 to 109 lbs.	110 to 129 lbs.	130 to 149 lbs.	150 to 169 lbs.
TIME FROM 1st DRINK / TOTAL DRINKS 1 2 3 4 5 6 7 8	TOTAL DRINKS 1 2 3 4 5 6 7 8	TOTAL DRINKS 1 2 3 4 5 6 7 8	TOTAL DRINKS 1 2 3 4 5 6 7 8
1 hr			
2 hrs			
3 hrs			
4 hrs			

BAC Zones: 170 to 189 lbs.	190 to 209 lbs.	210 to 229 lbs.	230 lbs. & Up
TIME FROM 1st DRINK / TOTAL DRINKS 1 2 3 4 5 6 7 8	TOTAL DRINKS 1 2 3 4 5 6 7 8	TOTAL DRINKS 1 2 3 4 5 6 7 8	TOTAL DRINKS 1 2 3 4 5 6 7 8
1 hr			
2 hrs			
3 hrs			
4 hrs			

SHADINGS IN THE CHARTS ABOVE MEAN:
☐ (.01%-.04%) Seldom illegal ▨ (.05%-.09%) May be illegal ■ (.10% Up) Definitely illegal
▨ (.05%-.09%) Illegal if under 18 yrs. old

Figure 4.1 Chart showing Blood Alcohol Concentration (BAC) according to weight, number of drinks consumed, and time from first drink.

To read: find the column which includes the person's weight. Look at the total number of drinks and compare that to the time shown on the left. If the BAC is in the grey zone, the chances of having an accident are 5 times higher than if the person had had no drinks—and 25 times higher if the BAC is in the black zone.

cirrhosis. However, cirrhosis appears to be more a result of the poor diet of the alcoholic, rather than a direct result of alcohol. Moderate use of alcohol does not appear to have a harmful effect on the liver of healthy, well-nourished people.

Common symptoms of alcoholic influence include:

- Odor of alcoholic beverage on the breath
- Swaying, unsteadiness, or staggering
- Poor muscular coordination
- Confusion, lack of response to stimulation
- Sleepiness
- Disorderly appearance
- Speech impairment, such as slurred, confused, thick tongue
- Dizziness
- Nausea
- Unusual actions, such as being very talkative, aggressive, depressed, or jovial
- Visual disorders, such as a fixed stare, bloodshot or watery, glassy eyes
- Flushed face

The symptoms of certain illnesses, injuries, or forms of drug abuse can be confused with those of alcoholic influence. Many so-called alcoholic influence symptoms can be associated with illnesses and injuries such as concussions, heart attacks, epilepsy, diabetic comas, as well as certain forms of drug use and abuse.

The officer should examine and question the suspect carefully to determine whether medical attention is necessary. A chemical test for alcoholic influence can thus serve to protect the public by indicating the suspect's need for medical attention, that is, a low BAC may indicate that the suspect's abnormal behavior is due to some condition other than alcoholic influence. A very high BAC may indicate the need for medical assistance to minimize the possibility of respiratory or cardiac arrest.

Tolerance to Alcohol

It is well known that people react differently to alcohol, that is, some are better able to "hold their liquor" than others. Different individuals at the same blood alcohol level (BAC) can react differently. Although it may be said that the heavy drinker has learned to compensate for the effects of liquor (e.g., by standing with his or her feet farther apart to minimize swaying), tolerance has been noted in people with no previous exposure. Individuals with the same weight attain different BACs from the same amount of alcohol. The exact reasons for differences in tolerance to alcohol are not well understood, but the following reasons have been proposed:

- Delayed absorption
- Decreased penetration in the central nervous system
- Increased elimination
- Increased water content of the body
- Increased tissue tolerance

When several drinks are consumed in a very short period of time, peak BAC may not appear until one to three hours after the last drink. Sometimes a retest is given to see whether the reading goes up.

EFFECTS OF ALCOHOL ON BEHAVIOR

Many people think alcohol is a stimulant because its first noticeable effects are to reduce inhibitions and promote a feeling of well-being. The first step of impairment affects the part of the brain that controls one's ability to predict his behavior, and to regulate one's powers of attention. As a result, the person's self - confidence increases.

If alcohol is consumed in sufficient quantities, the functioning of the part of the brain that automatically controls a person's body functions can be so impaired that a person can lose complete control of himself, pass into a coma, and ultimately die if the respiratory center of the brain is seriously depressed.

Between the mild effects and severe effects of alcohol there is a progressive deterioration of performance. Speech becomes slurred and vision is impaired. Pupils generally enlarge, and reaction to visual stimuli becomes slower—bright lights and glare are bothersome. Distance predictions are impaired as well as the ability to see things to one side or the other of the visual field (side or peripheral vision). There is a greater inability to focus from far to near objects, increasing at a BAC of 0.06 percent. At a BAC of 0.10 percent, blurred vision can occur, reaction time increases, and physical coordination is impaired. The beginning of impairment of physical coordination can occur with a BAC as low as 0.02 percent. Motor tasks that require complex discrimination are impaired at BACs of 0.05 percent. In addition, sensitivity to most stimuli (visual, auditory, pain) generally decreases.

Stages of Intoxication

There are no precise BAC's that define the various stages—there is overlap. The BAC ranges indicate that not all people are equally affected at the same BAC value.

1. Sobriety
    *   No apparent influence—person appears normal

2. Euphoria—BAC of .02 percent to .08 percent
    *   Sociable, talkative
    *   Increased self-confidence, decreased inhibitions
    *   Loss of attention, judgment

3. Excitement—BAC of 0.08 percent to 0.25 percent
    *   Loss of judgment and predictability
    *   Impaired memory
    *   Increased reaction time
    *   Some muscular incoordination

4. Confusion—BAC of .20 percent to .30 percent
    *   Mentally confused, dizzy
    *   Exaggerated emotions

- Disturbed vision
- Decreased sense of pain
- Poor balance, staggering gait, slurred speech

5. Stupor—BAC of 0.25 percent to 0.40 percent
   - Inability to stand, walk or react to surroundings. Possible vomiting, and falling asleep

6. Coma—BAC of 0.35 percent to 0.50 percent
   - Unconsciousness, which if persisting for more than ten hours, generally becomes fatal

7. Death—BAC of 0.45 percent
   - Respiratory paralysis occurs

Effects of Alcohol on Driving Ability

Generally, as an increasing BAC will impair the performance of the individual, so will it affect the person's driving performance and behavior in traffic. Specific effects include:

1. Inappropriate behavior
   - Extremely slow speeds on open highways
   - Stops where none is required
   - Long stops at stop signs
   - Apparent confusion at signalized intersections
   - Open car windows, especially in cold weather

2. Poor control
   - Failure to dim lights for passing traffic
   - Vehicle over center line especially when making turns or approaching vehicles
   - Erratic movement, such as weaving, driving on the shoulder, stopping and starting, abrupt turns without signaling

3. Parking in unusual places, such as the traveled portion of the roadway

4. Repeated moving violations, such as failure to observe signals, signs, and markings; failure to grant right-of-way; and excessive speed

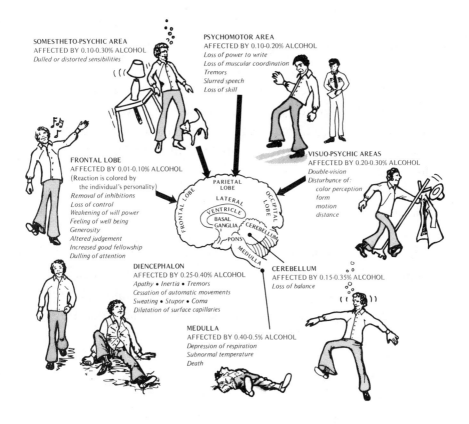

SOMESTHETO-PSYCHIC AREA
AFFECTED BY 0.10-0.30% ALCOHOL
Dulled or distorted sensibilities

PSYCHOMOTOR AREA
AFFECTED BY 0.10-0.20% ALCOHOL
Loss of power to write
Loss of muscular coordination
Tremors
Slurred speech
Loss of skill

FRONTAL LOBE
AFFECTED BY 0.01-0.10% ALCOHOL
(Reaction is colored by
   the individual's personality)
Removal of inhibitions
Loss of control
Weakening of will power
Feeling of well being
Generosity
Altered judgement
Increased good fellowship
Dulling of attention

VISUO-PSYCHIC AREAS
AFFECTED BY 0.20-0.30% ALCOHOL
Double-vision
Disturbance of:
color perception
form
motion
distance

PARIETAL LOBE
FRONTAL LOBE
OCCIPITAL LOBE
LATERAL VENTRICLE
BASAL GANGLIA
CEREBELLUM
PONS
MEDULLA

DIENCEPHALON
AFFECTED BY 0.25-0.40% ALCOHOL
Apathy • Inertia • Tremors
Cessation of automatic movements
Sweating • Stupor • Coma
Dilatation of surface capillaries

CEREBELLUM
AFFECTED BY 0.15-0.35% ALCOHOL
Loss of balance

MEDULLA
AFFECTED BY 0.40-0.5% ALCOHOL
Depression of respiration
Subnormal temperature
Death

Figure 4.2   Effect of alcohol on different parts of the brain.

EFFECTS OF DRUGS AND OTHER CHEMICALS

Although alcohol is technically a drug, the term drug is generally reserved for other substances. The symptoms that can be produced from the use or abuse of certain drugs and chemicals are similar to those of alcoholic influence. When an officer observes a driver operating a vehicle in an unusual and erratic manner, pulls such a driver over, and detects none of the physical signs of alcoholic influence, e.g., smell of an alcoholic beverage, nor has reason to suspect injury or illness, the officer should be alert to suspect driving under the influence of drugs. Thus, the erratic and unusual driving behavior of an individual who is under the influence of some drug can be very similar to that of a person under the influence of alcohol.

Effects of Alcohol Combined with Other Drugs

When alcohol is combined with some drugs, the effect is not simply additive but sometimes supra-additive. In other words, there is sometimes more impairment from an alcohol-drug combination than one would expect from a simple addition of the effects of each dose alone.

Stimulants

Stimulants do not counteract the major depressing effects of alcohol. They are only temporarily effective with regard to the grosser aspects of alcoholic influence. They may be used for temporary arousal in severe intoxication, but the arousal effect is brief.

Depressants

The depressant effects will be added together, and, in some instances, the resultant effect will be greater than the expected combined effect of the two drugs. The trainee should be alert to the fact that depressants are used widely and indiscriminately, and their use with alcohol could cause a serious problem for the driver.

Narcotics

Animal studies have indicated additive and supra-additive effects of narcotics and alcohol; human studies are understandably lacking. In examining the drunk driver suspect, the trainee should be alert to the possibility that the individual's behavior may be due to a narcotic or to a combination of narcotics and alcohol.

EFFECTS OF OTHER PHYSICAL IMPAIRMENTS

There are naturally occurring physical conditions affecting the driver and pedestrian that can impair traffic performance. Often the symptoms of these conditions resemble those associated with alcoholic or drug influence.

Fatigue

We all become generally fatigued from time to time and experience the effects of fatigue which can significantly impair performance, especially driving performance. Traffic accidents due to fatigue impairment are a common problem where, on limited access highways, the traffic situation is monotonous and boring. Some of the specific effects of fatigue are:

- Need for increased time to perceive and react to situations in the environment
- Need for stronger levels of stimulation for awareness
- Tendency to fix attention and vision straight ahead
- Mild forms of hallucinations
- Semiconscious behavior—poor directional control of a vehicle

In such cases the officer should inform the driver that he or she must rest or drink a cup of coffee, tea, a soft drink, or eat a small amount of a quick energy food.

Illness and Injury

There are many forms of illnesses and injuries that can impair traffic performance, many producing symptoms similar to alcoholic influence. Some examples of these physical conditions are:

- Epilepsy
- Narcolepsy (falling asleep)
- Diabetic coma
- Cerebral (brain) hemorrhage
- Heart attack
- Concussion

Some of the symptoms that can be produced from the above conditions are:

- Slurred speech
- Incoherence
- Loss of physical coordination—staggering

The officer should be alert to consider injury or illness as a cause of impairment in cases in which symptoms of violator impairment do not appear attributable to alcohol. Also, the officer should be particularly careful to medically verify the condition of an impaired individual who has been in a traffic violation in which the signs of alcoholic consumption are weak or nonexistent. It would be best to take the person directly to the hospital—otherwise, the officer risks a lawsuit.

Aging

Based on past experience with older drivers, physical capabilities (especially vision and hearing) diminish. Many older drivers fail to compensate for their impairments, or in some cases, overcompensate by unduly cautious and conservative traffic performance.

In either case, hazardous traffic situations can ensue. For example, the person who is unaware of his or her limitations produced by advancing age, may subject himself or herself to traffic situations in which the elderly person does not have full control. A report to the Department of Motor Vehicles should result in a retest of the driver. Issuing a citation to such drivers may, by adding points, eventually lead to a loss of his or her license.

FIELD TACTICS—DWI DETECTION GUIDE

Some patrol and traffic officers seem to have an uncanny ability to "spot" DWI vehicle operators. It has been found that those officers with the best DWI arrest and conviction rates have developed a series of indicators or "clues" which alert them that a driver might likely be under the influence of drugs or alcohol.

The National Highway Traffic Safety Administration has conducted an extensive field study of more than 4,600 patrol stops which they correlated with driver blood-alcohol concentrations (BAC). From this study they were able to develop a DWI "profile" consisting of 20 "clues" and "probability values" for detecting intoxicated drivers. What follows is the most systematically developed method available for visually predicting whether a vehicle is being driven by an intoxicated driver.

The percentage number with each visual clue is the probability that a driver exhibiting that conduct has a BAC of .08 percent or greater. For example, the 65 percent for the first clue on the list—Turning With Wide Radius—means that chances are 65 out of 100 that the driver will have a BAC of .08 percent or greater.

Each value shown is based on seeing only one clue. However, multiple clues are seen more often than not. When more clues are seen, add 10 to the largest value among the clues observed. For multiple clues, add 15 after adding 10 for the second clue to the largest clue value. These numerical values, although accurate, are provided primarily to emphasize the relative importance of a particular indicator or clue.

While the officer should certainly testify as to any erratic or unusual driving observed, the National Highway Traffic Safety Administration does not endorse the courtroom use of the numerical values assigned to specific driving clues. The numbers are most valuable as "probability indicators" which, along with department policy and the officer's judgement, can help the officer decide whether or not a stop for further investigation is appropriate.

Twenty DWI Indicators

1. Turning With Wide Radius – 65%

During a turn, the radius, defined as the distance between the turning vehicle and the center of the turn, is greater than normal. This clue is illustrated below.

Figure 4.3 Illustrates typical greater than normal turning radius.

2. Straddling Center of Lane Marker – 65%

The vehicle is moving straight ahead with the center or lane marker between the left-hand and right-hand wheels.

3. Appearing To Be Drunk – 60%

This clue is actually one or more of a set of indicators related to the personal behavior or appearance of the driver. Examples of specific indicators might include:

- Eye fixation—often straight ahead
- Tightly gripping steering wheel

- Face close to windshield
- Slouching in the seat
- Gesturing erratically or obscenely
- Drinking in the vehicle
- Driver's head protruding from vehicle
- Racing engine
- Failure to slow for blind intersection
- Excessive use of horn

The drawing below illustrates the first three "appearing to be drunk" indicators.

Figure 4.4 Illustrates three "appearing to be drunk" indicators: eye fixation, tightly gripping wheel and face close to windshield.

4.   Almost Striking Object or Vehicle – 60%

The vehicle is observed almost striking a stationary object or another moving vehicle. Examples include:

- Driving abnormally close to a sign, wall, building, or other object
- Passing abnormally close to another moving vehicle
- Causing another vehicle to swerve to avoid a collision

5.   Weaving – 60%

Weaving occurs when the vehicle alternately moves toward one side of the roadway and then the other, creating a zig-zag course. The pattern of lateral movement is relatively regular as one steering correction is closely followed by another. Weaving is illustrated by the drawing below:

Figure 4.5 Drawing illustrates typically weaving" on roadway.

6.   Driving on Other Than Designated Roadway – 55%

The vehicle is observed being driven on other than the roadway designated for traffic and possibly disregarding traffic lane markings. This includes:

- At edge of roadway
- On the shoulder
- Off the roadway entirely
- Straight through turn-only lanes or areas

An example of driving straight through turn-only lanes is illustrated by the drawing below.

Figure 4.6 Shows driver swerving to right after drifting left toward approaching traffic.

7.   Swerving – 55%

A swerve is an abrupt turn away from a generally straight course. Swerving might occur directly after a period of drifting, when the driver discovers the approach of traffic in an oncoming lane, or discovers that the vehicle is going off the road. Swerving might also occur as an abrupt turn is executed to return the vehicle to the traffic lane. In the illustration below, a swerve to the driver's right is executed to return to a lane after a period of drifting left toward opposing traffic.

8.   Slow Speed (More Than 10 mph Below Limit) – 50%

Often drivers who are aware that they've had too much to drink are consciously "overly cautious" in an attempt to compensate for their condition. This happens more often than one might guess—as the study indicated—50 percent of the time.

9.   Stopping Without Cause in a Traffic Lane – 50%

The critical element in this clue is that there is no observable justification for the vehicle to stop in the traffic lane. The stop is not caused by traffic conditions, traffic signals. an emergency situation, or related circumstances. Intoxicated drivers might stop in a traffic lane when their capability to interpret information and make decisions is severely impaired. As a consequence, stopping (without cause) in the traffic lane is likely to occur at intersections or other "decision" points.

10. Following Too Closely – 50%

The vehicle is observed following another vehicle while not maintaining the legal minimum safe separation.

11. Drifting – 50%

Drifting is a straight-line movement of the vehicle at a slight angle to the roadway. It is similar to weaving, except less exaggerated. As the driver approaches a lane marker, center line, or edge of the roadway, the direction of drift might change. As shown in the illustration below, the vehicle drifts across the lane marker to another lane, then the driver makes a correction and the vehicle drifts back across the lane marker. Drifting might be observed within a single lane, across lanes, across the center line, onto the shoulder, and from lane to lane.

Figure 4.7 Drawing shows driver drifting from right edge of roadway to center divider and starting back.

12. Tires on Center or Lane Marker – 45%

The left (driver's side) tires of the observed vehicle are consistently on the center line, or either tire is consistently on the lane marker. Often, the intoxicated driver tries to "ride" a roadway marker line to keep the vehicle from swerving or drifting.

13. Braking Erratically – 45%

In these cases, the driver is observed braking unnecessarily and frequently, maintaining pressure on the brake pedal ("riding the brakes"), or braking in an uneven or jerky manner.

14. Driving Into Opposing or Crossing Traffic – 45%

The vehicle is observed heading into opposing or crossing traffic under one or more of the following circumstances:

- Driving in the opposing lane
- Backing into traffic
- Driving the wrong way on a one-way street
- Failing to yield the right-of-way

Failing to yield the right-of-way is illustrated in the drawing below.

Figure 4.8 Drawing illustrates failure to yield right-of-way.

15. Signaling Inconsistent With Driving Actions – 40%

A number of possibilities exist for the driver's signaling to be inconsistent with the associated driving actions. This clue occurs when inconsistencies such as the following are observed:

- Failing to signal a turn or lane change
- Signaling opposite to the turn or lane change made
- Driving with four-way hazard flashers on
- Signaling consistently with no accompanying driving action

An example of this last clue is illustrated in the drawing below where the driver is signaling for a left turn, but is actually turning right.

Figure 4.9 Note that in drawing driver is signalling for a left turn, but starting to turn right.

16. Slow Response to Traffic Signals – 40%

The observed vehicle exhibits a longer than normal response to a change in a traffic signal. For example, the driver remains stopped at the intersection for an abnormally long period of time after the signal has turned green, and may be slow to respond even after drivers behind honk their horns.

17. Stopping Inappropriately – 35%

Here the observed vehicle stops at an inappropriate location or under inappropriate conditions. Examples include:

- Stopping in a prohibited zone
- Stopping at a crosswalk far short of the stop limit line
- Stopping well past the stop limit line
- Stopping well into an oncoming traffic lane

The drawing below illustrates an example of the last two clues.

Figure 4.10 Shows that driver has stopped passed the limit line and well into oncoming traffic.

18. Turning Abruptly or Illegally – 35%

The driver executes any turn that is abnormally abrupt or illegal. Specific examples include:

- Turning with excessive speed
- Turning sharply from the wrong lane

- Making an illegal U-turn
- Turning outside a designated turn lane

This latter indicator is illustrated in the drawing below where the vehicle is making an abrupt left turn from the normal right-turn lane.

Figure 4.11 Drawing depicts driver making an illegal left turn from the normal through or right turn lane.

19. Accelerating or Decelerating Rapidly – 30%

This clue includes any speed-up or slow-down that is considerably more rapid than that required by the traffic conditions. Rapid acceleration might be accompanied by braking actions. Rapid deceleration might be accompanied by an abrupt stop. Also, a vehicle might alternately accelerate or decelerate rapidly.

20. Headlights Off – 30%

At night, when the use of headlights is required, the vehicle is observed being driven with both headlights off. Also, sometimes an intoxicated driver will turn on the vehicle's parking lights, only, even when headlights are obviously needed.

Note: the 20 indicators or visual clues are listed above in descending order of probability that the person observed is driving while intoxicated. (Courtesy of the Institute of Police Technology and Management (IPTM), University of North Florida, Jacksonville)

Locating the DWI Offender

DWI violations can occur anywhere at any time, and, therefore, the officer should always be vigilant to detect offenses. However, violations can be expected to occur more often at certain times and places such as in the vicinity of night clubs, bars, taverns, and recreational or resort facilities dispensing alcoholic beverages. Also be alert in the vicinity of public events such as sporting events, fairs, music or folk festivals—especially where young people in groups would be inclined to abuse alcohol or drugs. The times when most offenses occur are weekends, holidays, paydays, and evening hours, especially Friday and Saturday. As might be expected, more drunk drivers are on the road an hour or two just before and after the bars close.

The Driving While Intoxicated (DWI) Stop

Driving under the influence of alcohol—or drugs—is a misdemeanor. This is true even if the driver was involved in an accident, providing that no one was injured or killed. Driving while intoxicated, on the other hand, is a felony if there was a violation of a traffic law and the violation is the proximate (real or actual) cause of injuries or death to anyone other than the driver.

In stopping the suspected drinking driver, the standard procedure for traffic stops is observed, along with the following precautions:

1. Leave additional distance between the patrol unit and the suspected violator, as the drinking driver may panic upon observing the police vehicle.
2. Be alert for unusual maneuvers such as braking in the middle of the street, pulling to the left to stop, stopping and starting suddenly, backing up in unusual ways.

3. Observe the suspect's vehicle closely, as it may not have been taken out of gear due to the confused state of the driver.

When selecting the site for the traffic stop, choose a wide, flat, well-lighted area whenever possible. This provides the maximum safety for field testing purposes.

The Driver

The prescribed method for the officer-violator contact should be followed, with the officer being alert for the following indications of intoxication:

1. The odor of an alcoholic beverage about the driver or the vehicle
2. Uncoordinated actions by the driver, such as the inability to properly alight from the vehicle, fumbling and searching for a driver's license, and the inability to remove it from the wallet holder
3. Slurred speech, bloodshot eyes, clothing in disarray, and the use of one's automobile for support.

In addition, the officer should closely observe the gait and stance of the driver. A broad, duck-footed stance with a continuous movement in the shoulders to correct the tendency to sway may indicate an experienced drinker who has learned to cope with the physical reactions to alcohol in this manner.

Field Testing

After careful observation of the suspected drinking driver, if the officer feels that intoxication is a possibility, a field test should be conducted. Field testing, if possible, should always be conducted on a smooth, flat surface in a well-lighted area. In addition, the officer should be alert to the possibility of subjects falling or otherwise injuring themselves due to an intoxicated state. If available, a back-up officer is preferred to assist for safety purposes.

Finger-to-nose Test

Subject stands erect, eyes closed, arms outstretched, index fingers extended. On command, subject attempts to touch the tip of his or her nose with the extended index finger—first with one hand, then the other. This test demonstrates the subject's ability to coordinate movements.

Balance Test

The subject is given verbal instructions and a visual demonstration to: (1) stand erect with heels and toes touching, (2) both arms outstretched from sides with palms upward, (3) head back and eyes closed, and (4) stand still and not to sway. The subject is told to hold this position until told to stop. The officer should observe any swaying motion or loss of position.

Figure 4.12 Balance test. Subject is told to stand erect with arms outstretched, head back and eyes closed. Swaying motion or loss of balance could indicate intoxication.

Raised Foot, Leg Lift Test

The subject is given verbal instructions and a visual demonstration to: (1) stand erect with both arms to sides, (2) raise right or left leg (as directed) about 6 to 9 inches extended in front with the knee straight, (3) remain in that position and (4) count rapidly from 1001 to 1030 while looking at the raised foot. Test the subject using first one leg then the other.

The officer should note and document any sudden dropping of the foot and leg, along with the ability to count accurately while maintaining balance on one foot.

Figure 4.13 Raised foot or leg lift test. Officer should note subject's need to drop foot and leg to maintain balance, and ability to accurately count while maintaining balance on one leg.

Heel-to-Toe—Walking the Line Test

The subject is given verbal instructions and a visual demonstration to: (1) begin placing the right foot in front of left foot on a straight line so the heel touches the toe, and (2) remain in that position. When told to begin, the subject is to (3) walk nine steps heel-to-toe on the line, (4) turn around and take nine steps back, heel-to-toe. The subject is to make the turn by (5) keeping one foot on the line and to (6) count the steps aloud. The entire test is demonstrated prior to asking the subject to attempt it. The officer should note and document any deviations from a straight line walk, loss of balance, and note any quick stepping movements to regain balance to avoid falling down.

Figure 4.14 Heel-to-toe—walking-the-line test. Officer should note any loss of balance, ability to count steps taken or deviation from a straight-line, heel-to-toe walk.

Counting Backwards Test

The subject is told to start counting from 90 backwards to 70 and stop. The officer should note any mistakes in counting, slurred, slow, or unduly deliberate speech.

Nystagmus Testing

Nystagmus is the rapid involuntary oscillation of the eyeballs. Even though many law enforcement agencies still administer this test to a DWI suspect, in some jurisdictions it has been challenged for accuracy when used to measure true intoxication. Therefore, because of some doubt, many agencies are no longer formally presenting the presence of nystagmus as evidence in court. However, many officers still look for nystagmus, along with other balance and coordination tests to assist in the preliminary determination of "under the influence."

The Report Form

The violation of driving while intoxicated must be documented in detail to assist the prosecuting attorney's office. All observations of the suspect driver before the stop and during the investigation need to be reported on proper forms. Accuracy is extremely important, and if forms are not complete, dismissal of the defendant is possible. Therefore, the Alcohol Influence Report Form should be filled in both front and back in all cases.

If an individual refuses to submit to the chemical test or any other test, a special form is used.

Evidence

In making the DWI arrest the officer should be alert for the following physical evidence which lends support to a charge of drug or alcohol intoxication:

- Alcoholic beverage bottles
- Beer cans
- Flasks
- Cups or glasses containing liquid
- Foil wraps from narcotics
- Pill containers
- Loose pills or marijuana

This evidence should be handled as all evidence in criminal cases and, in addition, can be submitted to the lab for identification of contents if necessary.

D.U.I. ARREST SUPPLEMENTAL REPORT

Location			RD	Date		Time	DR #

Name Last		First		Middle		DOB	CDL #

VEHICLE INFO:	Year	Veh. Make	Veh. Model	Veh. Style	Veh. Color	Veh. License	State

EYES:	BREATH:
PUPILS:	EXITING VEH:
FACE:	WALKING:
SPEECH:	STANDING:

Are you taking medicine or drugs/type?	What have you been drinking? how much?	With whom were you drinking?

Where (if A.B.C. licensed premises give full address of business	Time Now?	Time of first drink?	Time of last drink?

Actual time	Where were you stopped by officers?	Where were you going when stopped?	What have you eaten today?

Where did you eat?	When?	When did you last sleep?	How long?

Do you feel the effects of drinking?	Veh. have any mechanical defects?	Is your license suspended?	Have you ever been arrested for DUI?

Any medical or physical defect that would cause subject to appear intoxicated, when in fact he or she was not? Yes No If yes, explain in additional narrative	Roadway Conditions: Location of sobriety test, conditions	traffic heavy moderate light

If T/C involved, ask the following 7 questions:	Were you driving the vehicle? ☐ Yes ☐ No	If No, who was?	Was engine hood warm? ☐ Yes ☐ No
Did you bump your head? Yes No	Have you been drinking since the accident? ☐ Yes ☐ No ☐ N/A	What?	How much?

FIELD BALANCE AND COORDINATION TEST AND OBSERVATIONS:

TEST #1
Subject was given verbal instructions and a visual demonstration by me to: Stand erect with heels and toes touching, both arms outstretched from sides with palms upward, head tilted back and eyes closed not to sway, to stand still. Subject was told to hold this position until told to stop. In this position subject was observed to:

TEST #2
Subject was given verbal instructions and a visual demonstration by me to: Stand erect with both arms to sides, and raise directed leg in the air approximately 6" - 9" with knees straight, and remain in that position while counting rapidly from 1001 to 1030 while looking at your raised foot

Right leg raised:

Left leg raised:

TEST #3
Subject was given verbal instructions and a visual demonstration by me to: Begin by placing right foot in front of left foot on a straight line so the heel touches the toe, and remain in that position. When told to begin, subject is to walk nine steps heel to toe on a straight line, turn around and take nine steps heel to toe back. Make your turn by keeping one foot on the line. Count your steps aloud. (Entire test is demonstrated prior to subject attempting it).

WALK AND TURN TEST	Explain: Balance, Walking & Turning

TEST #4 COUNT BACKWARDS FROM 90 - 70.

MISSES #'S: 90 89 88 87 86 85 84 83 82 81 80 79 78 77 76 75 74 73 72 71 70

SLURRED ☐ SLOW, DELIBERATE ☐

Figure 4.15A DWI Arrest Supplemental Report form. To be completed by the officer at the scene during the course of the investigation (front).

ADDITIONAL EXAMS OR OBSERVATIONS

ATTITUDE

Polite ☐ Cooperative ☐ Excited ☐ Talkative ☐ Antagonistic ☐ Combative ☐ Other

	Name		DOB	Address		Phone (H)
WITNESS PASSENGER						(W)
WITNESS PASSENGER	Name		DOB	Address		Phone (H)
						(W)
WITNESS PASSENGER	Name		DOB	Address		Phone (H)
						(W)
WITNESS PASSENGER	Name		DOB	Address		Phone (H)
						(W)

Vehicle Location		Locked	Towing Agency if Towed	Owner's Request?
		☐ Yes ☐ No		☐ Yes ☐ No

CHEMICAL TEST ADMONITION (23157 V.C.)

I admonished the driver:

1. You are required by state law to submit to a chemical test to determine the alcoholic content of your blood.

2. You have the choice of taking a blood, breath, or urine test.
   WHEN APPLICABLE: Since you need medical treatment, your choice is limited to _____. These tests are only available
   _____ TEST(S) NAME
   at _____ FACILITY

3. If you refuse to submit to, or fail to complete a test, your driving privilege will be suspended for one year or revoked for two or three years. A two year revocation will result if the refusal occurred within seven years of a separate violation of driving under the influence and/or such a charge reduced to reckless driving, or vehicular manslaughter which resulted in a conviction or an administrative determination that you refused testing or were driving with an excessive concentration of alcohol on a separate occasion. A three year revocation will result if you had more than one of these violations or administrative determinations within the last seven years.

4. Refusal or failure to complete a test may be used against you in court. Refusal or failure to complete a test will also result in a fine and imprisonment if this arrest results in a conviction of driving under the influence.

5. You do not have the right to talk to an attorney or have an attorney present before stating whether you will submit to a test, before deciding which test to take, or during the test.

6. If you cannot complete the test you choose, you must submit to and complete a remaining test.

The above Chemical Test Admonition was read to arrestee by: (Name)_____
(Please sign if person is other than the officer certifying this statement.)

☐ Admonition given in Spanish or (Language)_____

Response to: Will you take breath test?_____ Urine test?_____ Blood test?_____
The person arrested refused to submit to or failure to complete any such test. The refusal or failure was indicated by the following statements or actions.

CHEMICAL TESTS: VIAL # _____ ARM _____

BLOOD: Date _____ Time _____ Location _____ By _____

BREATH: Date _____ Time _____ Location _____ By _____ Results #1 _____ #2 ____ #3_____

URINE: Date _____ Time No. 1 _____ Time No. 2 _____ Location _____ Disposition of Urine _____

REFUSAL: Read 13353 CVC ☐ Yes ☐ No. If yes, indicate time read. _____

Investigating Officer #1	Serial No	Investigating Officer #2	Serial No	Approving Supervisor		Records

Figure 4.15B Reverse side of DWI Arrest Supplemental Report Form. Note Chemical Test Admonition required by California and most all other jurisdictions.

OFFICER'S STATEMENT
SECTIONS 13353.2 AND 13353 VEHICLE CODE
☐ BAC .08   ☐ REFUSAL (Complete reverse)
(Complete in black ink.)

LAW ENFORCEMENT CASE NO. OR CITATION NO.

DRIVER LICENSE NO.   STATE

NAME (LAST, FIRST, M.I.)   DOB

RIGHT THUMB PRINT

MAILING ADDRESS   STATE   ZIP CODE

NOTE: PLEASE COMPLETE PHYSICAL DESCRIPTION OF DRIVER:
Sex: Age: Hair: Eyes: Ht.:   Wt.:

Vehicle License Number _____

☐ Violation occurred in a vehicle requiring a commercial driver license (Section 15210 VC).

The above named driver was ☐ observed driving ☐ in or about a vehicle blocking a roadway (Section 40300.5 VC) or ☐ involved in an accident on _____ at _____ AM/PM in _____ CA. I had reasonable cause to believe the driver was driving or in actual physical control of a motor vehicle while under the influence. The driver was **arrested** for violation of Section 23152 or 23153 VC on _____ at _____ AM/PM.

PROBABLE CAUSE for stop or contact **(Traffic Collision:** ☐ Yes ☐ No). Please **describe in detail** the facts and circumstances that led to the stop or contact: _____

Objective symptoms of intoxication ☐ Bloodshot/watery eyes ☐ Odor of alcoholic beverage ☐ Unsteady gait ☐ Slurred speech ☐ Other _____

Did you observe the person driving? ☐ Yes ☐ No (if not, show observer's name below or explain) _____

OTHER OBSERVER/WITNESS. If driving was observed, driver was arrested, or the accident was witnessed by another officer or person, please complete the following:

	NAME/ID NUMBER	ADDRESS/AGENCY	TELEPHONE NO.
Other Officer			
Citizen			
Witness			

.08 BAC SUSPENSION (13353.2 V.C.)
Driver submitted to and completed a chemical test(s) of: ☐ Blood ☐ Breath (see below) ☐ Urine.
(A DS 367A for blood and urine test results must be submitted within 20 days.) TIME OF TEST: _____ AM/PM.

BREATH TEST RESULTS
Breath test results were: BAC Test 1 _____ Test 2 _____ **(Attach a copy of the results.)**
BREATH TEST MACHINE OPERATOR'S CERTIFICATION
I certify under penalty of perjury, that the above breath test sample results were obtained in the regular course of my duties. I further certify that I am qualified to operate this equipment and that the test was administered pursuant to the requirements of Title 17 of the California Code of Regulations.
Executed at _____ , CA, on _____
Signature **X** _____ , ID _____ , Agency _____

FORWARD THE FOLLOWING DOCUMENTS WITH THIS FORM: ☐ Order of Suspension or Revocation (issued: ☐ Yes ☐ No)
☐ Driver license (☐ attached—if not attached, explain) _____

NAME OF OFFICER (PLEASE PRINT)   BADGE NO.

AGENCY   AREA   PHONE NO.
(   )

Executed at _____ on _____
                CITY   COUNTY   STATE   DATE
I certify, under penalty of perjury, that the information on both sides of this form is true and correct.

Signature of Officer **X** _____

Reverse side of form must be completed for Chemical Test Refusal.

Figure 4.16 California Department of Motor Vehicles (DMV) Officer's Statement - Chemical Test Form. To be completed by officer at time breath, blood or urine testing.

CHEMICAL TEST REFUSAL
(SECTION 13353 VEHICLE CODE)

CHEMICAL TEST ADMONITION (23157 V.C.)

I admonished the driver at _____ AM/PM:
1. You are required by state law to submit to a chemical test to determine the alcoholic content of your blood.
2. You have the choice of taking a blood, breath, or urine test.

   WHEN APPLICABLE: Since you need medical treatment, your choice is limited to _____ . These tests are
   TEST(S) NAME

   only available at _____ .
   FACILITY

3. If you refuse to submit to, or fail to complete a test, your driving privilege will be suspended for one year or revoked for two or three years. A two year revocation will result if the refusal occurred within seven years of a separate violation of driving under the influence and/or such a charge reduced to reckless driving, or vehicular manslaughter which resulted in a conviction or an administrative determination that you refused testing or were driving with an excessive concentration of alcohol on a separate occasion. A three year revocation will result if you had more than one of these violations or administrative determinations within the last seven years.
4. Refusal or failure to complete a test may be used against you in court. Refusal or failure to complete a test will also result in a fine and imprisonment if this arrest results in a conviction of driving under the influence.
5. You do not have the right to talk to an attorney or have an attorney present before stating whether you will submit to a test, before deciding which test to take, or during the test.
6. If you cannot, or state you cannot, complete the test you choose, you must submit to and complete a remaining test.

If the above Chemical Test Admonition was read to arrestee by another officer, please show:

Name _____ I.D. No. _____ Telephone No. ( ) _____

Admonition was given in ☐ Spanish ☐ Other Language *(Specify)* _____

Response to: Will you take a breath test? _____

Urine test? _____

Blood test? _____

The driver refused to submit to or failed to complete any such test. The refusal or failure was indicated by the following statements or actions: _____

DRUG ADMONITION SUPPLEMENT

Complete the following when the breath test has been completed and you believe the driver is under the influence of drugs. The driver MUST be given a choice of the blood or urine test even if the officer knows the drug will not show up in the test chosen. The officer CANNOT limit the test to be given.

I believe the driver to have been driving under the influence of a drug and/or an alcoholic beverage. In addition to the test results and information listed on the front, my belief is based on the following facts: _____

DRUG ADMONITION: Blood and Urine Only

1. The breath test you have just taken is designed to detect only the alcoholic content of your blood.
2. Because I believe you are under the influence of drugs or a combination of drugs and alcohol, you are required by state law to submit to a blood or urine test to determine the drug content of your blood.
3. If you refuse to submit to, or fail to complete a test, your driving privilege will be suspended for one year or revoked for two or three years. A two year revocation will result if the refusal occurred within seven years of a separate violation of driving under the influence and/or such a charge reduced to reckless driving, or vehicular manslaughter which resulted in a conviction or an administrative determination that you refused testing or were driving with an excessive concentration of alcohol on a separate occasion. A three year revocation will result if you had more than one of these violations or administrative determinations within the last seven years.
4. Refusal or failure to complete a test may be used against you in court. Refusal or failure to complete a test will also result in a fine and imprisonment if this arrest results in a conviction of driving under the influence.
5. You do not have the right to talk to an attorney or have an attorney present before stating whether you will submit to a test, before deciding which test to take, or during the test.
6. If you cannot, or state you cannot, complete the test you choose, you must submit to and complete the remaining test.

Response to: Will you take a blood test? _____

Urine test? _____

The driver refused to submit to or failed to complete any such test. The refusal or failure was indicated by the following statements or actions: _____

If the Drug Admonition above was read to the arrestee after the driver submitted to a breath test by another officer, please show:

Name _____ I.D. No. _____ Telephone No. ( ) _____

Figure 4.17 California DMV Chemical Test Refusal Form. To be completed by the officer after driver refuses to take either breath, blood or urine test.

Transporting of Driver and Passengers

The officer should keep in mind that the arrested individual is in a state of intoxication and is likely to act in an irrational manner and perhaps fall or injure him or herself. You should use caution in transportation to prevent injury to yourself, as well. If necessary, intoxicated passengers can be arrested for being drunk in an automobile or drunk in public. If they are not, they may leave in a taxi.

CHEMICAL TESTING

The following types of tests are available for determining the blood alcohol level of an individual:

1. Blood Test: Often used in accident cases where a breath test cannot be readily obtained
2. Breath Test: The most common—very accurate and easiest available
3. Urine Test: Not as often used

Chemical tests are administered by trained police personnel or laboratory technicians at the booking area. Breath tests are most commonly chosen by the offenders. The Intoxilyzer® is one brand commonly used. Other tests can also be requested.

Figure 4.18 The Intoxilyzer® 5000 alcohol breath tester. Suspect DWI driver blows through a tube into the machine for an immediate printed BAC report.

Chemical Test Admonishment

The chemical test admonishment document can be used to advise the suspect of his or her obligations to complete the chemical test chosen. The subject's choice is confirmed and well documented with authorized signatures. Warnings of the consequences of refusing to take or complete the test are clearly stated. Also, a statement is included on the form to advise the suspect that breath samples cannot be retained and one of the other tests can be selected which will provide samples for future review.

Implied Consent Laws

Most states have an implied consent law that requires a person to take the chemical test for intoxication if requested to do so after the suspect's arrest for DWI. Failure to consent to the test procedure causes the person's driver's license to be automatically suspended. In addition, most implied consent laws have provisions establishing the blood-alcohol limits necessary for conviction.

COURT TESTIMONY

The following material is being presented in order to better acquaint officers with the proceedings in a trial for drunk driving. The material covered in the following questions will be included in every drunk driving case in which you are called to be a witness for the People. The form and wording of the questions will vary, depending upon the facts and the attorney prosecuting the case. However, the general information contained herein will always be covered.

Prior to testifying, it is, of course, beneficial for the officer to discuss the case with the prosecutor. The officer may contact the attorney handling the case on the day before the trial. At this time, the officer should be informed as to whether the case will actually go to trial, in order to avoid sitting around in court when the case is to be continued. Also at this time, the officer should advise the prosecutor of any exceptional facts about the case.

It is suggested that during the period of time between the date when the case is listed on the calendar and when the trial actually begins, the officer should discuss in person with the prosecutor the general testimony to be given in the case.

ORANGE COUNTY SHERIFF-CORONER DEPARTMENT
INTOXILYZER 5000 PRECAUTIONARY CHECKLIST

(TO BE COMPLETED BY OFFICER, ALSO COMPLETE OFFICER'S BREATH TEST OBSERVATION BELOW)

DATE OF TEST _____ ARRESTING AGENCY _____ CASE NUMBER _____

OFFICER'S NAME _____

SUBJECT'S NAME _____ SUB. DOB _____

NOTE: Subject must be under continuous observation from 15 minutes prior to the first breath sample until the final breath sample is collected. During this time, he/she must not eat, drink, or smoke anything and must not belch, burp, vomit, or regurgitate. If any of the above occurs, the test must be discontinued and the observation restarted or the subject must choose another chemical test.

OFFICER'S OBSERVATION OF SUBJECT FOR BREATH TEST STARTED AT: _____ ; ENDED AT: _____ .

OFFICER'S INITIALS: [____]

OPERATOR'S OBSERVATION OF SUBJECT FOR BREATH TEST STARTED AT: _____ . OPR. INITIALS: [____]

TO BEGIN TEST: (OPERATOR MUST EITHER RESPOND TO OR COMPLETE EACH ITEM)

1. Ask subject "Do you have any breathing problems?" ☐ yes ☐ no OPR. Initials: [____]
   If yes, describe: _____

2. Record the following: **Instrument S/N 64-00** __ __ __ __ SIM. LOT# _____ VALUE 0. _____ %

3. Press green start button and follow Intoxilyzer 5000 instructions. SIM. TEMP. _____ °C
   (Use keyboard to enter information requested by display; press return after keyboard entries. After "N" is typed for "Review Data? Y/N", data is no longer entered with keyboard; write requested information in the appropriate spaces.)

WRITE CLOCK TIME	RECORD RESULTS

	AIR BLANK	CAL. CHECK	AIR BLANK	OPR. BREATH	AIR BLANK
of timepiece used for observation statement	0. _____	0. _____	0. _____	0. _____	0. _____

4. Demonstrate to the subject how to give a proper breath sample. Check that breath tube is warm. OPR. Initials: [____]

5. Discard operator's mouthpiece; place subject's mouthpiece into breath tube.

6. Ask the subject "Have you belched, burped, regurgitated, or vomited during the last 15 minutes?"
   Response: ☐ yes ☐ no OPR. Initials: [____] (If yes, press the green start button to discontinue the test.)
   RECORD RESULTS

SUB. BREATH	AIR BLANK	SUB. BREATH	AIR BLANK	SUB. BREATH	AIR BLANK
0. _____	0. _____	0. _____	0. _____	0. _____	0. _____

* Complete only if 2 breath results do not agree within a 0.02%.

7. Ask the subject "Have you belched, burped, regurgitated, or vomited during the test?" ☐ yes ☐ no OPR. Initials: [____]
   Comments: _____

8. Discard subject's mouthpiece. Insert test card when directed by the Intoxilyzer 5000.

9. I completed my continuous observation of the subject at _____ (time), by which time the breath sampling on the subject had been completed. OPR. Initials: [____]

10. After card is printed, press green start button once to reprint card or twice to complete test. Obtain the subject's right thumbprint on test card. Sign test card, include date and time.
    ATTACH TEST CARD TO INTOXILYZER 5000 PRECAUTIONARY CHECKLIST.

ADDITIONAL COMMENTS: _____

Operator's signature _____ Agency _____ Date/Time _____

Figure 4.19 Form to be completed by specially trained Intoxilyzer® operator at time of test. *(Courtesy of Orange County, CA Sheriff-Coroner's Department)*

Costa Mesa Police Department
ADMONISHMENT REGARDING CHEMICAL TEST

You are required by state law to submit to a chemical test to determine the alcoholic and drug content of your blood. You have the choice of whether the test is to be of your blood, breath, or urine. If you refuse to submit to, or fail to complete, a test, your driving privilege will be suspended 6 months, or revoked for 2 or 3 years. A 2-year revocation will result if you have been convicted within the last 5 years of driving under the influence, including such a charge reduced to reckless driving. A 3-year revocation will result if you had more than one of these convictions within the last 5 years. Refusal or failure to complete a test may be used against you in court. Refusal or failure to complete a test will also result in a fine and imprisonment if this arrest results in a conviction of driving under the influence. You do not have the right to talk to an attorney or have an attorney present before stating whether you will submit to a test, before deciding which test to take, or during the test. If you cannot complete the test you choose, you must submit to and complete a remaining test.

Which chemical test do you choose? (circle one)

Blood Test   **Breath Test**   **Urine Test**

You are further advised that the breath-testing equipment does not retain any sample of the breath and, therefore, no breath sample will be available after the test which could be analyzed by you or any other person. Because no breath sample is retained, you will be given an opportunity, if you **desire,** to provide a blood or urine sample that will be collected and retained, at no cost to you, and that may be subsequently analyzed for the alcoholic content of your blood, by either party, in any criminal prosecution.

Do you desire to provide a blood or urine sample to be retained?

◻ No   ◻ Yes   (circle one)   Blood   Urine

_____
Arrestee's Signature

_____
Admonishing Officer's Signature

1060-42(PD 273) revised 7/86

Figure 4.20 Typical DWI chemical test admonishment and test selection form. *(Courtesy of Costa Mesa, CA Police Department)*

While testifying, the officer will be much more effective if testimony is directed to the jury or the judge, as the case may be, and not solely to the prosecutor asking questions. In a jury trial, a conversational tone of voice between the officer and that member of the jury sitting farthest away will make the officer appear to be addressing the entire jury.

Points to Be Covered by Officer's Testimony on the Stand

When on the stand, the officer should be prepared to answer questions relating to the case. He should be thoroughly familiar with details regarding the following points:

1. Customary DWI report
    *   Facts attracting attention of officer
    *   Unusual driving by defendant
    *   Symptoms of alcoholic influence
    *   Coordination tests
    *   Manner of speech (slurred, incoherent)
    *   Blood or breath tests
    *   General conduct of defendant at the scene, and at the station
    *   Statements of defendant

2. Accident follow-up report—if accident involved
    *   General description of accident scene
    *   Names, addresses, and phone numbers of witnesses not involved who can identify the driver and testify to his or her behavior while driving
    *   Admission of driving by defendant
    *   Coordination tests
    *   Manner of speech
    *   Blood or breath tests
    *   Statements of defendant

3. Degree of intoxication

An officer should recognize the difference between a suspicion and an opinion. Suspicions are formed immediately. The officer has a duty to be suspicious if the defendant's driving, conduct, speech, and attitude seem to indicate some form of intoxication. Opinions are formed after seeing the defendant walk, talk, stand, and move, but before coordination tests are given. Tests are given to confirm the officer's opinion.

Cross-Examination

After the prosecutor has the officer tell his or her story, the defendant's attorney has the right to question the officer.

1. Purpose of cross-examination by defendant's attorney.
   - To show officer in error
   - To show officer forgetful
   - To show officer unobservant
   - To show officer opinionated
   - To show officer untrustworthy
   - To show officer angered
   - To show officer discourteous

2. Points to remember under cross-examination
   - Do not become angered at attorney.
   - Do not be afraid to say "I don't know," if such is true.
   - Do not answer questions too quickly.

Protection of the Officer by Prosecutor

The officer should remember that:

1. the prosecuting attorney deserves your trust
2. truth never needs protection
3. deliberate, straightforward, clear-cut answers are most effective

Legal Use of Notes on the Witness Stand

The officer may use notes on the witness stand if notes are authorized by state statute and written by the officer (or under the officer's direction) while the incident is still fresh in the officer's mind. The defense attorney must be allowed to inspect these notes in their entirety and may read them to the jury.

Common DWI Defense Tactics

The defense attorney may use the following tactics to influence the jury.

1. Erratic driving
    - Making an illegal turn, etc., does not necessarily mean that the driver was impaired.

2. Failure to stop immediately
    - The driver may have had the vehicle's windows up.
    - Conditions (e.g., rain) may have prevented the defendant from stopping immediately.
    - The police unit may have been too far from the DWI suspect's vehicle to judge accurately.

3. Odor of alcohol
    - Pure alcohol has no odor.
    - Odor of alcoholic beverage might mean that the driver had only one drink prior to being stopped by the officer.

4. Flushed face
    - Driver was excited about being stopped.

5. Bloodshot eyes
    - Driver might have eyestrain or defective vision.
    - Most people have some symptoms of bloodshot eyes.

6. Slurred speech
    - If the officer was able to obtain information from the suspect, he or she could not be too bad.

7. Fumbling for license

- It is possible that plastic stuck to the license, therefore making it hard to remove it from the holder.
- The driver was just nervous about being stopped.

8. Failing Field Test
   - Driver had a physical handicap.
   - Driver may have been nervous.
   - Roadway may not have been level.
   - Lighting may not have been adequate.
   - Officer did not explain and demonstrate the field test first.

In order to present your case fairly and convincingly in court, you must be sure that every word of testimony is correct to the best of your knowledge. For this reason, careful attention to details must be made from the first moment you notice the unusual driving behavior until the case is concluded in court.

Chapter Five

TRAFFIC POINT CONTROL

When working traffic control, your most important job is to let drivers and pedestrians know what it is you want them to do. If they do not understand your signals, they will have trouble and so will you.

The instructions that follow will help to make your signals clear to motorists and pedestrians, alike. When, as an officer directing traffic, it is your job to tell people how, when, and where they may move in vehicles or on foot. You must, therefore, pay attention to both cars and pedestrians and see to it that they are all given an equal chance to move.

What the officer actually does is to tell them how to behave. If you are not on hand to make decisions and direct movements when traffic is heavy, drivers and pedestrians might try to move and take foolish chances. This would cause repeated traffic jams or "gridlock," where no one can move. Motorists could also, without realizing it, get into dangerous situations which they did not anticipate.

Drivers are not often in a position where they can hear you when you want them to stop, so you cannot tell them what to do. You have to use a type of "sign language" which is clearly and universally understood by everyone. You could, of course, motion drivers to stop, start, or turn in many different ways. If each officer were to use his or her own signal system, different from all other officers who direct traffic, obviously chaos would result. Perhaps some of the drivers approaching your corner would understand, but most of them would be puzzled. If they had never experienced such motions before, they might choose to ignore them. Therefore, it is imperative for all officers to use the same system when directing traffic. Equally important, the gestures should be made so that the driver can see them from a long way off.

DIRECTING TRAFFIC BY HAND

When working as a traffic control officer, you must let people know that you are in charge by standing where they cannot fail to see you. This is usually right in the center of the crossing. You must stand there authoritatively and not look as if you have merely been caught in traffic and are just waiting for a chance to get out. You should stand straight with your weight equally distributed on each foot. When not using your hands to signal, you should let them hang easily at your side. You should not face vehicles authorized by you to move, but rather stand with your side toward them.

Right: Ready for business   Wrong: Just waiting

Figure 5.1 Stances for the police traffic officer.

Stopping Traffic

To stop traffic, two motions are used. First, the officer points with the arm and finger and holds this point until the driver sees the officer, or at least until the driver has had plenty of time to do so. Then the officer raises his or her pointing hand (but not his whole arm) so that the palm is toward the driver. He holds this until the driver stops.

The officer has to stop traffic from both directions to give traffic on the cross street a chance. Because you cannot look both ways at once, you stop the traffic coming from one side first, then from the other. After you have halted traffic with one hand, you hold that hand in the stop position and turn to the other side and repeat the process. You do not lower either arm until cars coming from both ways are halted.

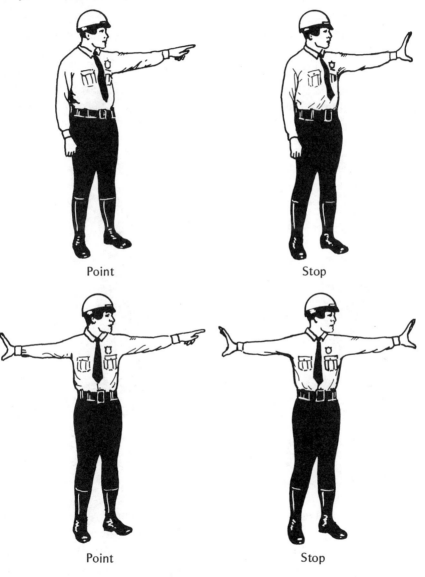

Point   Stop

Point   Stop

Figure 5.2 Arm positions for stopping traffic.

Starting Traffic

To start traffic, stand so that your side is toward the traffic to be started. You then point with your arm and finger toward the car you want to start and hold it until you get the driver's attention. Then, with your palm up, you swing your hand up and over your chin, bending your arm only at the elbow. If you get the attention of the driver first by pointing, you will not have to make the signal a second time. After traffic has been started from one side, drop that arm and start traffic from the other side in the same way. The officer should use the same signals to give the go-ahead to slow and timid drivers.

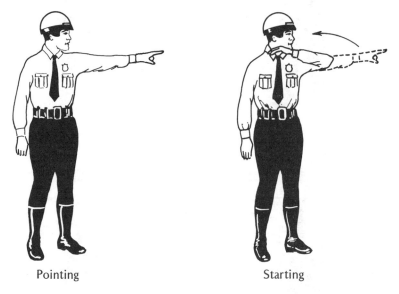

Pointing   Starting

Figure 5.3 Arm positions for starting traffic.

Right Turn

Signals for a right turn movement are not usually required at an intersection. When it is necessary, the arm the officer signals with will be determined by the car's direction. If it approaches from the right, you point toward the driver with your right arm. You give the driver time to see the gesture and then swing your arm to point in the direction the driver is going. The officer keeps pointing in that direction until the driver begins to turn.

If the car approaches you from the left, you point with your left arm. When the driver sees your point, you swing your arm in the direction the driver is to go. Because of your position, you will not be able to make a complete swing with your arm. You may find it more comfortable to bend your left arm at the elbow and indicate the direction the driver is to take with your thumb and forearm.

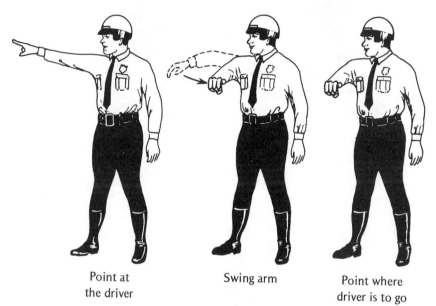

Point at   Swing arm   Point where
the driver   driver is to go

Figure 5.4 Arm positions when directing a right turn.

Left Turn

In helping a driver to make a left turn, you may first have to halt traffic in the lane or lanes through which the turning car must cross. If the car is approaching from your left, you give the stop signal with your right arm to stop traffic in the lane through which the turning driver is to pass. You hold the stop signal with your right arm and then give the turning gesture with the left arm.

If the car approaches from the right, you turn around so that you face the direction the car making the turn is to follow. You halt traffic with your right arm and give the turning gesture with your left arm.

Halt opposing
traffic with
right hand

Hold opposing
traffic and point
to turning driver

Give turn
signal with left
hand

Figure 5.5 Arm position when directing a left turn.

On a street with only one available lane in each direction, one driver wishing to make a left turn can delay many cars behind him or her unless the officer handles this movement properly. If traffic is approaching the left-turning vehicle from the opposite direction, the driver cannot make the turn until there is a gap in the traffic flow. While the driver is waiting, the officer should signal the driver to move into the intersection close to the officer so that the cars behind the driver can continue straight through or make right turns. The officer points a finger at the driver, motions him or her to move forward, and then points to the place on the pavement where the officer wishes the driver to stop. As soon as the driver begins to move, the officer should signal the cars behind the driver to move straight through or turn right. The officer can permit the left turn when there is a natural break in the opposing traffic, or can stop the opposing traffic and signal for the left turn.

Direct
driver into
intersection

Figure 5.6 Arm position when guiding a driver into an intersection.

Two-Officer Signaling

There is sometimes need for more than one officer at a busy intersection or control point. One of the two officers must originate all signals and gestures. In other words, one officer is leader and makes all decisions as to changes in traffic flow. The other officer assists by helping to make those decisions known.

Signaling Aids

The whistle is used to get the attention of drivers and pedestrians. It is used along with the appropriate gesture as follows:

1. One long blast with a **stop** signal
2. Two short blasts with a **go** signal
3. Several short blasts to get the attention of a driver or pedestrian who does not respond to a given signal

Stop   Go   For the daydreamer

Figure 5.7 Use of the whistle in directing traffic.

The officer should be judicious in using the whistle at all times. Whistle blasts directed at pedestrians usually need not be as shrill as those used to command the attention of motorists.

The voice is seldom used in directing traffic. Arm gestures and the whistle are usually sufficient. There are numerous reasons why verbal commands are not used. Verbal orders are not easy to give or understand and often lead to misinterpretations which are dangerous. An order which is shouted can antagonize the motorist. Occasionally, however, a driver or pedestrian will not understand the arm signals. When this happens the officer should move reasonably close to the person and politely and briefly explain the command. In all instances, the officer should address such people properly as Sir, Ma'am, or Miss. You should not shout or lose your temper, even though there may be provocation.

A flashlight can be used to halt traffic in an emergency. To stop traffic the officer slowly swings the flashlight at arm's length across the path of the approaching car. The beam from the flashlight strikes the pavement as an elongated spot of moving light which can be readily seen by the motorist. The officer should not stand directly in front of the approaching car. After the motorist has stopped, arm signals are given in the usual manner. Illumination from headlights will make arm signals visible.

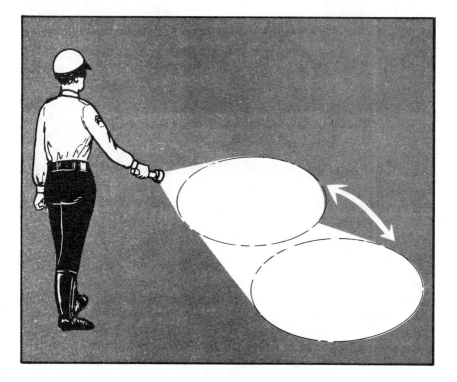

Figure 5.8 Use of the flashlight in emergency situations.

Figure 5.9 Arm signal illuminated by an approaching car.

CONTROLLING THE INTERSECTION

Sometimes there is not room enough in the street for all the drivers who want to use it. Left to themselves, they may get in each others way and a traffic jam will form. This can be so bad as to bring traffic to a standstill ("gridlock"), and impatient drivers may have accidents trying to free themselves from the jam. To keep traffic congestion from becoming a traffic hazard, somebody must act as an "umpire" to decide how cars will move, so that the delay to all concerned will be as short as possible.

The officer is the umpire when assigned to direct vehicle movements. If an officer is on the job, drivers will be glad to wait until he or she tells them it is their turn to move because they know the officer is trying to make the best possible use of the street and that he or she can prevent the jams which they all dread. Traffic signals often help to prevent jams, but there are not signals at every intersection where a jam may occur. Signals cannot always do the job alone, especially when a few drivers try to take advantage of others by committing violations which call for enforcement action.

The minute an officer takes his or her station, the officer becomes responsible for the smooth flow of traffic and for preventing or breaking jams at his post or intersection. You, as a traffic control officer, are expected to handle all of the following tasks as needed.

1. Regulate cross flow, that is, tell whether east and west or north and south traffic will move and for how long a time
2. Control turning movements, especially left turns
3. Coordinate vehicle movement at the intersection with movement in adjacent blocks and at neighboring intersections
4. Detour traffic in emergencies
5. Supervise signal obedience, if necessary directing traffic to disregard signal indications
6. Protect pedestrians crossing streets or highways
7. Restrain pedestrians from jaywalking and illegal crossings
8. Prevent illegal parking, double parking, or standing (parked with driver inside) of vehicles near the officer's post, especially if it interferes with traffic movement
9. Provide for the safe passage of emergency vehicles
10. Assist people seeking information
11. Handle accidents at the intersection or within your area of control, at least until an accident investigation unit can take over
12. Carry out general police work within his area

Officer's Position in the Intersection

One of the first problems is: Where does the officer stand? When you are working at regular intersections where no signals are operating, you usually stand near the center (position 1). From there you can see what is going on around you, and you can be seen by drivers and pedestrians on all the streets coming into the intersection.

However, the center of the intersection is not always the ideal place to stand. This position may not be good when signals are operating at irregular intersections, at one-way street crossings, when traffic is especially heavy in one direction, or when you have special rules to enforce. The most common alternate positions are at the corner (position 2) where your post best meets the particular requirements or at the center of one street (position 3) where it enters the intersection.

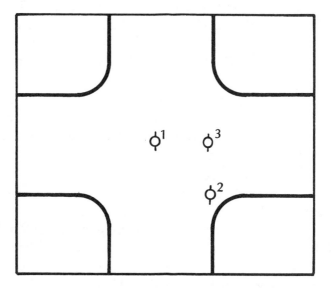

Figure 5.10 Position of officer directing traffic in an intersection.

An officer should take an alternate position only after considering the limitations of your effectiveness at that position. Some of the points to keep in mind when choosing a place to stand are:

1. Can you see and be seen by all approaching lines of traffic and by pedestrians?
2. Will you interfere with the free movement of traffic and thus be forced to shift positions continually?
3. Can you handle all turning movements from that point?
4. Can you direct pedestrian movement from that point?
5. Are you safe there?

Extent of Regulation

Another problem to be faced is: to what extent should the officer regulate the traffic? Too much regulation wastes time and energy. It may even cause congestion, slowing traffic through an intersection when, if left alone, it would adjust itself.

The same type of caution which makes some motorists reluctant to overtake an officer on the highway appears when they approach one at an intersection. They are careful to an exaggerated extent, thus slowing the flow of traffic. Many will wait for an individual go-ahead signal before proceeding. Officers must, therefore, guard against needless regulation.

Directing Cross Traffic

In directing cross traffic at intersections, the problems range from very light traffic, needing little or no control, to difficult situations involving more or less complete blockage of exits from the intersection.

Uncontrolled Operation

The cars on both streets may be so few that most of them can go right across the intersection without waiting. Those which must stop or slow down can go on after a short pause. The officer should leave this situation alone. If traffic needs no control, you should not stand where it may appear that you are directing traffic.

Simple Interruption

The cars on the main street or main line of travel come so often that a car on the cross street is forced to wait a half minute or more for a gap in the stream of cars before it can cross the intersection. Stepping into position, and waiting until there is a slight gap or slackening of travel on the main street, the officer should halt this traffic, allowing the car on the cross street to go through. After it has crossed, you should start traffic on the main street once more.

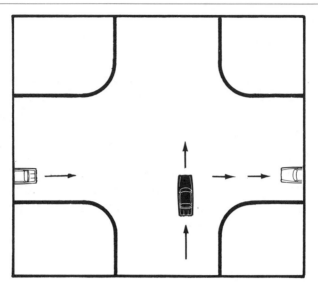

Figure 5.11 Intersection where no traffic control is needed.

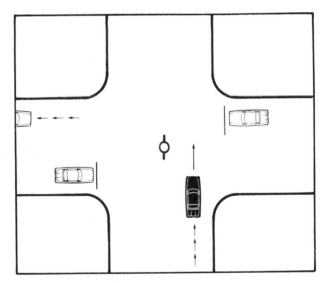

Figure 5.12 Direction needed to move cross-street traffic.

Grouping for Interruption

When there are several cars approaching on the cross street, the officer should stop the first to arrive until a small group has been formed. After this is done, you should halt the main street traffic and let the group enter. You should keep this cross-street traffic moving as long as cars come continuously. At the first gap, you should start the main street traffic going again. Do not keep cars on cross streets, in hopes of gathering a group for the crossing, for more than about a minute, nor try to clear stragglers who lag behind a group.

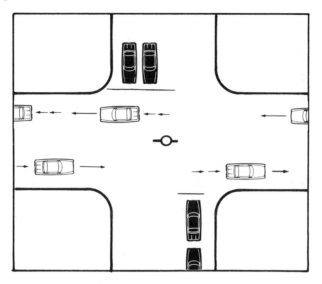

Figure 5.13 Formation of a group on the cross street.

Simple Alternation

When traffic on the cross street is continuous, the officer may have to halt it to let the main street traffic go. You should let cross-street traffic run until it thins out a bit and then halt it to let traffic on the main street run, so that it will not fill the block back to the next corner. Sometimes there is about as much traffic on the cross street as on the main street. When this situation exists, you should let the traffic flow on each street about the same length of time.

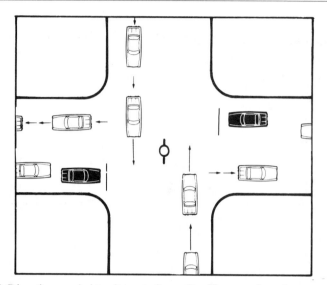

Figure 5.14 Direction needed to alternate flow of traffic on main and cross streets.

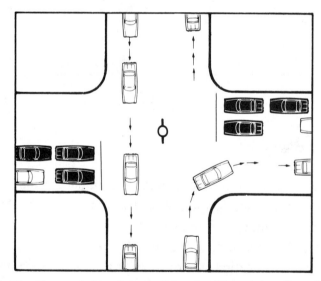

Figure 5.15 Direction needed to alternate flow of traffic on when flow of traffic is heavy.

Critical Alternation

As the traffic on both streets gets heavier, it should be allowed to run longer in each direction. This is necessary to reduce the time lost in frequent change of flow. In this situation the officer must be alert to prevent trouble. You should not let any car enter the intersection unless there is a place for it to leave. This means that you must watch the exit lanes, where cars are going, as well as where they are coming from. In other words, be careful not to fill any exit lane to its full capacity. The blocking, by filling up a lane which causes cars to jam in the intersection, usually occurs suddenly and needs to be avoided by careful attention.

Directing Turning Movements

Right turns, if made from the right lane, do not cut across the path of other cars. Therefore, they are easy to handle. In practice, the officer will find that they almost take care of themselves.

If a driver wishes to make a right turn across a line of traffic moving in the same direction on the driver's right, he or she is in the wrong lane. Except in unusual conditions, the officer should not stop the moving traffic to let him or her turn. To rescue this driver from an improper position in the roadway only serves to encourage further violations. One unusual situation altering this general rule is found in instances where a bus has stopped at the curb to load or unload. The motorist will then find it necessary to make his or her turn from the next lane.

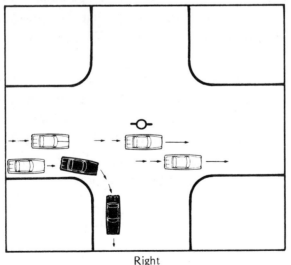

Right

Figure 5.16 Right turns from proper lanes take care of themselves. Do not permit right turns from wrong lanes.

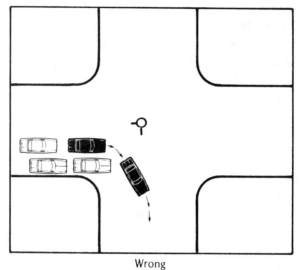

Wrong

Figure 5.16 Continued

Cross traffic rarely has to be stopped to let right-turning traffic join or merge with it. If the cross traffic does not offer natural gaps that permit a turn, it should be interrupted to give the car trying to turn an opportunity to do so. This is comparable to interrupting through traffic for cross traffic—except that through traffic needs to be stopped in only one direction. Traffic in the other direction can keep going.

Right turns need to be delayed or prohibited only when the street the turning car enters is filled up; when they interfere too much with pedestrian traffic; or when the traffic which they will join is very heavy and cannot be stopped to let them in. In these cases, drivers wishing to turn right may be halted until they can turn or be instructed to go on across the intersection.

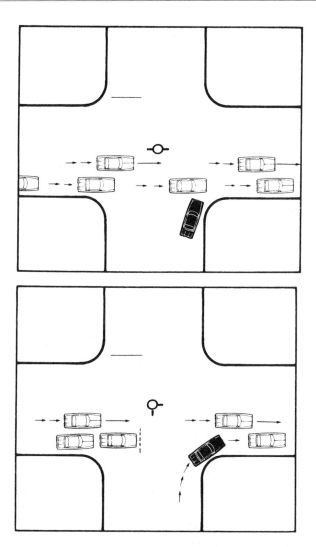

Figure 5.17 When a right turn joins heavy cross traffic, one lane of cross traffic may have to be interrupted.

Left turns cut across several lanes of traffic, and therefore, offer many possible conflicts. They require much attention when the officer is directing traffic. The officer should prohibit a turning movement and direct a driver to go straight ahead or, in some cases, to turn in another direction when:

1. The driver is in the wrong lane, and cars going straight through in the same direction in an adjacent lane would have

to be stopped. This should be done without encouraging further violations.

2. The street into which the driver wishes to turn is blocked, perhaps by an accident, and will be blocked for some time or is already full of waiting cars.
3. Pedestrian traffic, through which the driver must cut, is so heavy that no natural gaps are found and pedestrians cannot be stopped long enough to allow passage.
4. A car waiting for a gap in traffic would block those cars behind who want to go straight through, for an unreasonable time.
5. Stopping through traffic for left turns will fill up the block with waiting cars.

A driver wishing to turn left may have to be halted and made to wait until a gap appears or until the officer can make a gap in:

1. Through traffic approaching from the opposite direction
2. Cross traffic from the driver's left, either vehicles or pedestrians
3. A heavy stream of cross traffic which the driver must join in making the turn
4. Pedestrian traffic which the driver will cross in turning into a cross street

A single left-turning vehicle can be directed to come to a stop near the center of the intersection. When a momentary break occurs, this driver can then be directed to complete the turn.

Two vehicles in opposing streams of traffic, both wishing to turn left, can sometimes be permitted to turn at the same time if the intersection is wide enough. Ordinarily, it is safer and easier to use the same procedure followed for a single left turn and alternate each vehicle's movement. Such left turns can often be merged with right turns from the opposite direction.

When holding several cars for left turns, the officer should signal them to stop in correct position for the turn. You should try to keep them from starting the turn or from blocking crosswalks. They should be directed to complete the turn when the first break comes—through traffic should be halted, if necessary, until all cars waiting to turn have done so.

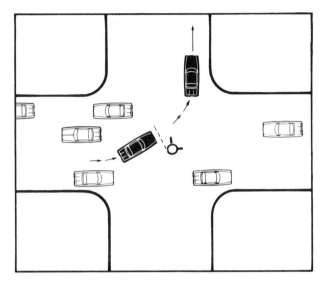

Figure 5.18 Single left-turning vehicle held in the intersection until there is a gap in through traffic.

When alternating through traffic at a cross street and a line of cars is waiting to turn left, the officer should hold them until through traffic in the same direction is stopped for cross traffic. Then the officer should direct the line of left-turning cars to move through the intersection before starting cross traffic.

Combining Movements

With experience and practice, you'll learn to combine various movements through the intersection which do not conflict with one another. You can permit right turns in any direction while almost any other movement is in progress. For instance, a steady stream of cars going straight through the intersection is not hampered by

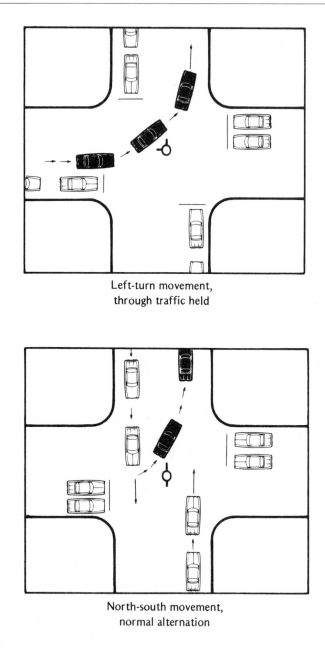

Left-turn movement,
through traffic held

North-south movement,
normal alternation

Figure 5.19 Directing a left turn through an alternating flow of traffic.

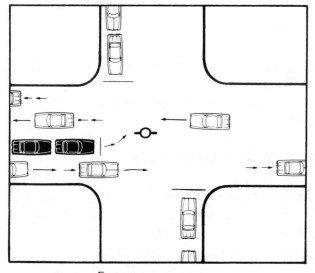

East-west movement,
left turn held

Figure 5.19 (continued)

right turns into or out of that stream if the officer watches for the openings into which cars entering the intersection can merge with the through stream.

In the same manner, a car going straight through is not in conflict with a car also going the same direction and turning left, or with those turning right. Combining two left turns is a little trickier and should be attempted only when both streets are sufficiently wide, and when there are no cars going straight through the intersection at the time. When the officer must interrupt or stop other traffic in order to combine certain movements, you will usually gain little or nothing by doing so. You are better off in those cases to let each movement await its turn.

Restriction of Turns

Restricting turns should be avoided unless it is necessary. Usually, officers are instructed to restrict turning movements only during certain hours which experience has shown to have the heaviest traffic.

ANTICIPATING THE EMERGENCY

When traffic is light and "loose," directing it is not difficult. But at certain points, as it gets heavier and thicker, just a few more cars can complicate the job and perhaps jam the intersection. It is primarily to watch for this point and keep a jam from forming that officers are assigned to direct traffic. Here are some tips that should be of help:

1. The officer must watch all exits of the intersection. If one of these exits starts to fill up, the officer should begin directing the traffic. If the officer does not, traffic will soon be stalled.
2. The officer should keep checking the traffic stream on both streets, making certain that cross traffic has an opportunity to move. If there are not enough natural gaps or breaks in a stream of traffic, the officer must make one to allow the stalled line to move.

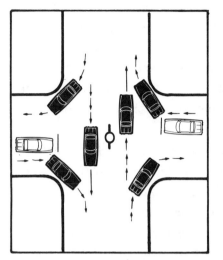

Right turns combine
easily with any
movements

Left turns can be
combined with some
through movements

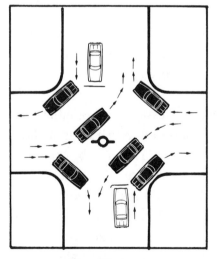

On wide street,
opposite left turns
will combine

Figure 5.20 Directing combined movements.

3. The officer must anticipate congestion. If you know when it is most likely to appear, you will be ready when it does. Never let a vehicle enter the intersection unless it has ample exit space. The best insurance is to keep a reserve space in all exit lanes. In this way, cars making movements cannot fill the lanes entirely and cause those following to halt in the intersection.

4. The officer should keep alert for blockage between intersections. If the officer does not, a lane will fill up and the intersection exit will be blocked. Double parking, unauthorized loading, and minor accidents are frequent causes of this type of congestion. The officer should investigate the reason for horn-blowing mid-block, and, if necessary, leave his or her post to clear the obstruction.

5. Make certain that motorists trying to make left turns do not hold up one or more vehicle lanes. Either help them complete the turn or prohibit the turn, as the situation requires.

6. The officer must know the intersection. Find out when traffic is heavy, where it comes from, and the direction in which it usually wants to go.

Blockage indicates that traffic is not adjusting properly because of its volume or because of selfish or thoughtless driver actions. In eliminating the temptation to jam, the officer must try to identify and remedy the specific source of trouble. When the flow returns to normal, he or she should resume the usual tactics of direction.

It is a lot easier to prevent a tie-up than to disentangle one after it is "tight." Once the area is blocked, the officer has a difficult job on his or her hands. By being always alert, you can avoid jams.

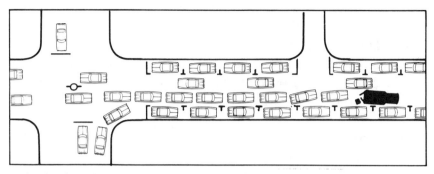

Figure 5.21 Mid-block obstructions, within a few minutes, cause a jam at an intersection.

If things begin to tighten up, the officer should prohibit turns or even detour traffic to ease congestion. But when you do this, you must consider what effect it may have on other intersections.

GENERAL RULES FOR SMOOTH OPERATION

After the officer has taken his or her position and has coordinated the go phase with the adjacent intersection, he should try to improve smoothness and continuity of flow by observing the following rules. It may take time to apply them correctly, but experience will show how valuable they are.

1. Use uniform signals and gestures.
2. Try to break traffic at natural gaps whenever possible. This will give following vehicles an opportunity to stop smoothly, and it is the logical time in which to make the change to allow cross traffic to flow.
3. When no normal break appears in the line of traffic to be halted, try to break the line behind a slow-moving vehicle such as a large truck. If this is done, starting traffic in that lane will not he hampered by it.
4. Keep stragglers and daydreamers alert, rolling and in their proper lanes. Three sharp blasts on the whistle will usually get the daydreamer's attention.
5. Do not get excited. If a jam starts forming in the intersection, look for the trouble spot immediately. Do not lose your

temper. Make the decision as to what is to be done and do it systematically.

6. Do not leave your position just to "bawl out" a driver.
7. Look cheerful. Be cheerful, but firm. Do not argue with drivers. The officer will be surprised at the extra cooperation he or she will get.

Control at Signalized Intersections

When the officer is assigned to a signalized intersection it is usually because the lights are not adequate to keep congestion from occurring during certain periods, especially when there are many left turns. The signals will relieve you of some of the physical effort of directing traffic, allowing you to pay closer attention to enforcement.

The biggest job you have is to keep alert for the symptoms of jamming and congestion already discussed. The officer can keep traffic rolling with minimum delay by anticipating the signal change and by using his or her whistle and proper hand signals.

Many signals have a simple on-off switch and another switch which turns off the automatic signal changer and permits the lights to be changed by a hand-operated button or plunger. A key to the control box should be available, and the sergeant should explain the mechanics of the switches and hand control. When traffic becomes too heavy to be handled by the automatic control device, it should be switched to hand-control position and operated by hand. Make sure to allow sufficient time in the caution phase to clear the intersection because cross traffic is usually ready to jump ahead at a light change. When the situation cannot he handled by lights at all, the signal should be turned off and traffic directed in person.

When dispatched to an intersection on a report of "traffic tied up," if the officer finds the lights out of order, the dispatcher should be notified at once. The officer should not try to adjust the lights. They should be turned off and traffic directed manually until the repair person arrives or until the jam is loosened so that natural flow without the lights can resume.

When an officer is first assigned to this type of intersection, a superior officer will probably brief the officer as to what conditions to expect. The officer may be ordered to switch off the automatic signals at a certain time to handle the heavier load of traffic expected at that time. In most instances, however, the lights are left in operation.

Control at Irregular Intersections

Irregular intersections, those where streets do not cross at right angles or where more than two streets join, sometimes require special handling. The first job is to note what turning movements are most common, where the traffic is heaviest, and other characteristics that may require attention.

The five or six-way intersection will often require the officer to conduct two major movements and allow minor movements between them. In other words, you should permit left turns after through traffic is stopped in one street and before it is started on another. This is because you cannot allow traffic to enter the intersection from more than two directions at once. The street having the heaviest traffic is kept open as much as possible.

The volume of traffic flow at "Y" or "T" intersections also determines how control is to be exerted. If left-turn movement is heavy, it may be necessary to set up three go movements, allowing traffic in each to move where desired and at the same time permitting right turns to be made from the other two directions. Note that the right-turn movements do not interfere with the main movement and thus can be permitted at any time.

Left turns are usually permitted at "T" and "Y" intersections unless there is danger or conflict and a nearby street permits the motorist to turn in the desired direction. Where the officer stands in the intersection will be determined by the main flow of traffic.

Off-set intersections are directed in much the same manner as regular intersections. Flow will be slowed because all movements through the off-set require double turns. If the off-set is greater than three times the width of the widest street, the situation should be handled as two separate "T" intersections and may take two officers working together.

Intersections of divided roadways, such as boulevards with median strips, are usually not controlled by a single officer. They are easily controlled by lights alone because the median strip separates the main lines of flow. The problem for a single officer

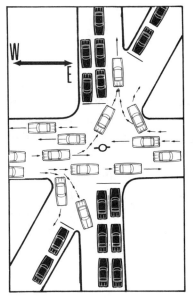

First movement, major flow
east-west

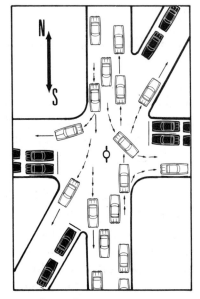

Second movement, major
flow north-south

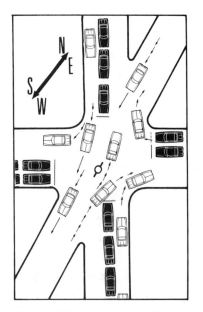

Third movement, minor flow
diagonal with right turns from
other directions combined

Figure 5.22 Directing traffic at irregular intersections.

in directing traffic at such intersections is in finding the best place to stand. The officer will usually be concerned with getting traffic across the boulevard, rather than with traffic on the boulevard itself. If the divided intersection is very wide, two officers may have to work together to handle it.

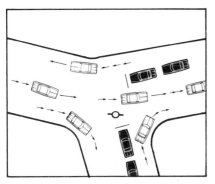

First movement, eastbound
combined with right turns
from other directions

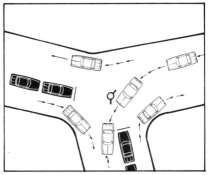

Second movement, north-
bound combined with right
turns from all directions

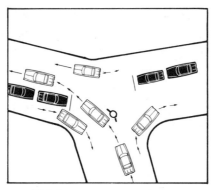

Third movement, westbound
combined with right turns
from all directions

Figure 5.23 Directing traffic at Y intersections.

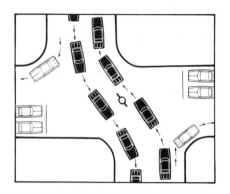

Flow slowed because of
double turns

Figure 5.24 Directing traffic at a "T" intersection.

SPECIAL CONDITIONS

An intersection on a hillside is more a problem of safety than of congestion. The officer should be careful to allow vehicles traveling downhill enough time to stop before changing the direction of flow. You should permit cars coming uphill, especially heavy trucks, to clear the intersection whenever possible. Such vehicles should not be stopped on the upgrade. Once halted, many heavy vehicles will take so long to start again that traffic following these vehicles will be unnecessarily delayed. These precautions must be kept well in mind in rainy weather, and especially under icy conditions. If the officer finds that traffic cannot safely stop on the grade because of slippery conditions, you should call radio dispatch and recommend that the block be closed to traffic, except for vehicles with chains, until conditions improve.

Breaking a Jam

A capable officer directing traffic will never allow cars to jam in an intersection, even if all exits become blocked. You simply let no vehicle into the intersection until it has an exit route.

But when a jam does occur in an intersection, it is the officer who has to "break" it. This will be easy if you are alert. First, you must size up the situation to see how serious the block is and how soon the cars which have blocked an exit may start moving. If the blockage will last only a minute or two, the job is easy. The officer can hold all approaching cars out of the intersection until the blocking cars move on and the jam breaks up by itself. But if the blockage will continue for some time, you must do something at once within the intersection to make an opening. Otherwise, neighboring intersections will become blocked as the streets fill up with cars.

When the cause of the jam is in the intersection itself, perhaps caused by conflicting turning movements, you must decide which vehicle is the "key" to the jam. You should direct adjacent cars to move sightly ahead, or back, as the situation permits, to free the key car. When an opening is made, you can release the key car and then the other cars one at a time, or in small groups, until the situation returns to normal. If the cause of the jam is temporary, resulting from locked bumpers or a minor accident, you should hold traffic until the blocked exit begins to open again.

The officer must stop any movement of cars that retards the free flow of vehicles into exits which are open. If it is necessary, the officer can order drivers to go where they did not intend to, for example, to turn right instead of going straight ahead, in order to keep vehicles moving.

Suppose an officer is sent to an intersection to break up the jam shown in Figure 5.25. You should proceed as follows:

1. Observe that the jam is caused by the black cars. They cannot move to the east and have therefore blocked an exit.
2. Stand on a bumper and look east to size up the situation. Cars are blocked a long way ahead. The trouble spot is not immediately apparent. It will be quite a while before the jam will loosen up by itself.
3. Look for the easiest car to move out first. This key car is 2. It will have to be turned west, but car 1 will have to back up first to let it turn.
4. Go to the driver of car 1 and say: "Please back up a bit... Thank you. Now, please stay right here for a minute. I'll tell you when to go."
5. Then, say to car 2, "I must ask you to turn west so that I can clear up this jam. Will you please back up first?"
6. Say the same thing to driver 3.

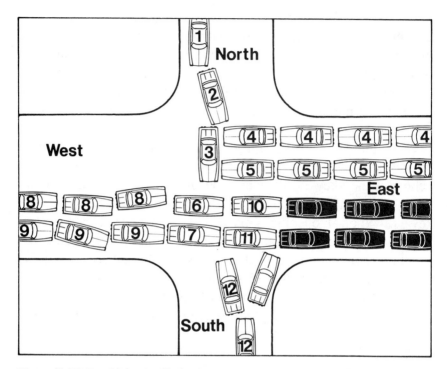

Figure 5.25 Breaking a traffic jam

7. Now let the 4s and 5s go west, or north, if they prefer. The officer must get these cars moving as soon as possible because they may be causing a block that makes a jam at the next intersection, to the east. When this westbound traffic has thinned out, you should stand in the middle of the intersection and be prepared to halt any further westbound cars before they get into the intersection.

8. Say to car 6, "I must ask you to turn north so that I can open up this intersection. Will you please back up first?"

9. Ask the same of car 7, but give the driver a choice of turning either north or south.

10. Stand in front of the 8s and 9s, motion the 8s to turn north and the 9s to turn south. The officer should keep this movement going until traffic thins out and there is no longer any danger of blocking the intersection to the west. Any approaching 8s or 9s should be halted before they reach the intersection.

11. Have car 10 back up and turn north as car 6 did.

12. Have car 11 back up and turn north or south as car 7 did.
13. With the intersection cleared, the officer should begin to move the 1s and 12s at the same time.

The officer can now alternate north-south and east-west traffic, but as long as the eastbound exit is still blocked, cars from the west will have to turn either north or south. You must be sure that whatever has blocked traffic is out of the way before letting the intersection take care of itself again.

If the exit lane in only one direction is open, it may be necessary to direct all cars entering on that street to turn and go back the same way they came. This would be done only if all other exits are going to be jammed for a considerable time. If traffic flow is almost entirely in one direction, the officer might be able to supply some relief by moving cars onto part of the left half of a street leading from the intersection, providing it is wide enough. But you must not block all lanes in this manner. Leave sufficient room for the passage of emergency vehicles and cars coming in the opposite direction. The officer should never use this technique if there is a possibility that he or she may have to get these cars out again because of a prolonged jam or if this extra lane of traffic will add to the jam at the next corner.

The officer must be alert for impatient drivers who try to bypass the waiting line and thus block the opposing line of cars. If this is allowed to happen, the jam will certainly become more difficult to handle.

Working Between Intersections

The usual reason for this assignment is the prevention of mid-block traffic jams which interfere with movement. The officer's work may be to assist the intersection officers by keeping motorists from double parking, parking in no-parking areas, or loading or unloading improperly.

When traffic is congested, stoppage of flow is a threat to the efficiency of street use. If double parking is tolerated and cars must pull into the opposite lane of traffic, flow is restricted. The same is true when trucks are loading or unloading in places and at times which restrict traffic movement. Usually, verbal orders to the motorists are enough to keep the roadway clear.

Working in Pairs or Teams

Two officers are sometimes needed at an intersection or control point. Such an assignment is usually made when the volume of traffic, particularly pedestrian traffic, is heavy because of the irregularity of an important intersection or because of the weather. It is important when working with other officers to have one officer in charge. This is usually decided by the superior officer making the assignment, but if it is not, or if an emergency arises which makes it impossible for such a designation, the officers must make the decision themselves.

When one officer is chosen as leader, the others serve as assistants, helping to enforce the leader's decisions as to flow movements. This prevents confusion. The assistant's job is to follow the lead of his or her partner. In some instances an officer may be stationed mid-block to guard against double parking, which will slow traffic flow. Other intersections may require an officer attending exclusively to the regulation of pedestrian movements, which would otherwise impede important turning movements and result in jams.

Sometimes the team or pair of officers are at adjacent intersections but not within sight of each other. For example, one may be on each side of railroad tracks which are frequently blocked by trains. In such cases, they should agree upon a plan of action with respect to prohibiting left turns, detouring traffic, etc., so that neither will simply pass his or her troubles on to the other.

Handling Emergency Vehicles

An important part of an officer's work is providing for the safe movement of emergency vehicles through the intersection or control point. This is a difficult task if the intersection is heavily traveled. The officer must halt all traffic and clear the intersection and make certain that an exit is open in the direction the emergency vehicle will travel.

The officer should be alert for emergency vehicles approaching the intersection at right angles to each other because their sirens make it impossible for one to hear the other. If they are in danger of colliding, one must be held back until it can safely proceed. Although such accidents are rare, they always tend to be serious.

After the emergency vehicle has passed the intersection, all movement must be held until the officer knows that no other emergency vehicles are following. Motorists may want to start moving as soon as the fire truck or ambulance has passed. If traffic is allowed to move immediately, the task of clearing the intersection for the following emergency vehicle will be difficult, if not impossible.

THE IMPORTANCE OF PUBLIC CONFIDENCE

The traffic control officer can make the job much easier if he or she understands the attitude of the public. Demanding obedience to directions and orders is absolutely essential. You must command the respect of the public in order to perform efficiently. But you must never let yourself show irritation or impatience.

The most successful and experienced traffic officers are always calm, if not cheerful. Nothing at all is gained by becoming angry or shouting insults at people. The officer will not only lose esteem in the eyes of the public but confidence in himself or herself as well. No one likes to be embarrassed, and an officer who is guilty of embarrassing others will probably learn that it only makes people resentful and more difficult to handle.

Chapter Six

TRAFFIC ACCIDENT INVESTIGATION

Traffic accidents have injured and killed more people and there caused greater economic loss than all other types of accidents combined. The importance of traffic accident investigation in relation to other types of police activity is apparent from a review of statistics.

Accident investigation is tremendously important as a public service to those people involved and to the public in general. Reports made as a result of accident investigation are the only source of complete, unbiased information that is available to interested parties. These include the people involved in the accidents, the insurance companies who protect their financial liabilities, and other persons and agencies who have a legitimate interest.

Accident investigation is the cornerstone of any program of traffic management. Without accurate information upon which to base a plan for traffic engineering and supervision, this function cannot be effective. The traffic administrator is the architect charged with designing and maintaining the traffic control model. He or she, along with the traffic engineer, is dependent on the research provided by competent accident investigators.

Accident investigation is not only important work, it is also interesting. The investigator deals with human problems, human frailties, and human suffering, and he or she renders a service to humanity. The officer's on-the-spot actions may save a life. Many more lives may be preserved indirectly as the result of the officer's efforts. Each investigation, therefore, presents a new challenge, calling for the utmost in accident investigation expertise.

Because accidents are not intentional, accident investigation is often more difficult than other types of police investigation. The American College Dictionary defines an accident as "an undesirable or unfortunate happening; casualty; mishap; anything that happens unexpectedly, without design or by chance." The element of surprise is a part of any traffic accident. It is certainly unusual when anyone has an accident by design, although records do show that is has been done.

Accident investigation offers a challenge to the investigator and gives him or her a chance to use initiative and common sense. Officers deal with persons in trouble and those who are emotionally upset. Officers also deal with those who have been injured and those whose loved ones have been injured or killed. And at the very least, officers work with those who are worried about the potential expense of property damage. A conscientious officer seeks to protect the wronged and to give immediate assistance to the injured. The public appreciates such actions in expediting traffic and assisting victims of the accident. The traffic investigator is doing something positive for citizens—assisting them in time of need.

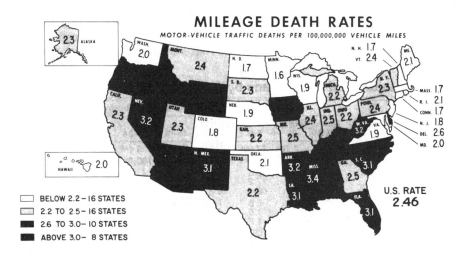

Figure 6.1 Motor-vehicle death rates of 100,000,000 vehicle miles travelled in each of the United States for 1994. (Rates are based on data from state traffic authorities and the Federal Highway Administration.)

QUALITIES AND ABILITIES NEEDED

Large and medium-size police departments have their own accident investigators. In smaller departments, the patrol officer often acts as an investigator. Even in large departments, however, the patrol officer must understand the procedures involved, for he or she must do preliminary work at the scene of an accident before the investigators arrive. Patrol officers are often called on to assist investigators with their duties.

In view of the importance of accident investigation, it becomes apparent that the successful accident investigator must possess certain qualities and abilities. This will assure that the task is accomplished satisfactorily from the standpoint of the individual, the public, and the department which the investigator represents.

Figure 6.2 Accident investigation can often provide an officer with a real challenge in sorting out the facts and sequence of events.

The first quality needed is enthusiasm. This means that the officer must be dedicated to this type of work and be interested in doing the best job possible. Each new investigation must be accepted as a challenge. When enthusiasm is lacking, the operation becomes routine—merely something to be accomplished with a minimum of time and effort. The completed investigation in such cases will often fall short of the quality that is necessary. It will be a recording, not an investigation.

Determination is another essential for the successful investigator. The officer must possess the tenacity to get the job done and done well, or the investigation will lack the completeness necessary for a thorough report.

A third quality which the investigator must possess is sincerity. He or she must believe in his or her work and its importance. He or she must have faith that the job being done is an important public service. If you believe fully that what you are doing is worth doing well, you will be content with nothing less than a genuine effort to achieve the best in each individual investigation.

In addition to these three basic qualities, certain other skills and abilities suggest themselves. Of great importance is a sense of responsibility and a desire to be an asset to the organization the officer represents. The officer must recognize the need to make a thorough investigation, to do a proper job of enforcement, to write a complete yet concise report, and to act as a representative of the department at the scene of the accident. In other words, investigation goes far beyond merely recording readily available information on an official form.

As an investigator, you will be expected to know more about the accident in point than a layman would. In fact, the investigating officer will probably know more about the accident than the participants themselves. This information must be written so that anyone who refers to the report will have as much knowledge of the circumstances as does the investigator. The officer's report must contain all pertinent facts of the incident, or it will fall short of its goal. If, after reading the report, the reader is left with a relevant question regarding the accident, the investigator has, in some measure, failed. Either the investigation itself was not sufficiently complete, or the information gathered was not properly conveyed by the report.

Proper representation of the department at the scene entails the ability to maintain control without an excessive display of authority. Wearing a badge is like living within a store display window. The officer does not have to remind people who he or she is; they recognize you the moment they see the uniform. Like an actor on a stage, the investigator is being observed all the time. The actions of the individual officer reflect not only upon himself or herself, but upon the entire department, and ultimately upon the whole police profession.

It is a logical conclusion that the investigator must possess investigative ability. You must be able to question and interrogate, be a good observer, reach sound conclusions, and make the investigation meaningful and valuable. You must be able to analyze situations and measure statements against physical evidence and probability.

Dealing as you do with people who are often emotionally upset, the investigator must possess the quality of leadership. You must, by your actions, be able to quickly restore order at the accident scene. You must have the ability to control emotionally upset, or injured, vehicle occupants and other individuals. You must use tact and skill in answering questions. An attitude of disinterest or levity is out of place at the scene of any accident. No matter how commonplace or routine the particular incident may appear to the investigator, you must always bear in mind that to the participants there is nothing routine about it so far as they are concerned. To them it is an unusual, sometimes frightening, and often sorrowful experience.   The investigator must approach the task with empathy. As another aspect of leadership, the investigator must be able to recognize how much authority can be delegated to volunteers, as well as properly evaluate their actions to determine if they will actually assist, rather than hinder in the investigation.

The investigator must have initiative. You must be able to work on your own. Many times you will not have anyone to direct you. It is obvious that you must be able to think logically and clearly under conditions of stress and pressure. You must persevere in your endeavor to conduct a thorough and complete investigation.

Knowledge of other police techniques will be of great value to the investigator. Part of your task will be to expedite traffic, so principles of traffic regulation must be applied. In some cases, fatal-accident investigation may be very difficult, as when the only person in the vehicle, the lone driver, has been killed. There are no witnesses to tell what occurred and the accident will have to be reconstructed from physical evidence alone. Instances are known of attempts to make it appear that victims of murder died as the result of a traffic accident.   Casual examination of the scene might lead to a false conclusion, allowing the perpetrator to escape. However, proper application of investigative techniques has often uncovered evidence that the incident was not what it appeared to be, and the responsible party has been brought to justice—all due to a sincere, intelligent, and complete investigation.

A basic knowledge of photography is valuable. The investigator must plan accident scene photographs for their evidential worth, rather than news value. You should know where a photograph will help in an investigation and where one will not.

The successful investigator will always be on the watch for new ideas and techniques. When one uncovers a new way of doing things, the information should be passed on. Progress in any field is a group effort, built upon the contributions of many individuals. The accident investigator today profits from the experience of past investigators, and you, in turn, can make a contribution by making available to others, the results of your own experience and knowledge.

The investigator must strive to get the facts, while conducting an impartial investigation, with no preconceived prejudice or opinion to prevent arriving at an honest conclusion. The officer should approach the investigation in terms of what each vehicle did, in relation to other physical conditions. With this viewpoint, he or she is less apt to be swayed by possible prejudices as to age, sex, race, color, or occupation.

Like any other endeavor, accident investigation has its pitfalls. The following list is offered in the hope that some of the more common mistakes may be avoided:

DON'TS FOR INVESTIGATORS

1. Do not discuss the accident with anyone outside the department or outside the line of duty. The investigation is part of the assigned job. It should be treated as such.
2. Do not take sides in an accident. The investigator is not a referee or an umpire, but a fact finder.
3. Do not tell any participant that he or she is in the clear.
4. Do not tell anyone you will be glad to be a witness. If you are to be a witness, you will be subpoenaed. When you do testify, you must testify honestly and impartially.

5. Do not mention garage or repair bills, or civil liability. These are not part of the investigation.
6. Do not enter into any discussion of a probable or possible fine. This is a function of the court.
7. Do not be too hasty in making decisions as to cause. Get the facts first; gather all of the evidence; analyze the situation; then, when you are sure, make the decision.
8. Do not conduct yourself as other than an impartial representative of the people throughout your entire investigation. Your sole purpose is to be a fact finder.

IMPORTANCE OF ACCIDENT INVESTIGATION

Many arrests will be made following an accident investigation. These include arrests for misdemeanor and felony drunk driving, manslaughter, hit-and-run, reckless driving, as well as auto theft and other crimes. Obviously, a great amount of care must be used in case preparation. Essential evidence must be recognized, identified, and properly preserved. The investigator must be careful to conduct a thorough investigation, prepare the case meticulously, and follow through by appearing in court in a professional manner.

If you should appear in an unfavorable light, the guilty may escape punishment, the innocent may suffer public embarrassment, and the officer will fall short of accomplishing his or her duty to the people whose rights you swore to defend, protect, and uphold.

In civil cases resulting from accidents, courts rely upon the investigating police officer for unbiased and informed testimony. Over a period of years, judges have come to give great weight to the officer's testimony. Investigators should always be conscious of this and realize that a poor investigation and a poor representation of evidence will soon destroy a trust it has taken years to acquire.

Officers will find that accident investigation will consume a great part of their time. The better they know the correct procedure, the more reliable their reports will be and the more satisfying the job.

Figure 6.3 Based on recommendations from the accident investigator for making slight engineering changes, signal phasing, or roadway marking changes, perhaps this type of accident could be avoided in the future.

Value of a Fixed Procedure

Some type of fixed procedure is extremely valuable in accident investigation. This should not serve to limit the investigator's actions—it should be flexible. Steps should be taken as conditions warrant, rather than by rote. By realizing the need for a fixed procedure, the investigator will be able to use it as a sort of mental check list. It will make the task easier for the officer by assisting in determining the accident cause(s) and in gathering data. It will enable the officer to make sure that nothing is overlooked in the investigation, provide a definite starting point, and help prevent duplication of effort. A planned procedure impresses the public with the efficiency of the investigator's department and builds favorable public opinion.

Many investigators, in the course of their experience, may have adopted other terms or may have interpreted the various types of accidents differently from those described here, but until such time as they discard the old and adopt the new, uniformity of reporting cannot, and will not, be accomplished. Until uniformity of reporting and interpretation can be achieved, it will be impossible to arrive at an adequate program of traffic supervision.

Types of Accident Investigation

Normal accident investigation will include investigation of those accidents in which the principals are present, vehicles are approximately as they came to rest, physical evidence is unaltered, and possible witnesses are present.

Late-reported, or late-investigated, accidents are those in which knowledge of the accident is gained and investigation, if any, is made after some lapse of time.

Hit-and-run accidents are those in which a driver causes damage or injury and knowingly leaves the scene without identifying himself.

Reasons for Accident Investigation

There are three equally important reasons for accident investigation. First is the basic police function—to protect life and property. This includes the civil aspects of accident investigation. The second reason is to determine the cause(s) of the accident. This is necessary in order to gather the information required for the department to perform its functions as set forth in the vehicle code. The third reason is to gather evidence for the prosecution of persons guilty of any violation of the law which contributed to the accident.

Since the success of any accident-prevention program hinges on thorough investigation and complete reporting, it becomes necessary to distinguish between attending an accident and investigating one. It is a comparatively simple matter to go to an accident scene and determine where and when it happened, what occurred, and who was involved, and record this information on a printed form. This, however, is not accident investigation. Granted, the investigator must have this information, but the critical part of the officer's task is to determine how the accident happened and why. It is these two areas where the real value of the investigator is determined.

Every action of the investigator, from the original accident call to the completion of the report, falls within one of the three reasons for investigating accidents. Steps in normal accident investigation will be grouped under these three broad headings in the order in which they most logically fall.

Figure 6.4 The basic questions that must be answered when investigating an accident are how did it happen and why.

PROTECTION OF LIFE AND PROPERTY

In a typical accident investigation, there are various steps which may be conveniently grouped under the broad heading of protection of life and property, which is one of the three basic reasons for investigation. Not all of these steps will be required in every accident investigation, nor will they always be done in any particular order. The important thing for the investigator to remember is that each investigation should be evaluated in the light of each of these steps, assigning top priority to that which is most important in each instance. The best procedure is a planned procedure that can be adapted to each event.

There are many reasons why the investigation should be made as soon as possible after the occurrence of the accident. It follows, then, that prompt arrival at the scene is extremely important. The first thing the investigator has to do is get to the scene safely, yet quickly (See: Emergency response, in the Index and Appendix C).

Since the accident has already occurred, the investigator can do nothing to prevent it. Take this fact into consideration and protect your life and the lives of others by driving at a safe speed in responding. Taking unnecessary chances may lead to the investigator's being involved in an accident, also.

Drivers of patrol vehicles must remember that they set an example for other drivers. Sirens and red lights are meant to protect the officer and other users of the highways. Their installation and use do not grant or infer the privilege of reckless driving. Operators of emergency vehicles soon learn that their safety depends on their personal judgment and defensive driving habits, rather than on the driving public. It is always better to be a few seconds late on an emergency call than to have an accident and injure someone, or not get there at all!

The officer is needed to protect the scene and other traffic, to preserve evidence that might be lost, and in some cases, to save life by applying first aid. Sometimes, another accident may occur because the highway is obstructed. Traffic congestion is usually present, and the officer must attempt to restore normal vehicular movements. Prompt arrival will prevent driver irritation and poor public relations. To those involved in an accident, time is fleeting. Also important is the fact that witnesses, who might be of great value, will become impatient and leave the scene once their curiosity is satisfied, and the investigating officer will not benefit from the information which might otherwise be received from them.

To accomplish these objectives you should plan an approach over the quickest, not necessarily the shortest, route. You must know the area—the short cuts, detours, construction zones, and areas of congestion. A few seconds spent thinking out the best route may save minutes of hazardous high-speed driving. The officer should start at once upon receipt of the call. A short delay in getting started will have to be made up on the road, and a long delay means that time is lost which can never be regained.

Upon arrival at the scene the officer should park safely and conveniently. Consideration should be given to the injured parties, conditions at the scene, evidence protection, and other traffic. Rather then parking opposite the accident, where the traffic stream will have to be crossed each time it becomes necessary to return to the patrol vehicle, the officer should try to park on the same side of the highway. By parking properly, the warning lights on the patrol car may be used to alert other drivers. Safety and availability of the equipment in the vehicle should be considered, as use will be made of the radio, flares, first-aid equipment, etc. Also, unguarded equipment may offer an incentive to potential looters. By parking safely, the investigator will help establish a safe parking and passing pattern for others at the scene of the accident to follow (See: Highway Flare Patterns, Appendix D).

It will be necessary to protect the accident scene to prevent the occurrence of further accidents and to preserve the evidence which the investigator will need. This may require using flares both day or night or under conditions of poor visibility. Thought should be given to the proper location of flares to give approaching drivers a chance to slow down before running into an obstruction and to channel them around the scene.

In some cases, bystanders will volunteer to assist, and if their aid is enlisted, they should be told what to do. Otherwise, their undirected efforts may hamper, rather than help, the investigation. Attempts should be made to keep onlookers in a safe location. At times this poses an extremely difficult problem for the officer.

Where gasoline or oil is spilled on the highway, it will be necessary to request fire equipment to evaluate the spill and decide on proper cleaning methods. Highway crews may be needed to sand the area to eliminate the hazard. Where fire hazard exists from gasoline, liquid petroleum gas, or similar fluids, care should be used in placing flares; onlookers should be warned of the danger of smoking, and, if necessary, the crowd should be cleared from the area.

Where there is injury, first aid will be necessary. When necessary, it should be given without delay. In other cases, when injury is minor, protection of the scene may warrant top priority. Placing flares and directing traffic while an injured person is bleeding heavily, would obviously be the wrong order of operations, as would bandaging slight injuries before protecting the scene where a high-speed road is blocked in an area of low visibility. Fire department personnel or paramedics should be ordered, if required. This is one of the first considerations when there is serious injury. Where there is a fatality, the coroner must eventually be notified. When there is uncertainty as to whether the victim is dead or alive, he or she should be treated as if alive.

The officer must care for the property of those injured. A tow truck may be needed, and it should be ordered as soon as it is convenient. If possible, the driver's preference as to towing service should be ascertained, and the tow car of his or her choice ordered. When the driver is unable to care for his or her own vehicle, the investigator must order it stored for safe keeping. In this case, a stored-vehicle report must be filled out and the contents of the car listed and inventoried—securing the signature of the tow-truck driver on the inventory form as a receipt for the vehicle and its contents.

GATHERING EVIDENCE AND DETERMINATION OF CAUSE

The remaining steps of the investigation come under the headings of gathering evidence for possible prosecution and determining the cause(s) of the accident. These two objectives are common to accident investigations and cannot be separated. Evidence as to the cause will indicate the violation involved. Evidence proving the violation will lead to the cause. From evidence and statements of witnesses and participants, the investigator must determine the cause of the accident, bearing in mind that there probably will be more than one cause in any but the most simple type of accident. Where more than one vehicle is involved, there may be one or more violations committed by each driver.

There are three factors which must be considered in any accident: (1) the highway, (2) the vehicle or vehicles, and (3) the people involved. All three should be checked for evidence. Although it is impossible to get all the facts about everything, still the investigator should strive to get all the pertinent facts. If a violation is indicated, an effort should be made to secure sufficient evidence to prove the occurrence of the violation.

Usually, early in the investigation, the officer will begin to form an opinion of what happened and will look for evidence to confirm it. At this point, the investigator must take care not to overlook evidence that does not agree with the theory. Evidence which tends to disprove a first impression may be very important. Things are not always what they seem. The officer must never attempt to distort facts to fit some theory. Your opinion must be adjusted to fit the facts. You must never be reluctant to accept negative or conflicting evidence, no matter how convinced you are that the accident happened in a different way. To do so would be like saying, "Don't confuse me with the facts, my mind is made up."

Figure 6.5 Gathering evidence and taking witnesses' statements at the scene is a vital part of a traffic investigator's job.

Every fact, every statement, and every shred of evidence must be analyzed and evaluated in order to get a true picture of what happened. Initially, the investigator is faced with a result. Step by step, he or she must work backwards from that result to find the causes. He or she must proceed from the "what" of the situation, in order to determine the "how" and the "why."

Questioning Driver and Witnesses

A logical first step is to locate and question the drivers and witnesses. This is done by making a quick preliminary check to see that all drivers are present, and then by attempting to locate witnesses. The investigator should get the operator's license of each driver and determine which vehicle each was driving. Many other persons may remain at the accident scene until the police arrive and then leave before the officer has an opportunity to question them. An early search for these people may provide the investigator with information which he or she would not otherwise obtain.

The officer who begins a search with the verbal query, "Were there any witnesses to this accident?" may not be very successful in finding any. The word "witness" has an unpleasant connotation in the minds of many people. They have been conditioned by motion pictures and other types of entertainment to visualize a witness in court being badgered and bedeviled by the opposing attorneys to the point of acute discomfort, and they want no part of it.

The indirect approach is much more productive. The officer should find out from the drivers what person they first saw or talked to after the accident, then approach that person and ask what he or she saw. If the accident took place before a witness arrived, he or she might still be able to furnish the officer with information as to who was already there. Thus, indirectly, a witness may be discovered. Sometimes the question, "Did you see the accident?" is effective.

Many times, while giving first aid or performing some of the other duties incidental to the investigation, the officer may overhear someone describing how the accident occurred. This person may or may not be a witness. They may have talked to someone who did see it, however, and in this way a witness may be located.

A check of the vehicles parked closest to the scene may be valuable. Drivers of these vehicles are most apt to be the first arrivals. At more serious collisions, locating witnesses can be critical to the reconstruction of the accident. Therefore, if witnesses cannot be found at the scene, making notes of license numbers of vehicles parked in the immediate area might later reveal a person who may have seen the accident.

However, witnesses should be located as soon as possible, as they are prone to leave when the excitement is over. Their statements may be valuable in offering leads to pursue during the actual interrogation of the drivers, and they may also suggest what physical evidence the investigator should look for.

In all contacts with witnesses or potential witnesses, the investigator must act with tact, diplomacy, and understanding. The officer must remember that these people have no legal obligation to tell the officer anything. Their assistance may be very valuable, if freely given, but if coerced into making a statement, they may feel resentment toward the interrogator which may destroy the value of any statement obtained.

Driver's Condition

Drivers must be thoroughly checked as to their physical condition. Intoxication is a state which may change rapidly. Tests for intoxication should be conducted without unnecessary delay (see Chapter 4). The condition of the driver at the time of the accident is more important than his or her condition an hour or two after the accident has occurred.

Hit-and-Run

Early in the investigation it should be determined whether it is a hit-and-run accident, because the procedures in this type of investigation are different from other types of accident investigations. Time is of the essence, and the sooner the hit-and-run procedures can be put into effect, the greater the chance of apprehension. Hit-and-run accidents are discussed in Chapter Seven.

Condition of Vehicle

The second factor to be considered is the vehicle itself. Much evidence may he uncovered by thoroughly examining and testing the vehicles involved. It should be determined whether all the visible damage is the result of the current accident. The exact location and extent of damage should be noted. Evidence of crumpled fenders and broken glass which does not tie in, may be the result of a previous accident. Fresh damage, not connected, may be the solution to an earlier hit-and-run.

The driver's statement may give the investigator a clue as to how to begin an investigation. However, it may not be a true or correct account. The damage which does not correspond to the statements may lead to the true account of the accident.

A check of the mechanical devices—brakes, lights, windshield wipers, turn indicators, and mirrors should he made to see if they are in good condition. In some cases, operator's licenses restrict the driver to the operation of vehicles equipped with certain safety devices; if such restrictions exist, the officer should check to determine whether safety devices were being employed as required. Other points to check are lack of safety devices on commercial vehicles, inadequate lighting equipment, defective windshields, and obscured vision.

The front end should be examined, providing the damage is not such as to make the test impossible. Brakes may be faulty or inadequate. A loss of control may suggest a worn steering assembly. However, a fresh break in the steering mechanism will probably be a result of the accident, rather than a cause. The condition of each tire on the vehicle should be noted. Tire failure is often claimed as the cause of an accident, but many times it is a result, rather than the cause.

The investigator should know whether or not vehicle failure contributed to the accident, for later, in the event of prosecution, the driver may claim vehicle failure as a defense. If the investigator has not checked, he or she will be unable to refute this type of false argument. However, if a thorough check has been made, it may answer any possible questions which may arise.

Scene of the Accident

The physical condition surrounding the accident is the third factor the investigator must consider. Any condition which might have contributed to the accident should be carefully observed by the officer, for example: holes in the roadway surface; loose material on the pavement; weather; visibility, including obstructions to vision, such as hedges, trees, poles, signboards; traffic-control devices; and warning signs. All observations should be made from the drivers line of sight. The operator of a truck looking down from 10 feet above the highway surface has a very different field of vision than the driver of a low-slung sports car. Skid marks, gouge marks, tire marks, and vehicle position should all be checked and the information recorded at the scene in notes, both for the accident report and for possible use in court when testifying.

In addition to making notes, the investigator should make a sketch of the area, both as an aid in the investigation and as a means of preserving the information. This sketch should be drawn with the north at the top of the page and all wording oriented to this direction. The scale should be large enough to make it clear, yet small enough to show the whole area. If necessary, second or third diagram can be drawn to include all evidence. Distances should he measured, rather than guessed at or stepped off. Everything that might have a bearing on the accident should be included in the sketch, such as:

1. Skid marks, their length and position
2. Distance traveled after collision
3. Width of street, shoulder, roadway, and intersection
4. Distance and height of view obstructions from intersection
5. Exact location of traffic control devices
6. Distance from pavement to any fixed object which was struck, including trees, light poles, broken glass and other debris, distance to victims, parts of vehicle, such as radiator water, oil or gasoline

The investigator should not neglect to locate and record the evidence that may be hidden beneath the vehicles. When making the sketch, vehicles should be treated as transparent, viewed from the top, and evidence should be recorded in its proper location.

Photographing the Scene

Photographs should be taken as needed. They may aid the prosecution, as they can present the facts and physical circumstances of a case in a manner that is simple and easily understood. Most people are visual-minded. As the saying goes, "One picture is worth a thousand words." A photograph of a large or perishable piece of evidence such as skid marks, footprints, or a body, is accepted as evidence in place of the original to show the location and type of injury. Photographs provided by experts show information gained by microscopic examination.

The photographer must he qualified and must know what he or she is doing and why. The more important the picture, the stronger will be the attempt to discredit or disprove it in court. A commercial photographer is not usually satisfactory for several reasons. In addition to being expensive, such a person may not know exactly what is required. Commercial photographers are often reluctant to appear in court and may not keep proper data to ensure that the photograph will be admitted as evidence. If a commercial photographer is used, however, the officer should specify the type of picture needed and should record exposure and other related data. It should be remembered that these types of photographs are not to be used for publicity, but as evidence in combination with the sketch of the scene as a part of the prosecution.

Pictures of many of the following subjects are often needed as evidence, or to complete the records of a case:

1. General scene from driver's viewpoint
2. Point of impact
3. Traffic-control devices
4. Skid marks, showing length and direction
5. Nature of roadway at location, showing any defects
6. Position of cars, victims, and parts of vehicles after impact—showing distances from point of collision
7. View obstructions or absence of them

8. Blood, flesh, hair, fabrics, scrape marks, etc., frequently useful in hit-and-run cases
9. Tireprints
10. Footprints
11. Defects of vehicles involved, such as missing headlight; stickers obscuring driver's vision; sagging springs, indicating overloading
12. Roadside, showing its characteristics
13. License number of vehicle for identification
14. Close up photographs of damage to all vehicles

Figure 6.6 Often overhead photographs help to put various aspects of an accident in better perspective by depicting the entire scene in one picture.

Even though photographs are taken, the investigator should also make a sketch. Photographs do not show measurements of distances. The accident sketch is the record of the investigator's detailed, personal examination of the scene.

Causes—Results—Key Events

When the information has been gathered, the investigator should determine the cause or cause(s) of the accident. One must be very careful in this procedure, as it is one of the most important parts of the investigation.

Collision vs. Non-collision Accidents

Broadly speaking, accidents may be classified as either one of two types: collision or non-collision. The collision accident may involve another vehicle, train, bicycle, fixed object, pedestrian, streetcar, animal-drawn vehicle, animal, or other type of object. The non-collision accident may involve running off the roadway, overturning in the roadway, fire, falling from a vehicle, or injury within a vehicle. In any event, these are not causes of accidents, but the result. For example, collision with another motor vehicle or running off the roadway may be called the key event, that is, the most significant event that happens to each vehicle involved.

Direct Cause—Mediate Cause—Key Event

The direct cause of an accident is the unconventional behavior of a vehicle which leads directly to the key event. An example of this would be a vehicle skidding on a curve. Mediate causes are connected with the accident, not directly, but through the direct cause. There may be more than one mediate cause. It is in the area of mediate causes that accident prevention can be effected. Thus, it is important to examine each factor that plays a part in the occurrence of the accident, that is, the contribution of the vehicle, the driver or pedestrian, and the highway.

Just as the key event is the result of the direct cause, and the direct cause is itself a result of mediate causes, so are mediate causes the result of earlier and more remote causes. There may be many of these, and they may be very remote indeed, such as the habits and attitudes of the persons involved. Improvements in traffic supervision may be effected by examining these earlier causes, but some of them are so remote that they are of little immediate concern to the investigator.

Take, for example, an uncomplicated accident where a vehicle runs off the road and overturns, injuring the driver. In this case, the result is an injury accident. The key event would be running off the roadway. The direct cause could be skidding on a curve, the result of a combination of mediate causes, including a slippery highway surface, excessive speed, smooth tires, improper brake application and inadequate traffic indicators of the hazard. These in turn may have many early causes—rain, poor driver attention; insufficient funds for providing adequate highway signs, construction, and policing; or driver's lack of education as to proper care of the vehicle.

DETERMINATION OF SPEED FROM SKID MARKS

In many investigations, knowing the initial speed of the accident vehicle is of great value to the investigator in reconstructing what happened and why. Drivers, for obvious reasons, may not admit accurate speeds. Many times, the speed estimate of witnesses will be unreliable due to their unfamiliarity with speed and its results. A scientific method which eliminates much of the guesswork is that of computing initial speeds from the measured length of skidmarks left by tires sliding on the pavement.

The actual computation of speed from skid marks is a specialized skill involving the use of a complex mathematical formula and is beyond the scope of this text. Students who are interested in pursuing this specialty will find the methods of computation outlined in Appendix B. This section covers the theory behind the computations and the methods of collecting evidence to be used in such calculations.

Excessive speed, or driving at a speed too great for conditions, is a common cause of accidents. When faced with an emergency, a driver will usually apply the brakes with maximum force. The driver may also swerve the vehicle sharply. The resultant skidmarks provide evidence which should be carefully studied by the investigator because the braking and skidding of vehicles conform to certain physical laws which serve as a basis for computing, with reasonable accuracy, the initial speed of the vehicle.

Not only will this evidence be of assistance in prosecuting violators, it may also serve to exonerate drivers who might otherwise be charged. A skid of 20 feet from a speed of 20 miles an hour does not mean that a skid of 100 feet—a skid five times as long—indicates five times as much speed, or a speed of 100 miles an hour. The actual speed in this case would be only about 45 miles an hour.

This type of evidence is particularly valuable in auto-pedestrian cases where not much damage is done to the vehicle. Where extensive damage results, all that can be measured is the amount of speed the vehicle lost in sliding. Energy absorbed in the collision is above and beyond that figure.

With emergency skidding, rotation of the wheels ceases almost instantly and wheels are said to be "locked." Locking the wheels will not stop the vehicle at once. Instead, the tires will slide upon the surface until all the kinetic energy of the vehicle has been transformed into heat energy of stopping, represented by the sliding of the tires. Since, by the law of conservation of energy, energy cannot be created or destroyed, the energy of motion must be equal to the energy of stopping. While this energy transformation is taking place, as the wheels slide, a heavy deposit of rubber will be left on the pavement. This can be readily identified, and the length of the skidmark left by each wheel can be measured.

Skid marks from locked wheels are the result of the efficiency of the brakes and the tire linings being greater than the efficiency of the tire on the surface of the pavement. This causes the wheels to lock and slide. The ratio of force to the weight of the vehicle is expressed as a percentage of the weight and is termed coefficient of friction.

On dry, hard surfaces, braking forces which can be attained are fairly uniform. The coefficient of friction will vary slightly with changes in speed. In contrast, on wet surfaces, due to the lubricating effect of the water and many other factors, the coefficient will vary with different speeds. Therefore, use of the formula for computing speed from skidmarks should generally be confined to dry pavements.

It is recognized that even with a freely rolling wheel, small particles of rubber are being deposited on the surface of the pavement; however, these deposits are so small that clearly defined markings are difficult to see. Even with a heavy brake application, if the wheels continue to rotate, it is often difficult to detect any markings on the pavement. Under emergency conditions, however, maximum braking force is generally applied, which causes the wheels of the vehicle to lock. On dry pavements, the locked wheels will leave a heavy deposit of rubber on the surface which can be accurately assessed as to length, location, direction, and number of wheels affected.

Under conditions where a heavy braking force is exerted, the retarding force is greatest just before the wheels are locked. This type of tire marking is labeled impending marks. The wheels are just about to cease rotating and the tire mark's are usually less visible than markings made by a locked wheel. In some instances, it is possible to see the design of the tire tread in the impending marks. Usually, this type of mark leads directly to, and is connected with, the locked wheel markings.

A general characteristic of the locked-wheel type of marking is that the path of the vehicle is usually a straight line. This is true because it is impossible to change direction by use of the steering apparatus during the time the wheels are locked.

In many collisions, there may be a sudden and violent change of direction due to impact with another vehicle or a fixed object. This change of direction is usually visible, but many times it results in a confusion of tire markings which are difficult to describe accurately.

In some instances, a sudden and severe change of direction is effected by the operator attempting to turn the vehicle from a straight path of travel. When this occurs it is possible that clearly defined tire markings will be visible in the pavement, and it is also possible that braking may or may not be in effect. In this case, a new force has been added to the vehicle which is called centrifugal force. This new force is acting upon the vehicle in such a manner as to resist the change of direction which the operator is attempting to impart by turning the wheels.

Investigators should be aware that it is possible to leave tire markings on the pavement which closely resemble locked-wheel or impending marks without any brake application. Such markings are many times identified by a variety of terms which are confusing.

These types of descriptions do not lend themselves to intelligent interpretations or evaluations in reconstructing the facts of the collision.

In order to rectify the situation, a uniform terminology must be developed and used. To arrive at a conclusion as to speed, based upon the evaluation of the physical evidence left upon the surface of the roadway, it is necessary that all deceleration factors be considered. The primary deceleration factor is the braking mechanism. Secondary factors are the surface upon which the vehicle is traveling, its grade percentage, and its condition.

Figure 6.7 A sudden change in a vehicle's direction is often indicated from skid marks.

First among the uniform definitions of skid-mark terminology is the tire skid mark which is defined as a mark left by a tire due to the sliding of the tire over a surface. There are three basic methods of leaving visible tire skid marks:

- **Extreme Deceleration:** When the braking system is sufficiently powerful to cause the wheels to cease rotating, they will lock, and skid marks will be left on the surface. Even though the wheels are still turning, when braking force has been exerted in an amount sufficient to bring the wheels to a point where they are about to cease rotating, skid marks will be visible.

- **Extreme Change of direction:** This action may result from an intentional effort on the part of the operator or may occur as a result of an impact or contact with a fixed object or another vehicle. The resulting skid marks are usually visible to the investigator.

- **Extreme Acceleration:** This condition occurs when a propelling force or thrust is generated in an amount exceeding the pavement efficiency. If the power applied to the drive wheels is such that it will cause them to "burn rubber," skid marks will result.

The following basic terms have been adopted and will be used throughout this discussion to define the various types of tire skid marks:

- **Impending skid marks:** Left by a "braked" wheel rotating slower than the forward motion of the vehicle in a straight or curved line.

- **Locked wheel skid mark:** Left by a non-rotating wheel of a vehicle moving in a straight or curved line in the original direction of motion.

- **Side skid mark:** Left by a locked, braked, or rotating wheel of a vehicle sliding in other than a forward direction, except when known to be caused by centrifugal force.

- **Centrifugal skid mark:** Left by a rotating wheel of a vehicle rounding a curve or turning at such a speed that centrifugal force partially or entirely overcomes frictional resistance.

There are descriptive terms which can be used to describe skid marks after the basic term has been used. Some examples are intermittent to describe markings which are not continuous; dual wheel and single wheel to indicate the number of wheels affected and the type of equipment; curving line and straight line to describe direction and type. Any term which further describes the skid after the basic terminology has been used and can be employed to clarify the facts of the collision is acceptable. By using a standard terminology, investigators will be able to reach a common understanding, so that from the skid marks at the accident scene definite conclusions may be arrived at concerning the speeds involved, the direction of travel, and the point of impact.

In order for such evidence to prove of any value in determining initial speeds and to assure its acceptance by the courts, it is imperative that it be properly obtained and recorded. The investigator is concerned with how far the vehicle skidded. Therefore, it is necessary to measure the mark left by each tire of the vehicle. In some cases, this is fairly easy to do. In other instances, it is almost impossible, when the marks of front and rear wheels are superimposed. In the latter case, the investigator must measure the total length of the skid mark and deduct the wheel base of the vehicle from the total skid. In any event, the officer must establish that the marks were left by a certain vehicle. This is usually accomplished by an admission from the driver or by the testimony of a witness.

In measuring curved skids, the tape should follow the curvature of the skid marks, rather than cutting across in a straight line, as the distance the wheels were in contact with the road surface is needed to calculate speed. The investigator must see both ends of the tape (from 0 to 1 inch, as well as the higher number measured) so that his testimony will be admissible.

Sometimes, when wheels are locked, they will bounce and leave what is called a "skip" skid—a series of locked-wheel skid marks with short spaces between them, the result of the wheels being in the air. In these cases, only the length of the individual skid marks should be computed. The spaces where the wheels were not in contact with the road surface should be disregarded. Although the wheels are locked while in the air, none of the speed is being dissipated. This only occurs when the wheels are sliding on the surface.

In some instances, a person will apply brakes when faced with an apparent danger, leaving skid marks, release them as the situation changes, and then apply them again. In some cases, the driver will "pump" the brakes. Skid marks left in cases of this kind will have a gap between them. Each set of marks should be measured and used in the computation. If they are completely superimposed, it will be necessary to deduct the length of the wheel base from each set of marks.

Having measured the skid marks, the measurements must be recorded. For each wheel, the length of the impending skid should be listed, plus the length of the locked-wheel skid. It is also necessary to record the weather, the condition and type of pavement, and the percentage of grade—noting whether it is up or down.

When this information is secured, it is fairly simple to calculate the minimum initial speed at which the vehicle must have been traveling. This can be done in several ways. What the investigator must remember is that skid marks do not show all the speed. Whatever energy was used in braking effort before the wheels began to leave visible marks will not appear, nor will any of the energy left in the vehicle at the time of the collision. What can be determined is the amount of speed lost in the distance the vehicle slid. Since any calculation will show less speed than the actual speed of the vehicle, this deviation from the actual speed will be in favor of the driver. (See Appendix B for Calculating Speed from Skid Marks)

ENFORCEMENT ACTION

Having gathered evidence which will support a prosecution, appropriate enforcement action is the next step which concerns the investigator. In most traffic accident investigations, the offense involved will be an infraction or a misdemeanor which may or may not be immediately enforced at the scene. Each individual law enforcement agency has policies which dictate whether a qualified officer can issue citations at the scene of an accident. In some jurisdictions, the accident investigation facts are reviewed by someone designated to later determine whether or not charges will be filed. This procedure serves to reinforce the fact that an investigation must be complete, thorough, and conclusive.

Should the prosecutor wish to review the evidence before approving a complaint, the violator should be notified in writing of the charges as soon as the complaint is filed, rather than be served with a warrant as the first knowledge that court action is contemplated. This latter procedure does not enhance public relations. In case of felony violation, the officer is empowered by law to take enforcement action at the scene if he has sufficient reason to support an arrest.

Reviewing Procedures

It is a good practice for the investigator to confer with assisting officers and review the entire investigation just before leaving the scene. This serves two purposes. It provides assurance that all points have been covered and that all of the necessary information has been gathered. A re-check may disclose a piece of evidence or property of the participants that was overlooked. If two officers are conducting the investigation, they should compare notes to be sure that they both have all the necessary information. It is a form of control which takes little time, but may be very productive.

In some instances, when an investigation is made by one officer alone, it may be advisable to solicit the opinions of other investigators in order to bring the investigation to a well-balanced conclusion.

Observing the Scene

One possibility the investigator should not overlook is that of the "staged" accident. Such are designed to defraud insurance companies by means of nonexistent injuries supposedly sustained in a carefully engineered "traffic accident." Cases are known in which individuals, including attorneys, doctors, garage proprietors, and others have conspired to collect damages for fictitious injuries by carefully staging traffic collisions. This type of fraud is difficult to detect.

Officers should observe carefully the demeanor of the persons involved in an accident, be sensitive to good factual detail, and watch for inconsistencies or fabrications. If fraud is suspected, careful questioning should be carried on to determine its motive.

Motives may range from the desire for easy money to outright murder.

Some of the circumstances which suggest possibility of fraud are:

1. extremely nervous participants
2. a lack of witnesses
3. no plausible reason for the accident
4. one person freely admitting liability while the other seems to be feigning injury, and
5. "victims" preferring to seek their own medical care in preference to usual facilities

While these "indicators" do not constitute conclusive evidence of fraud, officers should not close their eyes to the possibility that such a conspiracy might exist.

Before leaving the accident scene, the investigator must be sure that it is left in a safe condition. This means that not only must the vehicles involved be removed, but also that all parts of vehicles, broken glass, and other debris must be cleared from the highway surface. Spilled oil must be sanded or covered with dirt, flares must be extinguished if still burning, and all evidence that there has been an accident, insofar as possible, should be removed. Otherwise, traffic may become involved in additional accidents caused by a curious driver who observes signs of an accident and pauses or stops. This last step is really concerned with the protection of life and property, but is repeated here for emphasis.

Follow-Up Work

In many cases, it will be impossible to complete the investigation at the scene. It may be necessary to contact additional witnesses who are not present in order to determine the true causes. Drivers or other persons may have been injured and will have to be interviewed at hospitals or at their homes after treatment. Sometimes, the initial investigating officer will follow up with these tasks, but in other cases further investigation will be done by officers specifically assigned to accident follow-up work.

Should it become necessary to interview injured persons, the officer should check with the doctor in attendance before attempting to talk to these people. In some cases, their condition will be such that it will not be advisable to interview them. In other cases, they may have been given sedatives or other treatment so that their statements will not be reliable. Each instance will have to be treated on its merits by the investigator.

The final step of the investigation will be that of making out the accident report on a standard form. In filling out the report, the investigator will be guided by department policy, bearing in mind that for the report to be good, it should answer all logical questions that might be asked by any one of the several agencies which will use it as a source of information. A good investigation will lose much of its value if the information is not transmitted by means of a thorough, accurate, and complete report, including the who, what, when, where, why, and how of the accident.

Special-Investigation Accidents

In addition to standard accident investigations, there are two other types of accidents which require special investigation—late-reported accidents and hit-and-run accidents.

Late-reported accidents are those which come to the attention of the investigator after a lapse of time. Usually the vehicles involved are no longer at the scene, and much of the evidence may have been altered or destroyed. The degree of follow-up work required for these accidents will depend upon their severity.

Serious injuries or fatalities, of course, will require a thorough investigation. Whereas minor property damage accidents may entail no more than completing a driver's report of the incident on the official form. Hit-and-run accidents will be further discussed in Chapter Seven.

PROSECUTION AFTER ACCIDENTS

There are many reasons for prosecution of drivers involved in accidents. It is the most equitable and effective type of enforcement. A great deal of time is spent in apprehending and citing drivers whose violations might cause an accident. If these drivers are prosecuted, it follows logically that in all fairness, prosecution should be instituted against those whose violation actually has caused an accident.

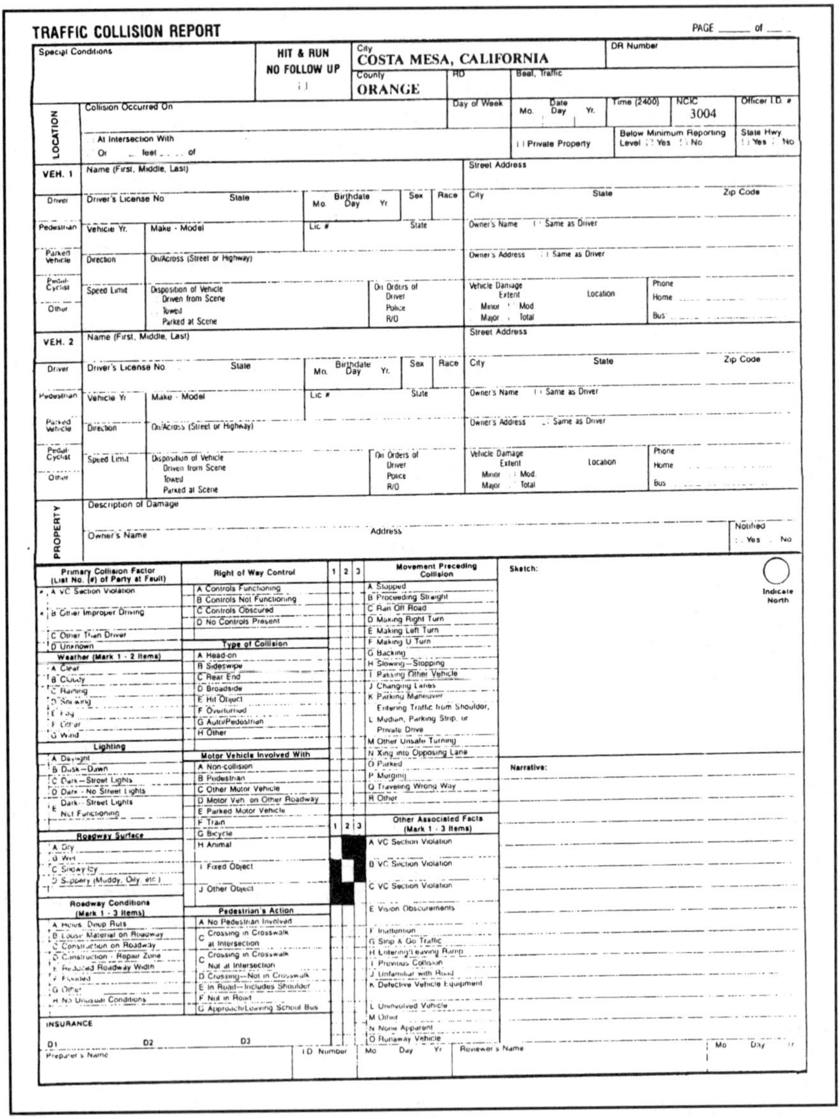

TRAFFIC COLLISION REPORT

PAGE ____ of ____

Special Conditions | HIT & RUN NO FOLLOW UP | City COSTA MESA, CALIFORNIA | DR Number

County ORANGE | RD | Beat, Traffic

LOCATION: Collision Occurred On | Day of Week | Date Mo. Day Yr. | Time (2400) | NCIC 3004 | Officer I.D. #

At Intersection With / Or ___ feet ___ of | Private Property | Below Minimum Reporting Level Yes No | State Hwy Yes No

VEH. 1 — Driver / Pedestrian / Parked Vehicle / Pedal-Cyclist / Other
Name (First, Middle, Last) | Street Address
Driver's License No | State | Birthdate Mo. Day Yr | Sex | Race | City | State | Zip Code
Vehicle Yr. | Make - Model | Lic # | State | Owner's Name | Same as Driver
Direction | On/Across (Street or Highway) | Owner's Address | Same as Driver
Speed Limit | Disposition of Vehicle: Driven from Scene, Towed, Parked at Scene | On Orders of: Driver, Police, R/O | Vehicle Damage Extent: Minor, Mod, Major, Total | Location | Phone: Home, Bus

VEH. 2 — Driver / Pedestrian / Parked Vehicle / Pedal-Cyclist / Other
Name (First, Middle, Last) | Street Address
Driver's License No | State | Birthdate Mo. Day Yr. | Sex | Race | City | State | Zip Code
Vehicle Yr | Make - Model | Lic # | State | Owner's Name | Same as Driver
Direction | On/Across (Street or Highway) | Owner's Address | Same as Driver
Speed Limit | Disposition of Vehicle: Driven from Scene, Towed, Parked at Scene | On Orders of: Driver, Police, R/O | Vehicle Damage Extent: Minor, Mod., Major, Total | Location | Phone: Home, Bus

PROPERTY: Description of Damage
Owner's Name | Address | Notified Yes No

Primary Collision Factor (List No. (#) of Party at Fault): A VC Section Violation; B Other Improper Driving; C Other Than Driver; D Unknown

Weather (Mark 1 - 2 Items): A Clear; B Cloudy; C Raining; D Snowing; E Fog; F Other; G Wind

Lighting: A Daylight; B Dusk—Dawn; C Dark—Street Lights; D Dark - No Street Lights; E Dark - Street Lights Not Functioning

Roadway Surface: A Dry; B Wet; C Snowy-Icy; D Slippery (Muddy, Oily, etc.)

Roadway Conditions (Mark 1 - 3 Items): A Holes, Deep Ruts; B Loose Material on Roadway; C Construction on Roadway; D Construction - Repair Zone; E Reduced Roadway Width; F Flooded; G Other; H No Unusual Conditions

Right of Way Control: A Controls Functioning; B Controls Not Functioning; C Controls Obscured; D No Controls Present

Type of Collision: A Head-on; B Sideswipe; C Rear End; D Broadside; E Hit Object; F Overturned; G Auto/Pedestrian; H Other

Motor Vehicle Involved With: A Non-collision; B Pedestrian; C Other Motor Vehicle; D Motor Veh. on Other Roadway; E Parked Motor Vehicle; F Train; G Bicycle; H Animal; I Fixed Object; J Other Object

Pedestrian's Action: A No Pedestrian Involved; B Crossing in Crosswalk at Intersection; C Crossing in Crosswalk Not at Intersection; D Crossing—Not in Crosswalk; E In Road—Includes Shoulder; F Not in Road; G Approach/Leaving School Bus

1 2 3 — Movement Preceding Collision: A Stopped; B Proceeding Straight; C Ran Off Road; D Making Right Turn; E Making Left Turn; F Making U Turn; G Backing; H Slowing—Stopping; I Passing Other Vehicle; J Changing Lanes; K Parking Maneuver; Entering Traffic from Shoulder, L Median, Parking Strip, or Private Drive; M Other Unsafe Turning; N Xing into Opposing Lane; O Parked; P Merging; Q Traveling Wrong Way; R Other

1 2 3 — Other Associated Facts (Mark 1 - 3 Items): A VC Section Violation; B VC Section Violation; C VC Section Violation; E Vision Obscurements; F Inattention; G Stop & Go Traffic; H Entering/Leaving Ramp; I Previous Collision; J Unfamiliar with Road; K Defective Vehicle Equipment; L Uninvolved Vehicle; M Other; N None Apparent; O Runaway Vehicle

Sketch: | Indicate North

Narrative:

INSURANCE D1 D2 D3
Preparer's Name | I.D. Number | Mo Day Yr | Reviewer's Name | Mo Day Yr

Figure 6.8 Short form used for minor non-injury collisions. The form is completed in the field and a carbon copy given to the drivers involved. *(Courtesy of Costa Mesa, CA Police Department)*

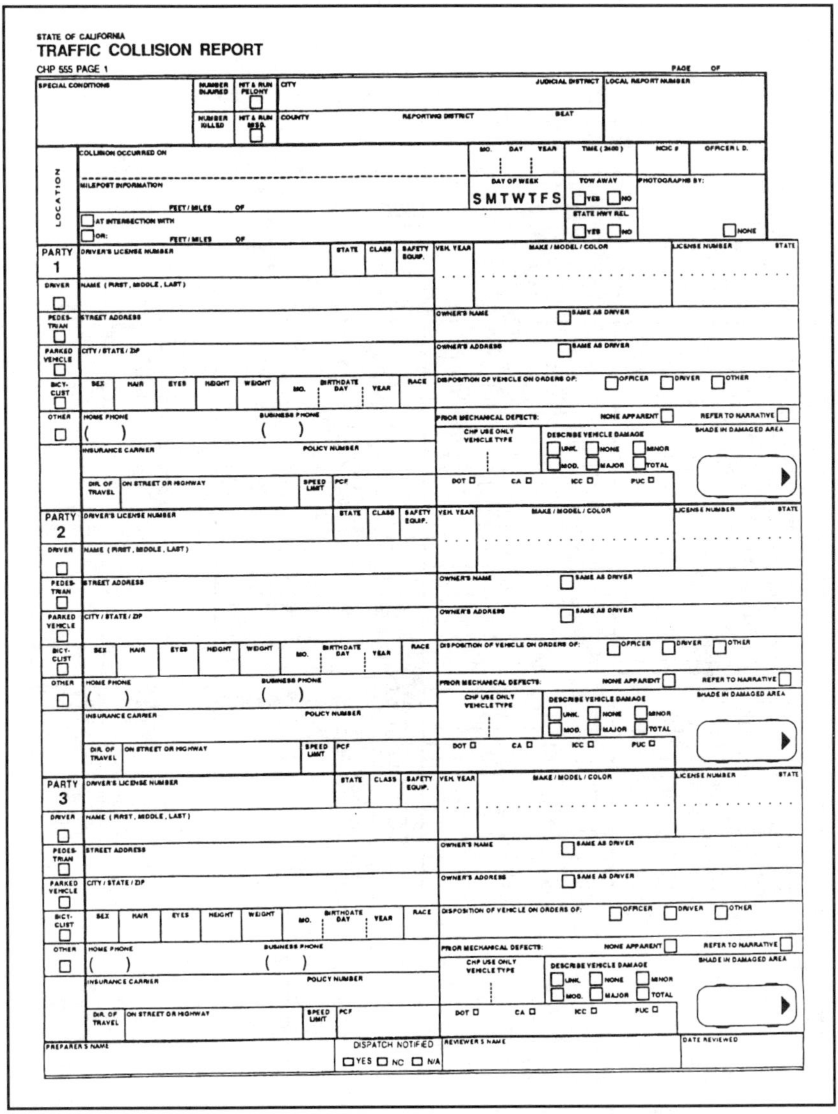

STATE OF CALIFORNIA
TRAFFIC COLLISION REPORT
CHP 555 PAGE 1

PAGE OF

SPECIAL CONDITIONS | NUMBER INJURED | HIT & RUN FELONY | CITY | JUDICIAL DISTRICT | LOCAL REPORT NUMBER
NUMBER KILLED | HIT & RUN MISD. | COUNTY | REPORTING DISTRICT | BEAT

LOCATION
COLLISION OCCURRED ON | MO. DAY YEAR | TIME (2400) | NCIC # | OFFICER I.D.
MILEPOST INFORMATION | DAY OF WEEK S M T W T F S | TOW AWAY YES NO | PHOTOGRAPHS BY:
FEET/MILES OF | STATE HWY REL. YES NO | NONE
AT INTERSECTION WITH
OR: FEET/MILES OF

PARTY 1 / PARTY 2 / PARTY 3
DRIVER | PEDESTRIAN | PARKED VEHICLE | BICYCLIST | OTHER
DRIVER'S LICENSE NUMBER | STATE | CLASS | SAFETY EQUIP. | VEH. YEAR | MAKE / MODEL / COLOR | LICENSE NUMBER | STATE
NAME (FIRST, MIDDLE, LAST) | OWNER'S NAME | SAME AS DRIVER
STREET ADDRESS | OWNER'S ADDRESS | SAME AS DRIVER
CITY / STATE / ZIP | DISPOSITION OF VEHICLE ON ORDERS OF: OFFICER DRIVER OTHER
SEX | HAIR | EYES | HEIGHT | WEIGHT | BIRTHDATE MO. DAY YEAR | RACE | PRIOR MECHANICAL DEFECTS: NONE APPARENT | REFER TO NARRATIVE
HOME PHONE ( ) | BUSINESS PHONE ( ) | CHP USE ONLY VEHICLE TYPE | DESCRIBE VEHICLE DAMAGE | UNK. NONE MINOR MOD. MAJOR TOTAL | SHADE IN DAMAGED AREA
INSURANCE CARRIER | POLICY NUMBER
DIR. OF TRAVEL | ON STREET OR HIGHWAY | SPEED LIMIT | PCF | DOT | CA | ICC | PUC

PREPARER'S NAME | DISPATCH NOTIFIED YES NO N/A | REVIEWER'S NAME | DATE REVIEWED

Figure 6.9A Standard accident report form (page 1). Used for all accidents involving injury, fatality, hit and run, or any collision requiring follow-up; including citation issuance. Each jurisdiction's form will vary slightly in format, but each requires similar basic facts. *(Courtesy of California Highway Patrol)*

STATE OF CALIFORNIA
TRAFFIC COLLISION CODING
PAGE

DATE OF COLLISION		TIME (3600)	NCIC NUMBER	OFFICER I.D.	NUMBER
MO.	DAY YEAR				

OWNER'S NAME / ADDRESS

PROPERTY DAMAGE   NOTIFIED ☐ YES ☐ NO

DESCRIPTION OF DAMAGE

SEATING POSITION

1 2 3
4 5 6
7

1 - DRIVER
2 TO 6 - PASSENGERS
7 - STATION WAGON REAR
8 - REAR OCC. TRK, OR VAN
9 - POSITION UNKNOWN
0 - OTHER

SAFETY EQUIPMENT

OCCUPANTS
A - NONE IN VEHICLE
B - UNKNOWN
C - LAP BELT USED
D - LAP BELT NOT USED
E - SHOULDER HARNESS USED
F - SHOULDER HARNESS NOT USED
G - LAP / SHOULDER HARNESS USED
H - LAP / SHOULDER HARNESS NOT USED
J - PASSIVE RESTRAINT USED
K - PASSIVE RESTRAINT NOT USED

L - AIR BAG DEPLOYED
M - AIR BAG NOT DEPLOYED
N - OTHER
P - NOT REQUIRED

CHILD RESTRAINT
Q - IN VEHICLE USED
R - IN VEHICLE NOT USED
S - IN VEHICLE USE UNKNOWN
T - IN VEHICLE IMPROPER USE
U - NONE IN VEHICLE

M / C BICYCLE - HELMET
DRIVER   V - NO   W - YES
PASSENGER   X - NO   Y - YES

EJECTED FROM VEHICLE
0 - NOT EJECTED
1 - FULLY EJECTED
2 - PARTIALLY EJECTED
3 - UNKNOWN

ITEMS MARKED BELOW FOLLOWED BY AN ASTERISK (*) SHOULD BE EXPLAINED IN THE NARRATIVE.

PRIMARY COLLISION FACTOR LIST NUMBER (#) OF PARTY AT FAULT	TRAFFIC CONTROL DEVICES	1	2	3	TYPE OF VEHICLE	1	2	3	MOVEMENT PRECEDING COLLISION
# A VC SECTION VIOLATED: CITED ☐YES ☐NO	A CONTROLS FUNCTIONING				A PASSENGER CAR / STATION WAGON				A STOPPED
# B OTHER IMPROPER DRIVING * :	B CONTROLS NOT FUNCTIONING *				B PASSENGER CAR W / TRAILER				B PROCEEDING STRAIGHT
	C CONTROLS OBSCURED				C MOTORCYCLE / SCOOTER				C RAN OFF ROAD
C OTHER THAN DRIVER *	D NO CONTROLS PRESENT / FACTOR *				D PICKUP OR PANEL TRUCK				D MAKING RIGHT TURN
D UNKNOWN *	TYPE OF COLLISION				E PICKUP / PANEL TRUCK W / TRAILER				E MAKING LEFT TURN
# E FELL ASLEEP *	A HEAD - ON				F TRUCK OR TRUCK TRACTOR				F MAKING U TURN
	B SIDESWIPE				G TRUCK / TRUCK TRACTOR W / TRLR.				G BACKING
	C REAR END				H SCHOOL BUS				H SLOWING / STOPPING
WEATHER (MARK 1 TO 2 ITEMS)	D BROADSIDE				I OTHER BUS				I PASSING OTHER VEHICLE
A CLEAR	E HIT OBJECT				J EMERGENCY VEHICLE				J CHANGING LANES
B CLOUDY	F OVERTURNED				K HIGHWAY CONST. EQUIPMENT				K PARKING MANEUVER
C RAINING	G VEHICLE / PEDESTRIAN				L BICYCLE				L ENTERING TRAFFIC
D SNOWING	H OTHER * :				M OTHER VEHICLE				M OTHER UNSAFE TURNING
E FOG / VISIBILITY FT.	MOTOR VEHICLE INVOLVED WITH				N PEDESTRIAN				N XING INTO OPPOSING LANE
F OTHER * :	A NON - COLLISION				O MOPED				O PARKED
G WIND	B PEDESTRIAN								P MERGING
LIGHTING	C OTHER MOTOR VEHICLE								Q TRAVELING WRONG WAY
A DAYLIGHT	D MOTOR VEHICLE ON OTHER ROADWAY	1	2	3	OTHER ASSOCIATED FACTOR(S) (MARK 1 TO 2 ITEMS)				R OTHER * :
B DUSK - DAWN	E PARKED MOTOR VEHICLE								
C DARK - STREET LIGHTS	F TRAIN				A VC SECTION VIOLATION: CITED ☐YES ☐NO				
D DARK - NO STREET LIGHTS	G BICYCLE				B VC SECTION VIOLATION: CITED ☐YES ☐NO				
E DARK - STREET LIGHTS NOT FUNCTIONING *	H ANIMAL :				C VC SECTION VIOLATION: CITED ☐YES ☐NO	1	2	3	SOBRIETY - DRUG PHYSICAL (MARK 1 TO 2 ITEMS)
ROADWAY SURFACE	FIXED OBJECT :				D				A HAD NOT BEEN DRINKING
A DRY					E VISION OBSCUREMENT :				B HBD - UNDER INFLUENCE
B WET					F INATTENTION * :				C HBD - NOT UNDER INFLUENCE *
C SNOWY - ICY	J OTHER OBJECT :				G STOP & GO TRAFFIC				D HBD - IMPAIRMENT UNKNOWN *
D SLIPPERY (MUDDY, OILY, ETC.)					H ENTERING / LEAVING RAMP				E UNDER DRUG INFLUENCE *
ROADWAY CONDITION(S) (MARK 1 TO 2 ITEMS)	PEDESTRIAN'S INVOLVED				I PREVIOUS COLLISION				F IMPAIRMENT - PHYSICAL *
	A NO PEDESTRIAN INVOLVED				J UNFAMILIAR WITH ROAD				G IMPAIRMENT NOT KNOWN
A HOLES , DEEP RUT *	B CROSSING IN CROSSWALK AT INTERSECTION				K DEFECTIVE VEH. EQUIP. : CITED ☐YES ☐NO				H NOT APPLICABLE
B LOOSE MATERIAL ON ROADWAY *									I SLEEPY / FATIGUED
C OBSTRUCTION ON ROADWAY *	C CROSSING IN CROSSWALK - NOT AT INTERSECTION				L UNINVOLVED VEHICLE				SPECIAL INFORMATION
D CONSTRUCTION - REPAIR ZONE	D CROSSING - NOT IN CROSSWALK				M OTHER * :				A HAZARDOUS MATERIAL
E REDUCED ROADWAY WIDTH	E IN ROAD - INCLUDES SHOULDER				N NONE APPARENT				
F FLOODED *	F NOT IN ROAD				O RUNAWAY VEHICLE				
G OTHER * :	G APPROACHING / LEAVING SCHOOL BUS								
H NO UNUSUAL CONDITIONS									

SKETCH

INDICATE NORTH

MISCELLANEOUS

CHP 555 PAGE 2

Figure 6.9B Standard accident report form (page 2) for additional accident details.

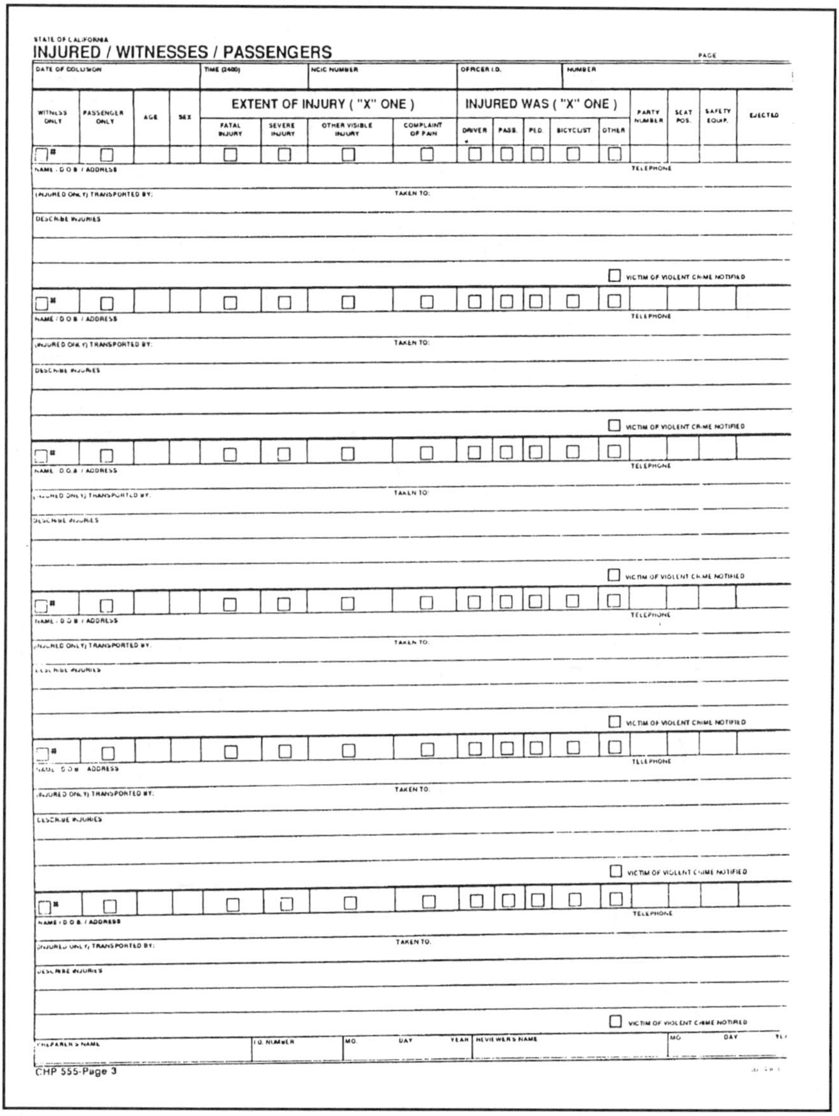

Figure 6.9C Standard accident report form (page 3) for accident victim injury details.

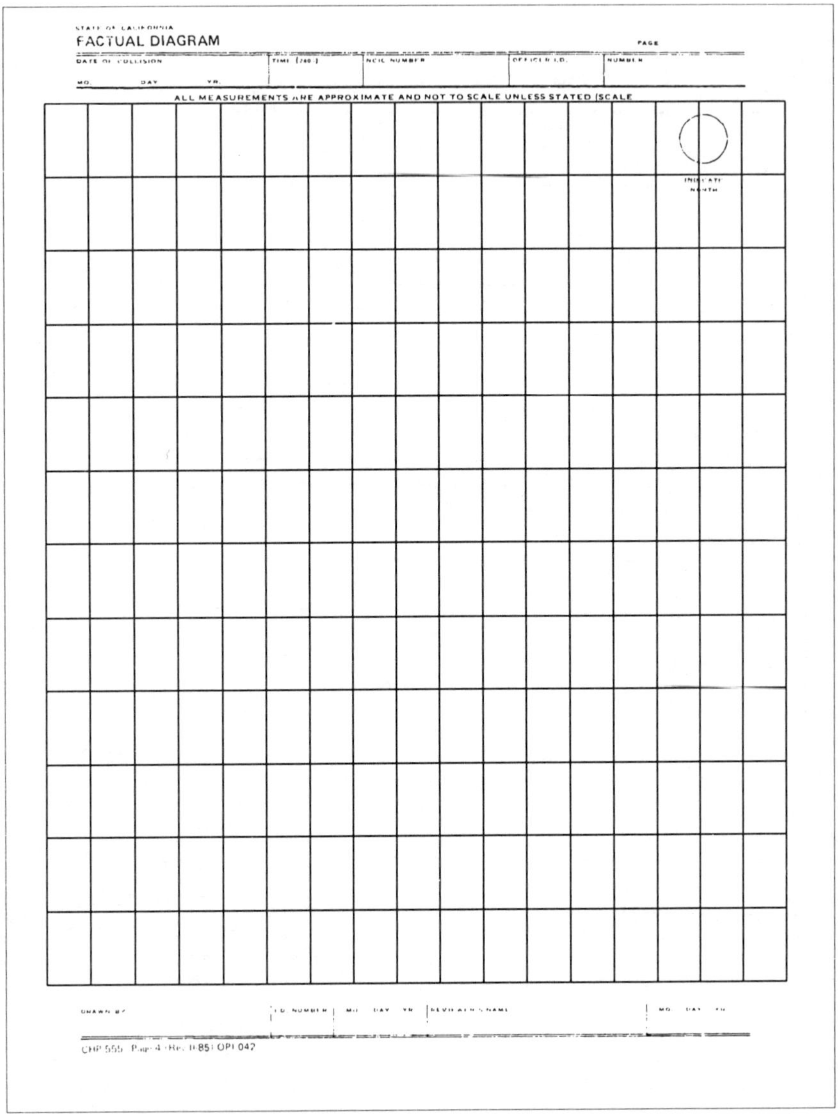

STATE OF CALIFORNIA
FACTUAL DIAGRAM
PAGE
DATE OF COLLISION | TIME (2400) | NCIC NUMBER | OFFICER I.D. | NUMBER
MO. DAY YR.
ALL MEASUREMENTS ARE APPROXIMATE AND NOT TO SCALE UNLESS STATED (SCALE
INDICATE NORTH
DRAWN BY | I.D. NUMBER | MO. DAY YR. | REVIEWER'S NAME | MO. DAY YR.
CHP 555 Page 4 (Rev. 11-85) OPI 042

Figure 6.9D Standard accident report form (page 4) for accident diagram.

By pointing out the relationship between accidents and violations, the public may be brought to realize the need for strict enforcement of all traffic laws as a preventive measure. There is, in fact, a direct correlation between the number of traffic citations issued and the number of traffic accidents which occur. Traffic accidents actually go down in direct ratio to the increase in the number of citations for the type of violations which are likely to cause accidents.

The philosophy of "Haven't they suffered enough already?" is no valid reason for failing to prosecute. The fleeing felon who is seriously wounded by the officer who shoots him as he attempts to escape undoubtedly suffers from his wound. Society, however, spares no effort to keep him alive in order that he may stand trial for his offense. Why then should personal suffering, no matter how great, limit the prosecution of the traffic violator?

People who witness, or who are involved in an accident where there is a violation of the law, expect the police to do something about it. They are perplexed if nothing is done. Prosecution of violators serves as an object lesson for the general public, acts as a strong deterrent, and lessens opportunities for further deaths, injuries, and economic losses. It presents the officer to the general public as someone who is doing something tangible on their behalf. It engenders a feeling of protection, which in turn, creates a very desirable relationship. To the violator, it points out that all traffic laws must be obeyed.

ACCIDENT INVESTIGATION IN RELATION TO PLANNING TRAFFIC SUPERVISION

Accident investigation is basic for planning traffic supervision and engineering— providing, as it does, a record of driver failure and deficiencies. Those agencies concerned with traffic legislation and driver improvement and education garner information from accident files. Improved laws and improved driver education result from accident investigation. Highway engineering improvements also take into consideration the accident picture. Based on accident studies, vehicle manufacturers have improved their products, resulting in safer vehicles. For example, hydraulic brakes, safety glass, better visibility, shock-absorbing driver compartments, shock-absorbing bumpers, anti-locking brakes, air bags, and seat belts are among the many safety advances which have occurred because of accident investigation and crash research.

If planning in these fields, as well as in the enforcement field, is to be sound, it must be based on a solid foundation of accurate accident reporting. Accidents follow a recurrent pattern as to time, location, and cause. To a certain extent, they are predictable. This suggests that they are amenable to a certain amount of control. If an occurrence can be predicted, something can be planned to prevent it. Another factor which implies that accidents can be controlled is the fact that accidents do not result from one cause, but from a combination of causes—a chain of events. If one or more of the causes can be eliminated, the chain leading to the accident may be broken, and thus, the accident may be prevented.

Take, for example, a relatively clear-cut accident wherein a drinking driver, traveling upon a slippery highway in the dark, comes to an unmarked curve at a speed which is more than his or her smooth tires will permit negotiating in safety. The driver runs off the road after a skid, overturns, and is killed. This accident has many causes. The elimination of any one of these causes might have prevented the occurrence. Through engineering, the curve could have been eliminated; the coefficient of the pavement could have been increased; or the curve could have been more prominently marked. Education of the driver regarding the danger of smooth tires might have had its effect. Strict enforcement of speed laws and laws relating to driving after drinking could have been a deterrent to the driver which would have saved his or her life. Planning is necessary in all three of the traffic safety fields—the three Es—Engineering, Education, and Enforcement.

If planning in order to prevent accidents is to be valid and productive, it must be based upon consideration of accident causes. The question then arises: Which accidents should be investigated and reported—fatal accidents alone; fatal accidents and those involving personal injury; or all accidents, in order to get the complete picture?

In many cases, the only difference between a fatal accident and one involving property damage alone is a matter of chance, a small difference in position, or a slight variation in speed. Would investigation of minor (in terms of severity) accidents be valuable in planning, or will planning be adequate if based on injury accidents alone?

The investigation and reporting of all known accidents encourages good public relations. No matter how minor an accident may appear to an outsider, it is an important thing to those people actually involved. They look to the police for help, and even though police are primarily concerned with the criminal aspects of the investigation, the parties concerned expect, and are entitled to, an impartial evaluation of the circumstances, so that the rights of everyone may be protected. The investigator should not attempt to establish civil liability or fix the blame, rather he or she should impartially record the facts so that in any future civil action the judge and jury will have available to them an unbiased, intelligent, and complete record from which they may reach a just conclusion.

Instead of basing an investigation upon the severity of the accident, the professional approach would be to consider the incident from an enforcement standpoint in terms of the possible violations involved. Thus, a one-car fatality in which the victim was alone in the car might take a minimum of investigation in spite of its grave consequences, as contrasted to a property-damage accident involving violations on the part of both drivers. As an enforcement officer, the investigator must not lose sight of the objective. Obviously, the same amount of time cannot be devoted to all minor accidents. There are too many of them. Evaluation of the occurrence in terms of possible violation appears to be a firm basis to use as a guide to gauging investigative effort.

If there was an injury, was it apparent? Did the suspect make any attempt to assist the victim? Was the victim conscious? How long from the time of the accident was it before the investigator arrived? Were there any other violations on the part of the suspect, such as excessive speed, driving while intoxicated, or any other illegal act? No particle of evidence should be overlooked.

The scene should be combed for physical evidence. Extremely small parts broken from the suspect's car can be matched with the vehicle in order to make a positive identification. Paint transfers or paint chips may be uncovered. Clothing should be preserved to be analyzed and properly marked for identification. Great care should be used so as not to handle clothing unnecessarily or roughly, as paint is invisible to the naked eye in many cases and might be lost. The clothing of persons fatally injured should be obtained from the coroner. Photographs of the accident scene, the victim, and the vehicle should be taken and other evidence photos obtained, as the circumstances warrant.

The area should be canvassed thoroughly for witnesses. Often women are good witnesses for describing clothes, and boys in their early teens will probably he very good in determining the makes of vehicles.

WITNESS AND DRIVER STATEMENTS

Taking statements from drivers and witnesses is an important part of many investigations. These may simply consist of asking what happened and recording it in the investigator's own words. It may be an informal written statement signed by a witness or, in serious cases, may take the form of a formally recorded statement taken by the prosecutor and transcribed by a stenographer.

Statements are valuable for several reasons. They give the investigator a clue as to what happened and in which direction the investigation should be started. Statements tend to dissuade a person from changing his story at a later date, and in some cases, he may be used to impeach a witness, i.e., show that he lied then or is lying now. Even if the person has not signed the statement, the mere fact that it was given to the officer may keep a witness from changing his or her story later. The statement may also be used to refresh the memory of a witness.

Statements assist the investigator in determining facts. They enable the officer to place the driver behind the wheel, determine probable point of impact if there are no skid marks, tie skid marks to a particular vehicle, and establish other circumstances of the accident.

One of the first considerations in taking statements is to talk to each person privately. Many people are reluctant to talk if several people are listening to what they say. They may be afraid of what the driver or others might do if the statement is not in the driver's favor. Spectators may interrupt by interjecting their own ideas, and arguments may start as a result of disagreements between participants.

Questioning Procedures

If possible, the investigator should have the witness or driver tell his story from the general location where the witness was at the time of the accident. This will serve as a check on reliability and establish whether or not the witness actually could see what he or she reportedly saw from the position at the time. A witness should be allowed to tell his or her story without interruption, except when it is necessary to keep him or her from rambling and wandering too far from the subject. The investigator must be sure he or she understands what the person means. Questions should be objective, positive, specific—not "Where do you live?", but "What is your address?" This will tend to save time and make the statements concise and pertinent. Statements should be supported with facts, and discrepancies should be pointed out. No attempt should be made to "coach" the witness, but the officer may suggest possible occurrences so that the witness, by indicating points of disagreement, can clarify his or her recollections.

After the person has finished his or her statement, if there are any points not covered, specific questions should be asked. When the investigator is sure the statement is complete, the witness should be asked to write a statement of observations. Once reviewed by the officer, the witness should sign the statement. Some people have difficulty putting their thoughts on paper, and their statements may not be adequate. If necessary, the officer may write the statement, using words directly stated by the witness.

After writing each pertinent statement, as the witness relates the events of the collision, the investigator should pause and show the witness the written remarks to confirm their validity. Once the entire document is written, the officer should include a statement indicating awareness by all parties that the report was actually written by the officer with permission of the witness.

If the witness refuses to sign, the officer must not insist upon a signature. It is better, rather, to use a positive approach in attempting to get the signature, and if this fails, drop the matter. The signature in itself is not that important. Once having given the statement to an officer, the subject will be less likely to change his or her story at a later date if he or she knows that it has been written down.

While listening to a witness's statement, the investigator should not be in too great a hurry to start writing, as some people are reluctant to talk if they know the conversation is being recorded and will not give a statement. Also, the first time they make their statement it may not be adequate and may have to be written again, which is time consuming.

Accuracy of the Statement

Ordinarily, by the time an officer is ready to take a statement, he or she will probably have a good idea as to cause and violation. Care should be taken to make sure the statement covers all the necessary elements as indicated. Particular attention should be given to make sure that all points, such as who the driver was, the direction of travel, the approximate speed, the condition of the pavement and the weather are covered. This will enable the officer to tie in the skid marks, if any, with the approximate speed, the condition of the pavement and the weather, and the appropriate vehicle.

A statement which does not add to the investigator's knowledge of the accident is wasted time, whereas, a properly taken statement may prove of great value. Even if the statement adds nothing to the case, it should be preserved with the remainder of the accident data. Witnesses have been known to change their stories. In a criminal trial, if a person from whom the officer has taken a statement at the scene in which he or she declares they saw nothing or knew nothing about the accident should turn up as a witness with testimony in the defendant's favor, the statement taken by the officer would probably invalidate the latter testimony and might mean the difference between winning and losing the case.

Chapter Seven

HIT-AND-RUN INVESTIGATION

Hit-and-run driving may be either a felony or a misdemeanor. In cases resulting in injury or death, it is a felony. It is a misdemeanor where only property damage is involved. In either case, the accident should be investigated just as any other accident, except that special hit-and-run investigative procedures should be followed.

The officer investigating the hit-and-run accident is really conducting two investigations in one—to determine the cause of the accident, and to determine the identity of the driver who has left the scene. It is one type of accident in which it is readily apparent that a violation has already occurred—that of evasion of responsibility. The officer, however, must not lose sight of the fact that leaving the scene is not a cause of the accident. The investigation must be thorough so as to uncover the cause of the accident as well as to locate the missing driver.

FELONY HIT-AND-RUN

The elements of felony hit-and-run, as established by many of our state vehicle codes, involves a driven vehicle "involved in" an accident resulting in injury or death that fails to stop immediately at the scene and furnish identification by giving the name and address of the driver, the name and address of the registered owner of the vehicle, and, upon request, fails to show a driver's license. In many jurisdictions, proof of currently valid liability insurance must also be shown. Failure to furnish aid, if requested or required is another element.

To prove a case of felony hit-and-run, therefore, it is usually necessary to prove each of the above elements. It must be shown that a driven vehicle was involved in an accident in which someone was injured or killed and that the driver had knowledge of the accident. Knowledge of the injury or death is usually not necessary.

However it must be proven that the driver either failed to stop or to identify himself or herself, or failed to offer aid if it was necessary or requested. The driver may stop, or return to the scene, but unless he or she identifies himself, the elements of the crime still exist. The investigator may prove knowledge of the accident, and identity of the driver and the offense by means of witnesses or by circumstantial evidence entirely. The owner of the vehicle, as a passenger, may be equally as guilty as the driver if the owner makes no attempt to stop at the scene and comply with the hit-and-run statute. The owner, under these circumstances, may be convicted of hit-and-run driving. Actual collision or contact between the vehicles involved is not necessary. The term "involved in" is broadly defined so that physical contact is not required. However, the driver involved must have committed the violation that caused the accident if there is no physical contact in order to be convicted.

THE TIME FACTOR

Time is important in a hit-and-run investigation. The longer it takes to locate the driver, the more time he or she will have to repair any damage to the vehicle, destroy evidence, and establish an alibi. Therefore, the initially responding officer faced with a hit-and-run investigation, should get information on the air for the benefit of other police units as quickly as possible, so that a wide search for the violator may be instituted at once.

It is not uncommon for a drinking driver to flee the scene of a hit-and-run accident, either in the vehicle or on foot. The motive here is to avoid being charged with driving under the influence. Unless the driver is located promptly, the BAC reading may not be as useful or incriminating. It should be pointed out, however, that if the driver is located and given a BAC test within a few hours following the accident, the BAC can be calculated for the time of the collision. It is, also, not uncommon for drivers of stolen vehicles or drivers involved in other crimes to flee the scene of a collision for obvious reasons.

HIT-AND-RUN PROCEDURES

At the scene of any accident a check should be made, first to ascertain if there are any injuries, then to determine if the drivers of all vehicles involved are present. As soon as it is determined that the accident is a hit-and-run, a description of the responsible vehicle, driver and occupants, direction of travel, area of possible damage, and probable paint transfers should be obtained. The names of witnesses should be secured at this time, and the preliminary information broadcast as soon as possible.

Having arranged for an immediate lookout, the investigating officer should question the witnesses more fully. The officer should get a complete statement and determine the amount of damage and injury. If there was a collision, how did the witnesses know? If a license number was obtained, how was it obtained, and by whom? It is essential to maintain a continuity of all evidence, so that if the driver is apprehended, the case will not be lost in court.

The officer should determine whether or not the suspect stopped at any time, and if so, did he or she converse with anyone? Any conversation should be recorded in the exact words, if possible, as an aid in questioning the suspect. Was any identification offered? Did the victim ask for any? The witness should be questioned as to whether they would be able to identify the driver. The best possible description of the driver, any passengers, and the vehicle itself should be obtained. Vehicle information should include the apparent damage, make, model and year, the color or color combination, and anything unusual or outstanding about the car. This should be as complete as the witness or witnesses can make it and may be supplemented by any physical evidence which the investigator discovers. Any new developments should be reported to the radio dispatcher so that other units involved in the search may be advised.

It should be determined whether or not the witnesses actually observed the accident. A person who did not see the accident itself might have seen the damaged vehicle leave the scene. Persons working in nearby areas or motorists arriving from the direction of the suspect's flight might fall in this category if they noticed or encountered the damaged vehicle.

The investigator should be alert for the return of the responsible driver to the scene of the accident to mingle with the crowd to see how the investigation is progressing—even going so far as to follow the officer very closely. The inquisitive person who displays an unusual interest in the progress of the investigation might well be the driver involved who is attempting to discover how close the investigation is coming to making an identification, and possibly to find an opportunity to destroy evidence.

FOLLOW-UP PROCEDURES

Follow-up activity will include checking garages, wrecking establishments, service stations, and body and fender shops, and putting them on the alert for a wanted vehicle.

Case #_____

DEPARTMENT OF POLICE
City of Miami, Florida
NOTICE

PH: 377-7364

It has been reported to this Unit that your car, License Tag_____, was

involved in an automobile accident on_____. As yet, we have no record of

your personal report on this accident as required by Metro Ordinance 30-228.

This information is necessary to complete our official records. Please report

immediately to this office upon receipt of this card, 1145 N.W. 11th St., Room 131.

_____
Special Investigator, Accident Investigation Unit

This office is open from 8:00 A.M. to 4:30 P.M. *weekdays only.*

Police Form #29

Figure 7.1 Initial information sent to registered owner of a vehicle involved in an accident by the City of Miami traffic division.

Should no apprehension of a suspect result, the officer might decide to revisit the scene periodically at the same time of day, then the same day of the week, and the same date of the month. Through this pattern, the officer may discover route salesmen, delivery drivers, or others who have a regular routine and may have been witnesses to the accident.

Case #_____

DEPARTMENT OF POLICE
City of Miami, Florida
SECOND NOTICE

PH: 377-7364

It has been reported to this Unit that your car, License Tag _____, was

involved in an automobile accident on _____. As yet, we have no record

of your personal report on this accident as required by Metro Ordinance 30-159A.

This information is necessary to complete our official records. Please report immediately

to this office upon receipt of this card, 1145 N.W. 11th St., Room 129.

If this card is not answered within 24 hours, a warrant will be sworn for your arrest.

_____
Special Investigator, Accident Investigation Unit

This office is open from 8:00 A.M. to 5:00 P.M. *weekdays only.*

Police Form #29-S

Figure 7.2 Second notice sent if registered owner does not comply with initial notice, giving driver last chance to report accident prior to enforcement action for failure to report an accident.

Once the vehicle is located and identification established, the driver will have to be found and connected to the crime. When located, the approach should be positive. The suspect may spontaneously make a statement which will identify him or her as the driver involved.

Hit-and-run investigation and apprehension is one of the most difficult, yet at the same time, most interesting jobs of the investigator. There is no apparent motive. The driver may have acted spontaneously through fear or nervousness. As stated previously, the driver may have fled to avoid apprehension because of intoxication or because of being wanted for another crime.

After Apprehension

After apprehension is made, it is vitally important that the broadcast for the wanted vehicle be canceled, and all establishments which have been alerted (such as body shops, service stations, etc.) should be notified. A word of thanks for their cooperation would be appropriate—they will likely prove helpful in a later case.

```
                        City Of Miami Police Department

                    Leaving The Scene and Hit And Run Reports

ACC. LOCATION _____ DATE:_____ OFFICER: _____
DRIVER WANTED:_____ AGE:_____SEX:_____RACE:_____
ADDITIONAL INFO. ON DRIVER:_____
_____

CAR WANTED—MAKE:_____TYPE _____YEAR ____COLOR _____
WANTED TAG_____STATE _____
REGISTERED OWNER _____
ADDITIONAL INFORMATION ON CAR _____

CAN DRIVER BE IDENTIFIED?____BY WHOM?_____
_____ TELEPHONE NO. _____
COLOR OF COMPLAINANTS VEH_____ WAS M.S.G. PUT OUT?____ M.S.G.#_____
WAS ANY EVIDENCE OBTAINED?___WHAT?_____
DISPOSITION OF EVIDENCE _____ RECEIPT # _____
```

Figure 7.3 Information card for hit-and-run case as a method of compiling information which can be referred to easily at a later date.

Good hit-and-run investigation and reporting means digging a little deeper to obtain more facts. It is the small detail that might be easily overlooked which, if found and checked, will start the chain of events leading to the apprehension of the violator. Success in this field is a group effort, calling for cooperation with other departments, as well as cooperation within the department. Cases are solved by common sense, attention to detail, hard work, perseverance, and appropriate technical knowledge.

Chapter Eight

TRAFFIC HOMICIDE

For the purposes of this chapter, the working definition of traffic homicide shall be "any death resulting from a traffic accident or situation in which a motor vehicle is involved." The field of traffic homicide investigation is a relatively new one. However, in view of the increasing number of fatal accidents, it is a vital one.

Many departments across the United States are finding it necessary to employ specially trained members of their traffic division as traffic homicide investigators. This is due to the increasingly complex investigation needed for successful prosecution of the offending driver.

Two types of investigators are in general use. First is the uniform officer who performs this function as part of the officer's regular duties and is usually a senior traffic officer. This type of investigator is used by state police agencies whose personnel are spread over large areas and by smaller law enforcement agencies whose traffic homicide reports are not frequent. Larger departments favor the use of plain-clothes officers who are assigned only traffic homicide duties or a combination of traffic homicide and nonfatal hit-and-run investigations.

Qualifications for the traffic homicide investigator include:

1. Extensive accident-investigation experience
2. Mechanical inclination
3. Training in drinking-driver enforcement
4. General police skills
   - Interviewing and interrogation techniques
   - Taking statements
   - Evidence collection and preservation
   - Scene sketching

- Felony case preparation
- Preparing and filing cases for prosecution
- Courtroom testimony
5. Completion of specialized training if available

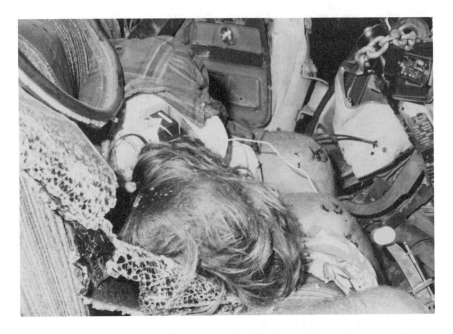

Figure 8.1 The traffic homicide investigator's job begins.

SPECIALIZED EQUIPMENT

The following equipment is utilized in traffic homicide investigation:

1. Tags and containers for evidence preservation
2. Investigator's "call-out" box containing
   - Steel measuring tape
   - Charting templates
   - Bright color spray paint canisters
   - Tape recorder and extra tapes
   - Camera (polaroid and regular)
   - Razor blade tools
   - Flashlight
   - Magnifying glass

3. Statement forms
4. Specialized forms for the traffic-homicide investigator
5. Coveralls and mechanics' hand tools (used to determine vehicle defects or failures)

Figure 8.2 The homicide investigator needs skill and training to resolve a case such as this one.

The following units are involved in support of the traffic homicide investigator:

1. Local or regional crime lab
2. Accident investigation department of the traffic division
3. Detective division
4. Coroner or medical examiner's office
5. State police or State Highway Patrol
6. Prosecutor on local and regional levels

TRAFFIC FATALITY REPORT

INFORMATION NEEDED	INFORMATION TO TELETYPE
	Attn: Accident Records Section FATALITY REPORT
Miami Traffic Fatality Number	Miami Traffic Fatality Number _____
	Urban
Total Fatalities for Miami. Year	Total Fatalities for Miami. Year_____
Name of Deceased......................	_____
Sex and Race	_____
Date of Birth	_____
Deceased's Address	_____
Location of Accident	_____
Time Accident Occurred	_____
Date Accident Occurred	_____
Weather and Road Condition at Time of	_____
Accident	_____
Was Deceased *Driver, Passenger,* or	_____
Pedestrian?	_____
Brief Description of How Accident	_____
Occurred	_____
	_____
	_____
	_____
	_____
Has Next of Kin been Notified?	_____
Investigating Officer	_____
Investigating Agency	Miami Police Department.

Note: Records unit will teletype this information to Department Of Public Safety, Tallahassee, as soon as possible.

Data Processing Use Only

Unfounded (Victim at Fault)	Actual (Victim Not at Fault)	If Victim Not At Fault Case Cleared by	
		Violator Over 18	Violator Under 18

Figure 8.3 Statistical report form for a traffic fatality. All jurisdictions report traffic fatalities on a required form to their designated state agency for statistical purposes.

THE TRAFFIC HOMICIDE INVESTIGATION

The specific investigation is conducted along with, but not as a part of, the accident investigator's routine inquiry as required by the laws of the various states. One major reason for this procedure is that most states require the driver to make statements for the accident report. These statements could be self-incriminating. Also, when similar statements are made to the traffic homicide investigator after the driver is advised of his or her rights, they are admissible.

The homicide investigation, by its nature, must go much further into the causative factors of the accident and the prospects for criminal prosecution, than the more routine traffic accident investigation.

The factors to be considered cover some of the same areas as those of the accident investigation. They include:

- Road conditions
- Weather conditions
- Vehicle condition
- Lighting of area
- Sobriety of involved drivers and pedestrians
- Mental or emotional condition of involved drivers and pedestrians
- Type and color of clothing worn by pedestrians
- Conditions at the time of the accident on arrival of first response officer, accident-investigation officer, and the traffic-homicide investigator

The homicide report, when completed, should include the following, as well as other considerations specific to individual cases:

- Investigator's summary
- Copy of the accident report
- Medical examiner's report
- Photographs
- Field and scale drawings
- List of witnesses
- Witnesses' statements
- Lab reports
- Vehicle-condition report
- Arrest or booking reports
- List of charges filed
- Press release (optional)

City of Miami, Florida

INTER-OFFICE MEMORANDUM

TO: Captain N. A. Horne   DATE: 12 April 19-- FILE:
        Commander, Traffic Section
                                     SUBJECT: Fatal:_____
                                                9 yrs, Pedestrian,
                                                SW 27 St & 32 Ct, 7:30 PM,
FROM: Officer Z. S. Siatkowski   REFERENCES: 10 March 1972
        Special Accident Investigator
        Miami Police Department   ENCLOSURES:

On Friday, 10 March 19 , at approximately 7:30 P.M., _____, Cu/M,
9 years, 3105 S.W. 27 Street, was observed walking east on the south road
edge of S.W. 27 Street. He was wearing dark-brown pants and a red corduroy
shirt and white sneakers.

At the same time, a vehicle described as being a Chevrolet with a black
bottom and white top, and a repair mark on the right side, was going east on
S.W. 27 Street and struck the boy from the rear. The vehicle slowed and then
left the scene, going east on S.W. 27 Street.

At 7:34 P.M., Officer D. Buerger received a radio call to proceed to the
scene and upon his arrival at 7:39 P.M., found the pedestrian D.O.A. The
scene was roped to preserve any evidence, and a call was put in for my
services.

Upon my arrival at 7:50 P.M., I was confronted with the facts of the accident and proceeded to conduct my investigation. The scene was photographed
by I.D. Technician R. Bloom. Measurements were taken and recorded by the
writer.

S.W. 27 Street is 17'7'' wide with an old asphalt surface. A dirt, rock,
and grass shoulder is 15'2'' wide on the south side and a 5' sidewalk ends at
property line. There is one street light hanging from a pole on the northwest
corner of S.W. 27 Street and 32 Court. The streets were dry and the weather
was clear.

Physical evidence found at the scene disclosed the following:

1. Point of impact was at the south road edge, 154' west of S.W. 32 Ct.
   After impact, the striking vehicle's right front tire left the road
   surface and left an imprint in the shoulder at the road's edge,
   traveled a distance of 27', then came back on the roadway. This imprint was made by a wide track tire.
2. At time of impact, the right-front top headlight of the striking vehicle was shattered and strewn onto portions of the road and shoulder from 12' to 40'7'' east of the impact. Inscribed on one piece of
   glass was the letter T and number 3 which indicated it had come from
   a General Motors product. The glass was collected and retained for
   physical examination at the Metro Crime Lab (See crime lab report).
3. The body of the boy came to rest 82' east of the point of impact in
   the south shoulder of 27 Street and was 7'4'' south of the south
   road edge. He was lying on his back (apparently turned over by Miami
   Fire Rescue Unit). His head was headed toward the east (See photo).

While on the scene, a Cu/M, _____, 2653 S.W. 34 Ct, came forward
and stated that his father had left home at the approximate time of the accident and is the owner and driver of a vehicle that fit the description pre--
viously stated. Officer J. Choate was sent to 2653 S.W. 34 Ct and reported
that the car was not there. He remained in the area, and at approximately
10:00 P.M., I was advised that the car in question was parked in the driveway
of 2653 S.W. 34 Ct.

In the company of Captain N. Horne and Sgt. W. McDonald, I arrived at the _____ home and requested to speak to the father. In the meantime, I.D. Technician J. Murray arrived on the scene to collect evidence from the car. There were no broken headlights; however, the right-front top headlight appeared to be freshly replaced (See report from J. Murray for findings).

During conversation with_____it was disclosed that he had his headlight replaced at about 7:00 P.M. that evening at a Phillip's 66 Gas Station located on S.W. 8th Street & 30th Avenue.

Sgt. W. McDonald went to that Station and spoke to a Cu/M,_____, 2436 S.W. 7 Street who stated he had replaced the light at about 9:00 P.M. that evening and showed Sgt. McDonald where he had thrown the old light. This evidence was collected and preserved and checked for a match-up with the glass pieces found on the scene (See crime lab report).

At no time did_____admit to being involved in this accident; however, he did admit to being in possession of the vehicle that evening. Based on physical evidence found at the scene, on the vehicle, and at the Service Station,_____was charged with leaving the scene of an accident involving a fatality.

Following is a list of witnesses this writer requests to be subpoened:

Officer D. Buerger	M.P.D.
Sgt. W. McDonald	M.P.D.
I.D. Tech. J. Murray	M.P.D.
Barry McCabe	Metro Crime Lab
Richard Werdelker	2712 S.W. 32 Ct Miami, Fla.
Jeannette Kiene	2712 S.W. 32 Ct Miami, Fla.
Rafael Hernandez	2653 S.W. 34 Ct Miami, Fla.
Luis Alfonso	2436 S.W. 7 St Miami, Fla.
Officer Z.S. Siatkowski	M.P.D.
Sgt. Bared	
R. Bloom	

Figure 8.4 Example of completed hit-and-run homicide investigation summary report. *(Courtesy of Miami FL Police Department)*

Chapter Nine

TESTIFYING IN COURT

A case often requires weeks, or even months, of painstaking effort and preparation on the part of several investigators—yet this case can be lost in court due to the improper presentation, demeanor, attitude, or appearance, of just one police officer who does not prepare properly to be a credible witness. A hearing or courtroom trial is a very important test of a law enforcement officer's real worth. Investigative skill and ability as an interrogator alone, are insufficient—the usefulness of an officer is impaired when he or she is a poor witness. A witness can lend credit, or discredit, to their testimony by their behavior in court, regardless of the substance of any testimony given.

THE COURTROOM

The courtroom should command the respect of the professional police officer. His or her conduct in the courtroom and in the areas of close proximity to the courtroom should reflect this respectful attitude.

An officer should not, under any circumstances, attract undue attention by his or her behavior, loud talk, or otherwise act unprofessionally in the courtroom, anteroom, or hallways near the court. Courtroom proceedings are serious and should be treated as such. Unbecoming behavior could very easily discredit a police officer as a witness, particularly if observed by the judge, lawyers, members of the jury, or other persons interested in the court.

The Officer in Court

An officer's testimony should begin with the inception of the violation. Therefore, the officer should make sure that all field notes are accurate and properly dated. Notes should be kept in a secure place and should be filed so that they can be easily retrieved.

Figure 9.1 The test of all criminal cases—can the case be made in court?

When an officer collects the evidence pertinent to a case, it should be collected properly, and correctly marked or tagged and preserved. Care must be taken that the "chain of custody" is maintained. This means that a written record must be kept of where the evidence is stored and in who's custody it has been in from the time it is found until presented in court. When all these precautions are followed, items of physical evidence will be much more likely to be acceptable in court.

Court Manners

There is a certain demeanor, or lack of it, that will often help to win or lose a case in court. The following suggestions are relevant to every type of court case, whether it is for a traffic citation or a major accident investigation.

1. It is a good idea to be in court five or ten minutes prior to the mandatory time.
2. Maintain a dignified and attentive bearing in the court and hearing room.
3. Do not whisper or talk unnecessarily to others sitting or standing nearby.
4. Do not approach the court clerk or prosecutor unless there is business to conduct which is pertinent to the case.
5. Stay in the courtroom. Continually coming and going will tend to disrupt court proceedings.
6. Walk erect with a military bearing. Do not swagger or act overly confident.
7. Do not smile at the jury or at court personnel. Maintain a businesslike manner.
8. Do not gather in the hallways, etc., to visit and talk with fellow officers. Be aware that others may be eavesdropping on your conversations. You can be required to testify to your casual comments if related to the case.
9. If, for some reason, you cannot be in court at the specified time, see to it that the prosecutor or proper court official is notified.
10. Always be neat—clothes pressed, shoes shined, and conservatively dressed.
11. Sit up straight and comfortably in the witness chair with both feet on the floor. Refrain from moving around, as it is disruptive for the judge or jury.

12. Speak distinctly and clearly. Use good English and avoid the use of slang and stilted language, e.g., say "saw," rather than "observed," etc.
13. Do not rush the testimony and think before speaking.
14. Avoid vulgarity unless it is necessary, such as if asked, "Officer, exactly what did the defendant say to you?" (if the defendant used vulgarity, it may be important for the prosecutor to bring out this fact.)
15. Ask to have a question repeated if you did not hear or understand it.
16. Make your answers as brief as possible.
17. Always tell the truth.
18. It is acceptable to respond with a "yes" or "no" answer. Check with the prosecuting attorney before you volunteer additional details or information.
19. Answer all questions directly and honestly, even if it is something favorable to the defendant. This will demonstrate lack of bias or prejudice.
20. Do not hesitate to correct mistakes or errors.
21. Only facts should be given unless an opinion is requested.
22. Do not appear to want to convict the defendant.
23. Notes should not be taken to the stand unless needed to remember the information. In this case, the defense attorney should have the opportunity to examine them.
24. Do not answer until the entire question has been asked, and do not anticipate what the question will be.
25. If there is an objection to a question, wait for the court's ruling before answering.
26. Remain objective—do not show personal feelings when testifying.
27. Do not be sarcastic or facetious.
28. Do not leave the witness chair too hastily. Wait for permission to leave and do so in an unrushed manner.
29. After testifying, do not leave the courtroom unless so instructed. Return to your seat and be ready to be recalled, if needed.
30. Always address the judge as "your honor." Use "sir" or "ma'am" when answering the prosecutor and defense

attorney, and refer to other persons as Mr., Ms., Mrs., or Miss, and other officers by rank.

CIVIL COURT ACTIONS

From time to time an officer will be called to testify in a civil action. In these cases, there are always attorneys present, and the officer will definitely have had access to a pretrial conference. The rules here regarding opinion evidence are sometimes more flexible in civil suits. Civil suits fall into these main categories:

1. Accident cases—Citizen v. Citizen
2. Illegal arrest suits—Citizen v. Officer
3. Any case in which the plaintiff is requesting money from the defendant for current or projected loss

PRETRIAL CONFERENCE

It is perfectly legal, and should be the policy in all cases to have a pretrial conference with the prosecutor or other witnesses involved in a case. Unfortunately, due to the workload of most prosecutors, this is not always done in all courts. If the prosecutor does not call a pretrial conference, the officer should in all cases refresh his or her memory by reviewing all documents (notes, reports, tapes, diagrams, etc.) prior to the trial date. If you feel there is a special need for a pretrial conference, call it to the attention of the prosecutor.

The purpose of a pretrial conference is not for the prosecutor to tell a witness what to say. It is for the prosecutor to learn just what facts the witnesses can testify to. Also the prosecutor can eliminate any testimony that might be improper according to legal rules of evidence, as well as any unneeded duplicate witnesses or testimony.

INVOKING THE RULE

In many criminal trials, "the rule" will be invoked. This simply means that all witnesses, other than the one testifying at the time, will be excluded from the courtroom while testimony is taken. All witnesses are ordered by the judge not to discuss this particular case with anyone. To break this ruling would jeopardize the case and will result in the witness who talks being liable for contempt of court.

The following exceptions do exist:

1. The police officer may discuss the case with the prosecutor, but it is best to let the prosecutor bring the subject up unless there is a very important point of which the prosecutor should be aware. The prosecutor, however, will not talk to the officer in the presence of other witnesses.
2. It would not be prudent for an officer to discuss the case with the defense attorney, because some innocent remark could be used against the officer during cross examination on the stand. It is best to be courteous to the defense attorney, but the officer must not talk too much.
3. The defendant is always allowed to remain in the courtroom during the proceedings, even if he or she takes the stand as a defense witness.

The invoking of the rule is usually at the request of the defense attorney. If the prosecution witnesses disagree on different points during a case, it will tend to discredit the validity of the testimony given and to add credibility to the testimony of the witnesses. However, when the rule is used, it can also be very useful to the prosecutor—particularly if there has been proper preparation on the part of the officers (pretrial conference).

THE PROSECUTOR

The prosecutor is, in effect, the state's attorney and represents the people. The officer should help him or her by relating all the facts to the prosecutor, in person, if possible. If an officer has information concerning the type of defense that will be used, it should be brought to the prosecutor's attention before the trial so the prosecutor can be prepared for it. An officer's job is to help the prosecutor as much as possible before the trial and to be a good witness during the trial. The prosecutor's job is to present the case to the court in logical, sequential manner, in order to obtain a successful outcome. He or she cannot possibly do a good job if an officer is unprepared or otherwise is a poor witness.

THE DEFENSE ATTORNEY

The defense attorney is sworn to protect the rights of the accused and to give the accused the best possible defense. Sometimes this involves a verbal attack on the veracity of the officers. Keep in mind that if you have done your job well and are prepared for trial, an attack on your veracity will accomplish nothing. As a matter of fact, often it will "backfire" on the defense attorney and the jury will place even more credibility in the officer's testimony. Remember, such an attack is designed to make the officer angry enough to become confused or make mistakes. It is a valid and much-used technique of the defense. Everyone is entitled by constitutional right to a vigorous defense.

THE JURY

The jury is made up of all types of people who bring with them their personal likes, dislikes, and prejudices. The prosecuting attorney will try to excuse any juror who the prosecutor feels cannot render a "fair and just" verdict. The defense attorney will try to excuse any jurors who he or she feels is prejudiced against the defendant. It is your job to impress the jury with your professionalism, honesty, objectivity and trustworthiness.

THE JUDGE

The judge is the arbitrator in all legal matters—his or her word is "law" in the courtroom. The officer should not show any emotion either way when the decision (verdict) is given. It is not an easy job to be a good judge. It means always acting impartially, deciding on the legality of matters under hot discussion by both attorneys, protecting the rights of all persons before the court and making sure that the proper procedures are adhered to. The good judge deserves the same high respect as does a good police officer.

Chapter Ten

THE TRAFFIC DIVISION

For the most part, traffic division personnel are more experienced officers who have expressed a desire to perform the special tasks related to accident investigation and prevention. The traffic unit, which may be a division or bureau, is a specialty detail considered by many officers to be one of the preferred assignments in any law enforcement agency. One of their very important tasks involves stopping a large number of motorists for traffic violations on a regular basis. This means that the knowledge and practice of good public relations techniques is very important. Many of the tasks performed by the traffic division requires a strong interest in, and a dedicated desire to learn, all types of accident prevention methods. Because of these aspects, the traffic commander is usually in a position to select the most sincere and capable officers to work in the traffic division.

CHARACTERISTICS AND ABILITIES

In selecting personnel for the traffic division, the commander should carefully consider the characteristics and abilities of the officers applying for entry into the unit. A number of special qualities are important in this division.

Interest and Intelligence

The applicant should show a sincere interest in the traffic problem. An officer should have a clear understanding of the traffic picture in the community and want to devote his or her police career entirely to this area of law enforcement. Seeking a transfer into the traffic unit because it is a prestigious position within the agency or because it offers better hours, etc., is not a valid reason for applying or for being accepted.

Above average intelligence, good technical knowledge, and common sense is required because traffic personnel must often make emergency decisions affecting the lives and property of accident victims. Traffic officers come into contact with more citizens each day than members of any other unit. They will also be required to answer many citizen inquiries and will be judged by their ability to reply to these inquiries.

Appearance

Since traffic personnel are observed on duty by more citizens than most other police employees, care should be taken to select personnel who will best represent the department. Personal appearance need not be the only deciding factor for selection, however, a commanding presence is an important asset for traffic officers.

Common Sense

All areas of police work require officers and other personnel to display an ability to use common sense. However, when working under emergency conditions, sound judgment is vital. Accident investigation is, of course, another area where good investigative techniques, as well as common sense, will be mandatory. Issuing traffic citations may seem to be a simple task, but public relations, psychology, and good judgment are all part of this routine function.

Energy and Good Health

Naturally, good health is necessary for all police personnel. Obviously traffic assignments require especially strong constitutions. Special units, such as those of motorcycle officers, do not enjoy the comforts of patrol vehicles and must be able to ride the heavy motorcycle for a full shift and often cover an overtime shift.

THE MOTOR OFFICER

Motorcycle units in the police traffic division hold a unique position. They are highly maneuverable and their high acceleration capabilities make them excellent tools in traffic enforcement in any congested area. On visible patrol, they are a very effective deterrent to potential traffic violators. In apprehending violators, the motorcycle is noted for excellent performance.

Many American communities use the motorcycle for traffic enforcement, parade, and escort duty. In many departments, the motorcycle officer is in a special class in terms of both prestige and pay. Hazardous-duty pay seems justified because, in some cities, mishaps have been sufficiently frequent and serious to cause concern among administrators.

However, some cities have ceased using solo motorcycles, or have reduced the numbers, because of the hazard they pose to personnel. For example, the solo motorcycle has little to commend it as an all-purpose vehicle. It is not a good all-weather conveyance, and its limited carrying capacity does not permit transport of prisoners, other personnel, or quantities of equipment. In some American cities, weather factors such as snow, ice, and rain limit the use of the solo motorcycle to less than half the year. Solo motorcycle officers must seek shelter during sudden rainstorms and may not return to patrol until streets are virtually dry. Yet it is during just such storms and on wet streets that the need for traffic supervision is perhaps the greatest.

The three-wheeled motorcycle is somewhat safer, is less wearing on the officer, and has proven its utility in traffic patrol in congested areas in the enforcement of time-zone, limited-parking regulations and in escort duty. It has been used for general patrol in certain cities, especially in downtown areas, in the vicinity of alley loading facilities and in highly congested dock and airport terminals and parking lots.

Some cities are now using small compact cars for such patrol, and for parking control enforcement, in place of three-wheeled motorcycles, because the cars have the advantage of protecting the officer and equipment from the weather, of being safer, and of allowing prisoners to be transported.

Detailed records should be kept of the relative costs of operating motorcycles and cars. Time lost because of automobile and motorcycle accidents should he included in the analysis. When time lost because of accidents is included, the total cost for motorcycles may be much greater. In any event, police executives should assess, very carefully, the need for motorcycle use and be certain that such conveyances can do the job well enough to offset the factors of increased cost, hazard, and lack of all-around utility. If motorcycles are used, care should be taken that all proper safety equipment is issued.

Figure 10.1 The motor officer is the backbone of the traffic division. *(Courtesy of Costa Mesa, CA Police Department Traffic Bureau)*

It can readily be seen that an administrator instituting a traffic program must contemplate the selection of personnel, the equipping of vehicles, and the effectiveness of using motorcycles. Proper research of these three factors can provide the police department with the foundation for an effective, efficient traffic division.

ACCIDENT INVESTIGATION VEHICLES

Special accident investigation vehicles are currently being used by many of our major cities. They may be standard police vehicles, but are more commonly, a "van" type vehicle. The following equipment should be considered for minimum installation:

1. Radio (with outside speakers)
2. Flood or spotlights
3. Emergency equipment
   - Flares
   - Torches
   - Flashers
   - Reflectors
   - Cones
   - Bumper pushing equipment
4. Fire extinguisher (large size)
5. Rescue equipment
   - Small crowbar
   - First aid kit (large size)
   - Blanket
   - Jacks
   - Cutting tools
   - Shovel and broom (for gathering evidence)
6. Inventory system (prevention of theft)
7. Steel tape measure (100 feet)
8. Yellow chalk or crayon (heavy-duty type)
9. Lighted clipboard (with plastic cover)
10. Basic accident forms
11. Sketch sheets
12. Statement forms
13. Accident analysis sheets
14. Case summary sheets
15. Citation book
16. Tracing and carbon paper
17. Envelopes and plastic bags for evidence collection
18. Tags with string attached
19. Photo equipment with high-speed film
20. Accident investigation manual
21. Typewriter

Most all of this equipment can be installed in a standard police vehicle or a station wagon if a van is not used.

Figure 10.2 Typical van used for more efficient accident investigation. All needed emergency and routine equipment, supplies, and communications are readily available.

USE OF HELICOPTERS

Helicopters are very expensive law enforcement tools. However, their assistance in apprehending suspects, controlling pursuits with less traffic conflict, finding lost children, backing up officers and often saving lives, makes them invaluable and indispensable in modern law enforcement. Helicopter units have often come to the aid of traffic and general law enforcement needs.

In large cities, a police helicopter can easily spot potential traffic problems and alert ground vehicles as to where the problems are and what should be done to correct them. In areas congested by freeways and dense traffic, the helicopter has proved to be especially effective in promptly transporting accident victims to a hospital emergency room. Statistics indicate that 20 percent of the traffic deaths are avoided by using this speedy method of transportation. In remote areas special medical emergency helicopter units can be used to rapidly transport accident victims to the nearest hospital.

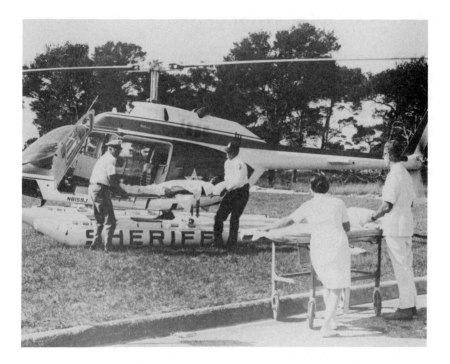

Figure 10.3   The police helicopter—highly useful and effective for traffic observation, vehicle pursuit control, fleeing criminal apprehension, general routine city patrol, and emergency transportation.

NON-SWORN PARKING ENFORCEMENT PERSONNEL

Many large American cities are using full-time male and female civilian employees to ticket parking violations. By utilizing these nonsworn personnel, city governments are enabling sworn officers to concentrate on major traffic violations. Because parking violations are part of the traffic picture, those assigned to this detail are usually supervised by the traffic staff.

SCHOOL-CROSSING GUARDS

School-crossing guards are usually part-time civilian employees who usually come under the direction of the traffic division. They are of great assistance to traffic officers, as traffic control at school-crossing areas is essential. If part-time civilian employees did not perform this function, a traffic officer would have to be assigned.

CIVILIAN ACCIDENT INVESTIGATORS

A new concept in accident investigation is that of using non-sworn civilian accident investigators, thus freeing sworn personnel for enforcement activities. According to this concept, the civilian accident investigators have summons power in the matter under investigation but no powers of arrest, beyond that of any citizen.

SELECTIVE TRAFFIC ENFORCEMENT

Basically, selective traffic enforcement is the placing of a sufficient number of officers and vehicles in an area where a certain offense has resulted in a large number of accidents so as to prevent this particular type of traffic violation. For example, at intersections where drivers running red lights have caused numerous collisions, traffic officers will be alert for this offense and will issue citations to violators. Within a short period of time, the average citizen will become aware of what is being done and, as a result, will be careful not to run the light.

One of the most common methods of selective enforcement is the use of radar and other devices to compute vehicle speeds to deter speed violators. It is quite obvious to civilian drivers just what traffic law is being strictly enforced when they pass the all-too-familiar parked police vehicle, with its speed measuring device conspicuously in view.

Figure 10.4 Each year during the Christmas season, many police traffic bureaus display wrecked cars in shopping malls as a "sobering" attention getter to warn against drinking and driving—an excellent public relations device. *(Courtesy of Costa Mesa, CA Police Department)*

Appendix A

THE STATE OF MAINE POINT SYSTEM

Maine's Legislature has enacted some rather unique laws which relate the driving privilege with safe driving in its state. A driver may lose his or her driver's license for various periods of time if convicted of certain moving violations over a period of time based on a point system. "Penalty points" are assigned for various violations according to the schedule list below. When the points reach a certain level, the offender's driver's license is suspended for a period of time, as indicated below.

Any driver whose record of conviction for motor vehicle violations would indicate that such driver is habitually reckless, negligent or disrespectful of traffic laws and the safety of other persons on the highways, may have his or her license suspended according to the following schedule:

- Eleven through 15 point accumulation—suspension up to 60 days

- Sixteen through 18 point accumulation—suspension up to 90 days

- Over 18 points—an indefinite suspension with the right to apply for restoration at the end of 6 months

As an example of the above schedule, if a driver was convicted of reckless driving (9 points) and a few months later was convicted of improper passing (6 points), they would thus have accumulated a total of 15 points, and would automatically lose their license for 60 days.

Any driver, whom the Secretary of State or Deputy Secretary of State has reason to consider as incompetent to operate a motor vehicle, such incompetence to consist of adverse physical or mental handicaps or adverse drinking or driving habits, shall be suspended without a hearing provided the Secretary of State or Deputy

Secretary of State shall, prior to suspension, review such evidence as may be available.

Anyone convicted of leaving the scene of an accident, taking a motor vehicle without the consent of the owner, reckless driving, operating to endanger, or speeding 30 miles per hour or more in excess of the posted speed will be suspended without hearing for a period of up to four months provided the Secretary of State or Deputy Secretary of State shall review the evidence. Any person convicted of the fraudulent use of a driver's license shall be suspended without hearing for a period of up to six months.

Any person operating a motor vehicle while in possession of his or her instruction permit and who is convicted of a motor vehicle moving violation shall have such permit suspended without hearing for a period of 30 days for the first conviction. 60 days for the duration of the validity of the permit, whichever is longer. Any driver whose license is suspended may, by Law, request and be granted a hearing but the suspension will remain in effect pending such hearing.

POINT SCHEDULE

Conviction	Point Value
Driving Under the Influence of Intoxicating Liquors or Narcotic Drugs	9
Liquors or Narcotic Drugs	9
Reckless Driving	9
Leaving the Scene	9
Taking a Motor Vehicle Without Consent	9
Operating After a Suspension or Revocation (Conviction Record)	9
Loaning or Altering License or Permit	9
Conviction for any Homicidal or Assault Committed by Means of a Motor Vehicle	9
Failure to Stop for Police Officer	9
Exceeding Posted Speed by at Least 30 MPH	9
Exceeding Posted Speed by More Than 20 MPH	5

Exceeding Posted Speed by	
at Least 15 MPH (but not more than 20 MPH)	4
Exceeding Posted Speed by at Least 10 MPH	3
Speed Less Than 10 miles per hour over Posted Speed	2
Operating after Suspension (Financial Responsibility)	6
Improper Passing	6
Passing a Stopped School Bus	6
Illegal Attachment of Registration Plates,	
Tags, or Inspection Stickers	6
Violation of Instruction Permit	6
Failure to Report an Accident	4
Permitting Unlicensed Operator to Operate a motor Vehicle	4
Operating Without a License	4
Violation of Restriction	3
Failure to Obey Stop Sign or Traffic Control Device	3
Failure to Yield Right of Way	3
Other Moving Violations	3
Littering from Vehicle	2
No Inspection Sticker	2

Note: Points will be erased from a driver's record when those points become three years old.

CALCULATING SPEED FROM SKID MARKS

The formula used in calculating speed from skid marks is $\dfrac{V^2}{S=30f}$, in which S represents the skid distance in feet, V the speed in miles per hour, and f the coefficient of friction. This formula may he rewritten without changing its value as follows: $V^2 = 30 \times S \times f$, which is more simple to use. What the investigator is concerned with is the speed. He simply substitutes known factors in the right-hand side of the equation, performs the multiplications, extracts the square root, and he has the minimum speed. This can be very easily done in a matter of a few seconds at the accident scene, which gives him a result close enough to guide him in his investigation. It is a quick method of determining whether there was sufficient speed involved to warrant running test skids or any further analysis.

If there is indication of excessive speed, particularly in a serious accident, test skids should be made to assure that the evidence will be as complete as possible in the event of prosecution. Although it is true that the weight of the vehicle involved, the condition of tires, or the condition of brakes (providing they are sufficient to lock the wheels) is not significant, the task of convincing a jury is much simpler if test skids are made by the same vehicle which was involved in the accident. In some cases, this will not be possible; however, if it can be done, the vehicle involved should be used. The tests should be made at the same location and in the same direction in which the accident vehicle was traveling. A minimum of three test skids at the same speed should be made and the longest skid mark used. These tests should be run at a legal speed, if in a restricted zone, is closely as possible to the speed the accident driver says he was traveling. Great care should he used in running tests skids, due to the danger involved. Under any conditions, it is not a good idea to run tests at high speeds. For all practical purposes, 30 miles an hour should be fast enough.

As an example of the use of skid marks in determining initial speeds, the following example will illustrate several principles. The investigator has measured 50 feet of accident skid marks, including locked wheel plus impending, on a dry, level asphaltic concrete pavement. The driver involved states he was going only 25 miles per hour. The quick method of estimating initial minimum speed is $V^2 = 30$ x 50 x 60, or 900. The square root of 900 is 30. Therefore, the minimum speed is 30 miles an hour. This can be done very simply without a test skill by arbitrarily assessing a 60 percent coefficient of friction.

Desiring to arrive at a the coefficient of friction, the investigator will run three test skids from the admitted speed of 25 miles an hour. These tests give skid distances of 28, 29, and 30 feet, respectively. The longest skid from the claimed speed is 20 feet shorter than the accident skid. This should be quite convincing to the driver that he was traveling faster than he admits, particularly if the investigator points out the discrepancy in the skidding distance.

Results of the test skids may be used in three different ways. One of these is by means of skid-speed chart, California Highway Patrol Form 185, as illustrated and described in the following illustration.

In the absence of a skid chart, the problem could be worked out by substituting known values in the equation for determining the coefficient of friction, , then substituting this in the $V^2 = 30$ x S x f equation and solving for the unknown speed. This will give a minimum speed of 32 miles per hour.

A method which saves time is direct substitution in the formula $V_a = \dfrac{S_a}{V_t \, S_t}$ where V_a equals accident speed, V_t, equals test speed, S_a equals accident skid distance, and S_t equals test skid distance. This too, gives a result of 32 miles per hour.

This method demonstrates that the quick approximation arrived at by using the assumed coefficient of friction of 60 percent gives a result close enough for practical use.

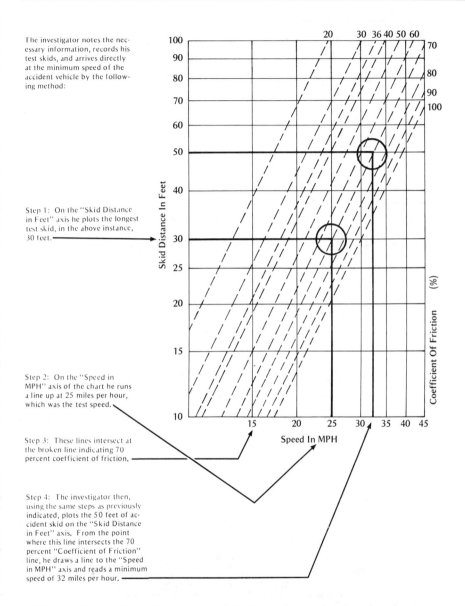

The investigator notes the necessary information, records his test skids, and arrives directly at the minimum speed of the accident vehicle by the following method:

Step 1: On the "Skid Distance in Feet" axis he plots the longest test skid, in the above instance, 30 feet.

Step 2: On the "Speed in MPH" axis of the chart he runs a line up at 25 miles per hour, which was the test speed.

Step 3: These lines intersect at the broken line indicating 70 percent coefficient of friction.

Step 4: The investigator then, using the same steps as previously indicated, plots the 50 feet of accident skid on the "Skid Distance in Feet" axis. From the point where this line intersects the 70 percent "Coefficient of Friction" line, he draws a line to the "Speed in MPH" axis and reads a minimum speed of 32 miles per hour.

If a vehicle other than the accident car is used to make the test skids, it is important that the speedometer be accurate, so that the evidence obtained will be reliable for presentation in court.

While the investigator will be able to closely calculate initial speeds by these methods, presentation in court will probably require expert testimony, including explanation of the various physical laws and mathematical formulas involved. The expert will rely on the information given him by the investigator to reach his conclusion. This information must be accurate, understandable, and complete, for without it this information skid-mark evidence will be of little value. With the proper measuring and recording of skid-mark evidence, accurate minimum initial speeds can be computed.

Highway Definition: Typical Freeway

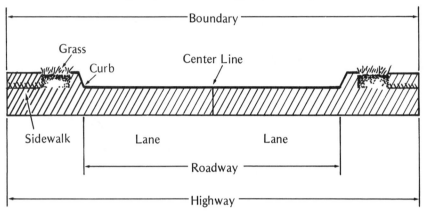

Highway Definition: Typical Surface Street

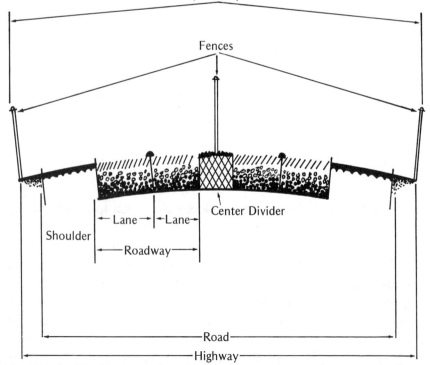

In complicated cases where not all the wheels slide, or where the skid marks are on different types of surfaces, it will probably be up to the expert to determine if any use can be made of the skidmark evidence. In these instances, however, it is important to record the evidence so that the expert may decide to what extent it is usable.

This same formula can be used to find the radius of a small circle by using inches instead of feet for measurements. This might help you find the size of a round headlight lens from a piece of glass found at the scene of an accident.

The drag factor or coefficient of friction of a pavement of a given *description* may vary considerably because quite a variety of road surfaces may be described in the same way and because of some variations due to weight of vehicle, air pressure in tire, tread design, air temperature, speed, and some other factors.

The following figures represent experiments made by many different people in all parts of the United States. They are for straight skids on clean surfaces. Speeds referred to are at the beginning of the skid. This table is reproduced from the Accident Investigator's Manual for Police, published by the Traffic Institute. See page 258.

Possible Ranges of Pavement Drag Factors for Rubber Tires

Description of Road Surface	Dry		Wet	
	Less Than 30 mph	More Than 30 mph	Less Than 30 mph	More Than 30 mph
	From To	From To	From To	From To
Cement				
New, Sharp	.80.00	.70.85	.50.80	.40.75
Traveled	.60.80	.60.75	.45.70	.45.65
Traffic Polished	.55.75	.50.65	.45.65	.45.60
Asphalt				
New, Sharp	.80.00	.65.70	.50.80	.45.75
Traveled	.60.80	.55.70	.45.70	.40.65
Traffic Polished	.55.75	.45.65	.45.65	.40.60
Excess Tar	.50.60	.35.60	.30.60	.25.55
Brick				
New, Sharp	.75.95	.60.85	.50.75	.45.70
Traffic Polished	.60.80	.55.75	.40.70	.40.60
Stone Block				
New, Sharp	.75.00	.70.90	.65.90	.60.85
Traffic Polished	.50.70	.45.65	.30.50	.25.50
Gravel				
Packed, Oiled	.55.85	.50.80	.40.80	.40.60
Loose	.40.70	.40.70	.45.75	.45.75
Cinders				
Packed	.50.70	.50.70	.65.75	.65.75
Rock				
Crushed	.55.75	.55.75	.55.75	.55.75
Ice				
Smooth	.10.25	.07.20	.05.10	.05.10
Snow				
Packed	.30.55	.35.35	.30.60	.30.60
Loose	.10.25	.10.20	.30.60	.30.60
Metal Grid				
Open	.70.90	.55.75	.25.45	.20.35

EXEMPLARY POLICE PURSUIT
and
EMERGENCY
RESPONSE DRIVING POLICY

(Courtesy Anaheim, California Police Department)

A. OBJECTIVES

The purpose of this procedure is to establish guidelines for the safe operation of police vehicles under the following conditions.

1. Routine police vehicle operation.
   a. Defined as CODE 1 operation of a police vehicle.
2. CODE 3 emergency response.
   a. Defined as a CODE 3 response to any call for service or assistance, not including pursuits.
3. CODE 3 pursuit.
   a. Defined as the CODE 3 pursuit of suspect vehicles.
4. Definition of CODE 1, 2 and 3.
   a. CODE 1 is responding to a call at the officers convenience.
   b. CODE 2 is responding immediately, obeying all traffic laws.
   c. CODE 3 is responding with red light and siren.

B. ROUTINE POLICE VEHICLE OPERATION

1. During routine police vehicle operation, officers shall always maintain complete control of their vehicle and obey all traffic laws.
2. Seat belts shall be worn by all officers at all times while the vehicle is in motion.

C. CODE 3 EMERGENCY RESPONSE

1. Section 21055, California Vehicle Code (CVC), provides that the driver of an emergency vehicle shall be exempt from provision of the Vehicle Code *only* under the following conditions:
    a. Responding to an emergency call.
    b. Immediate pursuit of a *suspected or actual* violator of the law.
2. Section 21055 CVC indicates that in order to be exempt, three conditions must always exist simultaneously:
    a. Vehicle must be an authorized emergency vehicle.
    b. A red light must be displayed and a siren sounded as reasonably necessary.
    c. One or more of the conditions listed in foregoing paragraph C.1 must exist.
3. At all times, officers shall keep the emergency vehicle under control and drive at a speed that is safe considering visibility, weather and road conditions. CODE 3 emergency response speeds shall not exceed the area speed limit by more than 1 5 miles per hour and never more than 50 miles per hour on city streets and 70 miles per hour on freeways.
4. Upon hearing a siren, a motorist should be expected to pull over to the right. Therefore, officers should pass on the left, even if it is necessary to cross the center line.
    a. Officers may cautiously pass on the right, only when there is no other course open and it is safe to do so.
5. A police vehicle should not follow too closely another emergency vehicle. Motorists yielding to the first may not observe the second and pull onto the roadway.
6. Officers will not enter any intersection in violation of traffic control signal device or a blind intersection *unless* they are prepared to make an immediate complete stop to avoid another vehicle or a pedestrian.
7. Officers shall not use their own private vehicle to pursue traffic violators.
    a. Officers should report serious violations to the police station.

8. In addition to safety factors already mentioned, when operating a vehicle under CODE 3 conditions, the officer shall:
   a.   Beware of pedestrians, especially children, who may run into the street to observe emergency vehicles.
   b.   Start slowing vehicle prior to arrival.
   c.   Ascertain that red lights and siren are functioning prior to going on duty.
   d.   Alternate the pitch of siren when approaching major intersections.
   e.   Be observant for other emergency vehicles.
   f.   Beware of the hesitant motorist who seems undecided in his action. This type of motorist is the cause of most accidents involving emergency vehicles.
   g.   Seat belts and helmets shall be worn during CODE 3 responses.

D. CODE 3 PURSUITS

1. This procedure is not intended to discourage an officer from attempting to apprehend a suspect in a pursued vehicle, but sets guidelines for these specific reasons:
   a.   To prevent injury or death of police officers.
   b.   To prevent injury or death to innocent citizens.
   c.   To prevent injury or death to a suspect.
2. Reason for pursuit must be known.
   a.   Officers starting pursuit must radio in the reason for the pursuit, and no units shall join the pursuit until authorization is given by the Communications Supervisor.
3. Radio messages in pursuit.
   a.   Once the officer has determined that an actual pursuit has commenced, he shall notify the station on the green channel and continue to use the green channel for communications regarding the pursuit until instructed by the station to switch to the red channel for inter-city coordination by Control One.
   b.   At the time of pursuit, the suspect vehicle requires the absolute attention of the lead unit. Whenever possible, the unit behind the lead unit shall radio in the location of the

vehicle being pursued, allowing the lead unit to give full attention to the suspect vehicle. In the absence of a second unit, the lead unit must, of course, radio the information. All units in the pursuit shall monitor the radio for messages directed to them. Radios shall be turned up and strict compliance shall be made with orders when given. The use of automatic yelp of the siren is discouraged as the high pitch has a tendency to drown out any incoming messages.

4. Assuming the position of lead unit in pursuit.
   a. The unit behind the suspect vehicle shall never be passed by another unit unless the lead unit approves the maneuver.

5. Spacing of unit in pursuit from suspect vehicle and spacing of other units from one another while in pursuit.
   a. All units while in pursuit-whether the vehicle in front of the unit is the suspect vehicle or another police unit-shall space themselves at a distance to ensure proper braking and reaction time in the event the lead vehicle stops, slows or makes any other moves.

6. Number of units in pursuit.
   a. In all pursuits, only two units shall be involved in the pursuit at any time. The Watch Commander, Operations Support Lieutenant, Communications Supervisor or Field Sergeant may approve additional units, if necessary. Paralleling a pursuit is not permitted unless approved by the Watch Commander, Operations Support Lieutenant, Communications Supervisor or Field Sergeant. This is not meant to discourage units from taking positions along or near the pursuit route to relay information.
   b. A pursuit initiated by a motorcycle shall be abandoned when a unit has taken the lead and a second unit is a backup. The motor unit may then proceed CODE 1 to the termination point for assistance, if needed.

7. Aerial surveillance.
   a. The helicopter shall notify radio as soon as he is in position to follow the pursued vehicle. The aircraft then becomes the pursuing unit and is responsible for coordinating the ground units. Once the pursued vehicle

is observed and followed by the helicopter, vehicles on the ground shall slow to a safe speed and follow the route of the pursued vehicle on the basis of information received from the helicopter.

8. Use of firearms.
   a. The use of firearms to stop fleeing vehicles is discouraged. Tests and research indicate that, even if justified, effectiveness is negligible.

9. Pursuit outside city limits of Anaheim.
   a. Whenever a pursuit is through our city by a unit of another jurisdiction, regardless of the violation, Anaheim police units shall cease pursuit when the suspect vehicle leaves the city limits, unless by some circumstance an Anaheim unit is the first or second unit behind the suspect vehicle or on express orders of the Watch Commander or Communications Supervisor.

10. Caravaning
    a. Caravaning of more than two police units is forbidden except on express orders from the Watch Commander, Communications Supervisor or Field Sergeant.

11. The traffic offender and misdemeanants.
    a. Occasionally an officer becomes involved in a high-speed chase with a traffic offender whose crime, at the outset, may have only been speeding or a misdemeanor. When the suspect realizes he is being pursued, he often increases his speed to avoid arrest. The officer is cautioned against this sort of high-speed chase when the offender tries to elude arrest and his *only* offense is a traffic violation or a minor misdemeanor. (Example of this would be one who does not pay for food at a restaurant or fails to pay for gas at a service station.) In pursuit of this individual, the police officer places himself(although he is afforded some protection with his red light and siren) and others in danger when the suspect goes through stop signs without stopping or drives recklessly, trying to avoid arrest. Our procedure in these cases is to attempt to get information on the vehicle, including the license number, and radio this information to the station where it can be relayed to other

units throughout the county. The officer shall slow down and, in some cases, cease the pursuit because *the apprehension of the violator is not as important as the safety of the citizen and the police officer himself* Some may say that when a suspect attempts to elude the police there may be deeper factors, such as possession of narcotics, a stolen vehicle, or a car containing stolen items. This is just an assumption and would not justify a high-speed chase which resulted in a serious accident. *REPEAT:* It is better to let the suspect get away than to jeopardize the lives of so many others. In most cases, where information is available on the suspect and vehicle, investigators can make an arrest at a later time and a complaint can be issued. A license check on the vehicle at the time of the offense may also allow for a stakeout or a check of the home of the suspect or a possible stop further up the road by other units. It has been departmental experience that apprehension can be made of suspects in most cases, even though they elude arrest at the time of the offense.

b.   All pursuits originating as a result of traffic infractions or misdemeanor traffic violations will be terminated within a reasonably short distance.

12. Pursuit of known felons.

a.   In this type of situation, many things must be taken into consideration in addition to the pursuit rules listed previously; first, the type of felony committed and whether a high-speed chase would be justified (which would endanger the lives of many and possibly cause a serious accident). Here again, the use of the police radio informing other units of the suspect's flight and route, the nature of the crime, and any other information that the officer can supply on the vehicle for follow-up action will suffice. Consideration should be given to dropping back in order to make the suspect vehicle slow down. In the case of a major felony such as murder or armed robbery, or if there is reason to believe the suspect might kill or injure someone if allowed to escape, then a pursuit might be justified, depending on the circumstances involved.

Even in these cases, the officer should follow the precautions outlined in this procedure and follow defensive driving practices, keeping his and the public's safety in mind.

13. Supervisory responsibility.
   a. The Watch Commander, Operations Support Lieutenant, Communications Supervisor and area Field Sergeant are responsible for the pursuit activities as outlined and have the authority to cancel a pursuit at any time it becomes necessary.
   b. Upon being notified of the pursuit, the Communications Supervisor shall assure himself of the following:
   (1) No more than the required units are involved in pursuit.
   (2) Available helicopter has been requested.
   (3) Proper radio frequency is being utilized.
   c. The field supervisor shall proceed to the termination point of the pursuit, if at all practical, to provide guidance and necessary supervision.
   d. All supervisors involved shall submit a critique and analysis of the pursuit.

14. Training.
   a. Critiques and analyses of pursuits shall be reviewed for subject matter which might be of benefit in training personnel for future operations.

15. Blocking or ramming.
   a. The use of a police vehicle to ram a suspect vehicle shall not be permitted. A police vehicle may be used to block a suspect vehicle when danger of injury or damage would be minimal.

16. Seat belts and helmets shall be worn in all CODE 3 pursuits.

E. SUMMARY

This procedure has been designed to promote safe and efficient methods to protect lives and property when operating a police vehicle under any driving conditions.

Appendix D

HIGHWAY FLARE PATTERNS

THE USE OF HIGHWAY FLARES (FUSEES)

Highway flares (fusees) are used as a temporary measure to control traffic for relatively short periods of time until the situation requiring their use can be corrected or until barricades, directional signs and flashers can be installed. Most flares are manufactured for a 15 minute or a 30 minute burning time.

HAZARDS OF FLARE USE

The greatest danger in using flares occurs during the lighting process; especially to the eyes, face and hands. Here are six simple safety rules to be observed.

1. Ascertain if there is a fire danger before lighting flares. Look for leaking gasoline, butane or other flammable substances and keep all fires at a safe distance, including the smoking of cigarettes, cigars and pipes by other officers and bystanders. Ascertain if wind conditions are such that a flare may start a grass or forest fire. Remember fuels such as butane are heavier than air and will flow into ditches and storm sewers and, if ignited in such confined places, a violent explosion could result.

2. To light a fusee point it away and down and strike the cover also downward and away against the igniting device. Flares have a tendency to pop when struck. The head and eyes should therefore be turned away at that time.

3. Molten material drips from flares; when being held there is always the danger of burning yourself or other people at the scene. Keep flares away from your body by extending your arm. Never hold the burning end higher than the part you hold

in your hand or above shoulder height. When running with a lighted flare hold it to the side, never to the front.

4. Burning flares give off smoke that can cause discomfort if breathed for prolonged periods. Stand upwind from flares and hold them downwind when using a flare to direct traffic.

5. When burning, flares become molten for some distance back from the actual name. Remember this when picking up a burning flare to move it or put it out. Grasp the flare by the end away from the flame and gently tap the burning end on the pavement to get the molten part out, then snuff out the flame. Don't step on flares. They may burn through the sole of your shoe and cause a severe injury.

6. When placing flares at an accident scene, always walk *toward* oncoming traffic as you place them. Never turn your back to oncoming traffic.

STACKING FLARES

When you are all alone at the scene and it is apparent that the obstruction cannot be readily cleared, certain time savers can be used. Place your flares in a criss-cross pattern or stacking so that when the first flare has nearly burned out, it will light the next flare. Remove the caps from the flares prior to stacking. This is shown in Figure F.1, below.

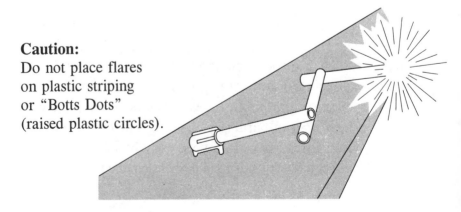

Caution:
Do not place flares
on plastic striping
or "Botts Dots"
(raised plastic circles).

Figure F.1 "Stacked" Flares

PROTECT THE SCENE

Upon arrival, flares at times will be already placed on the roadway. It will probably be necessary to re-arrange the pattern to get the desired channeling and to provide sufficient warning distance for the approaching drivers to bring their vehicle under control to pass the scene or stop.

When two officers are present, one should immediately begin to protect the scene and establish a pattern of traffic flow that is the safest possible. The second officer should ascertain the extent of injuries and render first aid where needed in serious cases. It will be extremely rare when both officers are needed to render first aid.

PLACEMENT OF FLARES

The positioning of flares as suggested is not the final answer. Where the officer places flares will vary depending upon the type of accident, fire hazards, weather conditions and desired traffic flow patterns. On a grade in windy weather, or if you suspect the movement of traffic will make your flares roll, use the cap from the flare to make it more stable. After lighting the flare, place the cap on the rear of the flare. See Figure F.2, below.

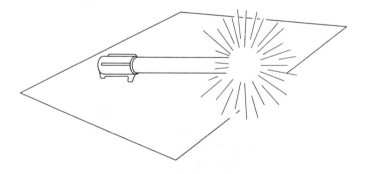

Figure F.2 Flare with cap replaced on rear

SPEED MUST BE CONSIDERED

The speed of vehicles using the roadway must be considered in developing a traffic flow pattern at the scene. It is well worth remembering, when placing flares, that vehicles travel in feet per second, approximately one and a half times their speed in miles per hour. For example, a car going 55 MPH is traveling approximately 83 feet per second. It also means the driver of this same vehicle will travel 60 feet between the time he spots the danger and the time he applies his brakes. He will travel an additional 1 87 feet after he has applied his brakes for a total distance of 247 feet. The stopping distance chart(Figure 1.4 page 9) will help to determine how far from an obstruction flares should begin.

FLARE USE AND REMOVAL

There is almost as much danger in having too many flares at the scene as too few. More flares than necessary, blending with all the flashing red lights and tail lights of stopping cars can lead to confusion. Panic stops, locked-brake skids and drivers crossing flare patterns can lead to additional accidents.

Accident scene obstruction, of course, should be cleared as soon as possible. Once the roadway is cleared and stopped traffic has been made to leave the scene, all flares should be extinguished except for a minimum necessary to mark any obstruction which may remain on the shoulder.

TRAFFIC FLOW PATTERNS MUST BE OBVIOUS

Flares set too close together from a distance will blend in to a single light and lose their value. Especially when setting flares in a straight line, they should be at least 20 to 25 feet apart nearest the accident scene with a gradual increase to a distance of 50 to 100 feet apart at the farthest distance needed. When it is desired to have traffic change lanes, set a gradual angle of alignment depending upon the speed of the passing traffic (see Stopping Distance Chart, Figure 1.3 page 9).

LIMIT THE NECESSITY FOR MOTORIST DECISION

Flare patterns should be set to direct traffic to one side only if at all possible. Heavy traffic requiring temporary lanes on each side of an obstruction confuses approaching motorists by giving them a choice and a decision to make. Avoid situations where decisions are necessary whenever possible. (See recommended flare patterns starting with Figure F.3)

VARIOUS FLARE PATTERN EXAMPLES

Every accident scene differs to the extent that recommended patterns may not be applicable in every case. The officer must always exercise personal judgement in each case. However, the following examples will serve as a useful guide for most situations commonly confronted.

TWO LANE ROADWAYS

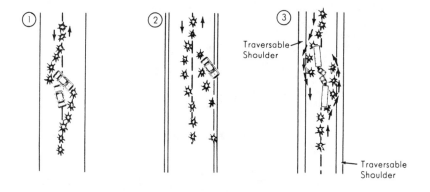

Figure F.3 Flare position for two-way roads. Diagram 1, shows a center-line obstruction, diagram 2 shows a road side obstruction and diagram 3 shows a road center obstruction under conditions which permit the use of shoulders.

TWO LANE CURVES

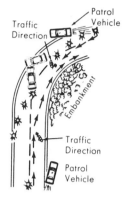

Flares must be placed at both ends of curve to be seen before entering curve.

Figure F.4 Flare pattern for stop and go, one lane at a time traffic control.

Figure F.5 Flare pattern for a blind curve; gradually diverting traffic away from and around one blocked lane.

INTERSECTIONS

If side road is controlled by stop signs, one flare in center of roadway about 100 feet in both directions should be sufficient.

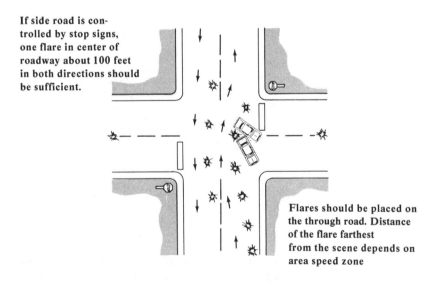

Flares should be placed on the through road. Distance of the flare farthest from the scene depends on area speed zone

Figure F.6 Two-lane roadway with one lace blocked at an intersection.

INTERSECTION CONTROL

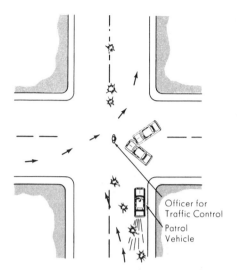

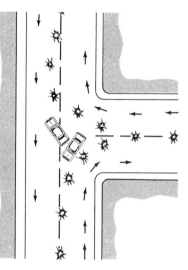

Figure F.7 Typical four-way intersection control flare pattern.

Figure F.8 "T" intersection control flare pattern.

HILLS AND GRADES

Figure F.9 On hills and grades first flare must be back over hill far enough so that approaching traffic will be alerted prior to reaching the top of hill.

EXPRESSWAYS WITH LIMITED ACCESS

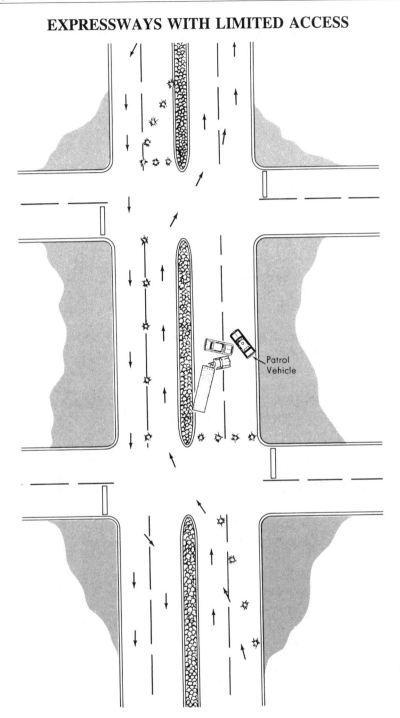

Figure F.10 Expressway (limited access available) flare pattern traffic control.

FREEWAYS AND DIVIDED HIGHWAYS

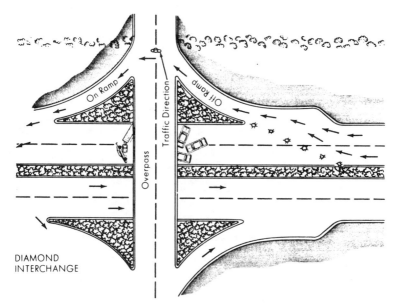

Figure F.11 Flare pattern for a freeway with on-off ramps available.

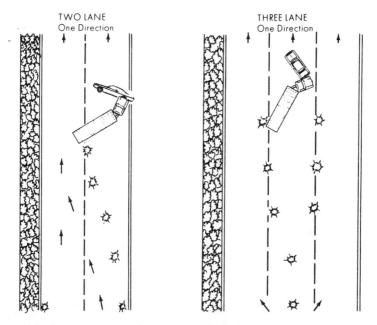

Figure F.12 Flare pattern for freeway or divided highway with two lanes and three lane in one direction.

Appendix E

VEHICLE IDENTIFICATION NUMBERS

(VIN CHARTS)
courtesy of

NATIONAL INSURANCE CRIME BUREAU

1994
VIN
LOCATION
POCKET GUIDE

Headquarters located at:
10330 South Roberts Road
Palos Hills, Illinois 60465-1997
(708) 430-2430   FAX (708) 430-2446

PASSENGER VEHICLES

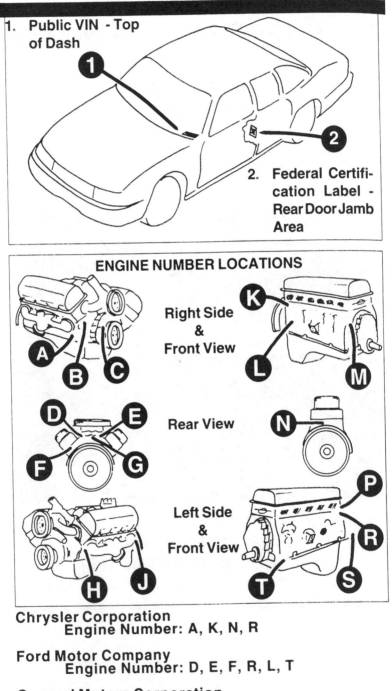

1. **Public VIN - Top of Dash**

2. **Federal Certification Label - Rear Door Jamb Area**

ENGINE NUMBER LOCATIONS

Right Side & Front View

Rear View

Left Side & Front View

Chrysler Corporation
    Engine Number: A, K, N, R

Ford Motor Company
    Engine Number: D, E, F, R, L, T

General Motors Corporation
    Engine Number: B, C, G, H, J, M, P, S

PASSENGER VEHICLES

TRANSMISSION NUMBER LOCATION

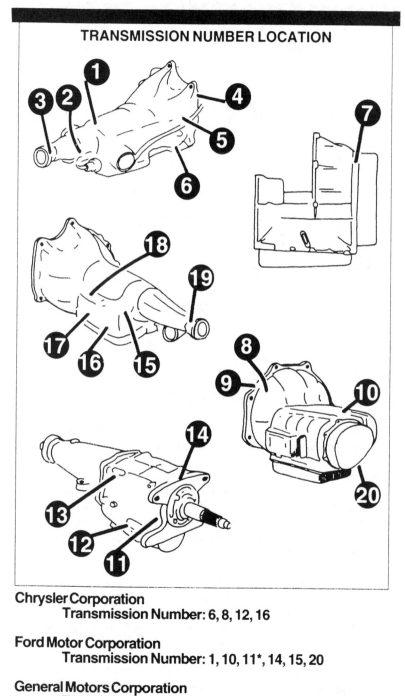

Chrysler Corporation
    Transmission Number: 6, 8, 12, 16

Ford Motor Corporation
    Transmission Number: 1, 10, 11*, 14, 15, 20

General Motors Corporation
    Transmission Number: 2, 4, 7, 9, 10, 11*, 12, 13, 16, 17
*Denotes Left Side

COMMERCIAL MOTOR VEHICLES

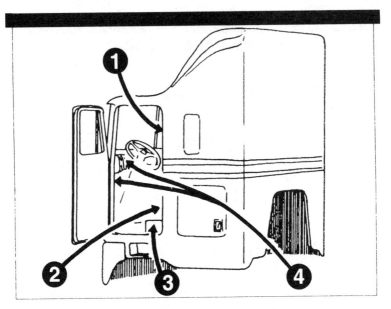

PUBLIC VIN LOCATIONS

1. Attached to interior surface of rear cab wall.

2. Attached to the door jamb or edge of door.

3. Attached to the base of the driver's seat.

4. Attached to the underside of the dashboard on the left side, or on the firewall in the area of the clutch pedal.

Prior to 1981, no uniformity existed in the configuration of VINs utilized on truck-tractors. Some VINs were as short as four characters, while others were much longer. Quite often only the suffix, or sequential portion, of the VIN was reflected on invoices, registrations, and titles. Since the 1981 model year, truck-tractors have utilized the seventeen character VIN, as have automobiles.

There is little consistency in the display of truck-tractor VINs. Some manufacturers attach a metal VIN plate, while others display the VIN on a mylar-type label affixed to the interior of the cab. Most manufacturers stamp the VIN into other portions of the vehicle; however, such stampings may not necessarily display the full VIN.

NICB publishes a Commercial Vehicle and Off-Road Equipment Identification Manual which is available to law enforcement agencies.

COMMERCIAL MOTOR VEHICLES

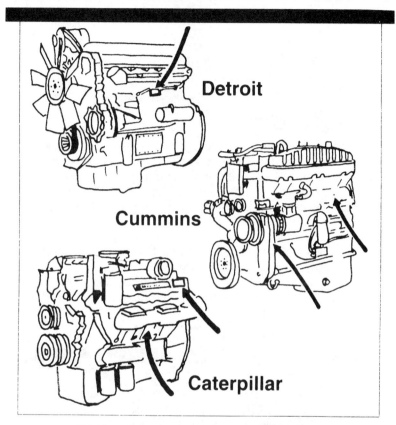

ENGINES AND TRANSMISSIONS

Engines and transmissions are identifiable by a manufacturer's serial number which normally does not contain any portion of the truck-tractor VIN. Serial numbers on engines and transmissions can generally be cross-referenced to the VIN through assembly and warranty records.

Caterpillar Engine Serial Number can be located in two places. A plate attached to the valve cover or a plate attached directly to the block on the left side.

Cummins Engine Serial Number can be located on the fuel pump side below the cylinder head stamped into the side of the block, or on a metal plate on the left side of the engine at the front.

Detroit Engine Serial Number is stamped into the block near the thermostat housing on the left side. There are two numbers at this location. The top number is the model number and the bottom number is the serial number.

TRAILER IDENTIFICATION

Trailer identification number formats prior to 1981 model year were non-standardized and consisted of various alpha and numeric configurations. Most identification numbers were displayed on a metal plate attached to the front or front sides of the trailer, although some manufacturers used less permanent means of identification, such as labels.

Use of the standardized character VIN format, beginning with the 1981 model year, has significantly improved trailer identification. Trailer vehicle identification numbers will normally be displayed on a metal plate attached to the front of the trailer at the lower center or at the lower left or right corner.

MOTORCYCLES

Left Side
Right Side

Motorcycle vehicle identification numbers will generally be stamped into the left or right side of the headstock or frame downtube.

Motorcycles display a Federal Safety Certification Label containing the VIN and date of manufacture which is attached to the headstock or frame. On some models, the complete VIN may be found only on the Federal Safety Certification Label.

An engine number will normally be stamped into a location on the left side, right side, top, or front of the crankcase. The engine number may or may not be identical to the frame VIN.

OFF ROAD EQUIPMENT

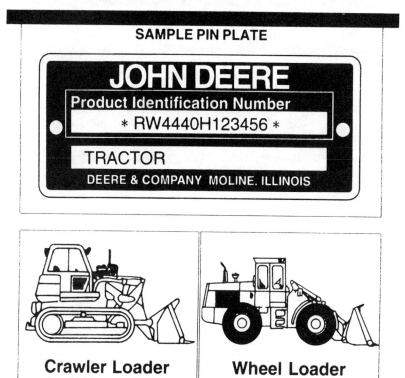

SAMPLE PIN PLATE

JOHN DEERE

Product Identification Number

* RW4440H123456 *

TRACTOR

DEERE & COMPANY MOLINE. ILLINOIS

Crawler Loader   **Wheel Loader**

The PIN is die-stamped into an aluminum foil or metal plate and is attached with drive rivets, pop rivets, screws, or adhesive.

PINs are displayed in various locations depending on the manufacturer, year, make, and model of the product. Local dealers can offer assistance in locating the PIN and describing the method of attachment.

Most equipment will also possess serial plates for most major components, i.e., engine transmission and attachments. Caution should be taken when attempting to identify a product to insure that the PIN plate is located, not a component part number.

The manufacturer's name and model number should be prominently displayed on the unit and should accompany requests for shipping or assembly information. The model number becomes a significant identifier along with the PIN when requesting information through the NICB or the manufacturer.

For more detailed information on the PIN location of off-road equipment, please refer to the NICB commercial Vehicle and Off-Road Equipment Identification Manual.

BOATS

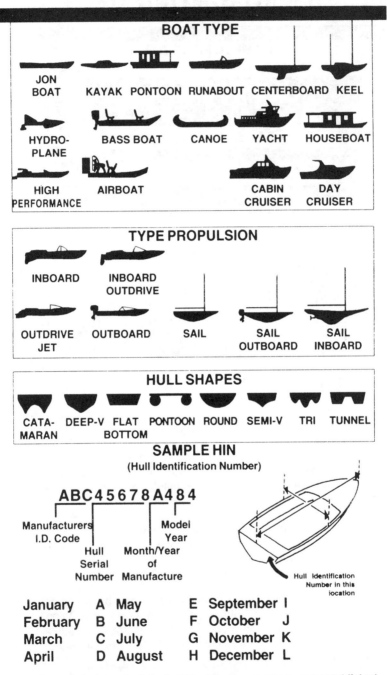

BOAT TYPE

JON BOAT KAYAK PONTOON RUNABOUT CENTERBOARD KEEL

HYDRO-PLANE BASS BOAT CANOE YACHT HOUSEBOAT

HIGH PERFORMANCE AIRBOAT CABIN CRUISER DAY CRUISER

TYPE PROPULSION

INBOARD INBOARD OUTDRIVE

OUTDRIVE JET OUTBOARD SAIL SAIL OUTBOARD SAIL INBOARD

HULL SHAPES

CATA-MARAN DEEP-V FLAT BOTTOM PONTOON ROUND SEMI-V TRI TUNNEL

SAMPLE HIN
(Hull Identification Number)

ABC45678A484

Manufacturers I.D. Code

Hull Serial Number

Month/Year of Manufacture

Model Year

Hull Identification Number in this location

January	A	May	E	September	I
February	B	June	F	October	J
March	C	July	G	November	K
April	D	August	H	December	L

U.S. Coast Guard standards for hull identification numbers were established in 1972 and made mandatory on August 1, 1984. (No uniform hull identification numbers prior to 1972.)

GLOSSARY

ADMONISHMENT: A warning or instructions regarding rights and requirements. Example: *Miranda* warning and DUI/DWI chemical test options.

ALLEY: An alley is any highway having a roadway not exceeding 25 feet in width which is primarily used for access to the rear or side entrances of abutting property.

AUTHORIZED EMERGENCY VEHICLES: Fire department (fire patrol) vehicles; police vehicles; such as ambulances and emergency vehicles of municipal departments or public service corporations operated by private corporations; and emergency vehicles of the Department of Transportation, as designated or authorized by the department or the chief of police of an incorporated city or any sheriff of any of the various counties.

BICYCLE: A bicycle is a device upon which any person may ride, propelled exclusively by human power and having two or more wheels.

BRAKE FADE: The gradual loss of holding strength in brakes used for a period of time or immediately following heavy use.

BUS: Any motor vehicle designed for carrying more than ten passengers and used for the transportation of persons; and every motor vehicle, other than a taxicab, designed and used for the transportation of persons for compensation.

BUSINESS DISTRICT: The territory contiguous to, and including, a highway where 50 percent or more of the frontage thereon, for a distance of 300 feet or more, is occupied by buildings in use for business.

CANCELLATION: Voiding and termination of a license which has been issued through error or fraud, and a new license obtainable only as permitted.

CITATION: Notification of a violation; a traffic ticket.

COEFFICIENT OF FRICTION: The drag factor created by a surface causing a body sliding across it to slow it down; represented by a number, usually a decimal less than 1.00; and used in calculating speed from skid marks.

CROSSWALK: That part of a roadway at an intersection included within the connections of the lateral lines of the sidewalks on opposite sides of the highway measured from the curbs or, in the absence of curbs, from the edges of the traversable roadway; any portion of a roadway at an intersection, or elsewhere, distinctly indicated for pedestrian crossing by lines or other markings on the surface.

DARKNESS: Darkness is any time from one-half hour *after* sunset to one-half hour *before* sunrise and any time when visibility is not sufficient to render clearly discernible any person or vehicle on the highway at a distance of 1000 feet.

DAYTIME: That time between a half hour before sunrise and a half hour after sunset-nighttime being any other hour.

DEPARTMENT: To be construed herein as referring to the Department of Highway Safety and Motor Vehicles, Department of

Motor Vehicles or the Department of Highway Patrol as defined by each state's Motor Vehicle Code.

DEPARTMENT OF TRANSPORTA-TION: To be construed herein as referring to the Department of Transportation as defined by each state's Motor Vehicle Code or Government Code.

DRAWBAR: A drawbar is a rigid structure forming a connection between a trailer and a towing vehicle, securely attached to both vehicles by non rigid means and carrying no part of the load of either vehicle.

DRIVER: Any person who drives or is in actual physical control of a vehicle, on a highway, or who is exercising control of a vehicle or steering a vehicle being towed by a motor vehicle.

DWI: Driving while intoxicated.

EXPLOSIVE: Any chemical compound or mechanical mixture that is commonly used or intended for the purpose of producing an explosion and which contains any oxidizing and combustive units or other ingredients in such proportions, quantities, or packing that an ignition by fire, friction, concussion, percussion, or detonator of any part of the compound or mixture may cause such a sudden genera-tion of highly heated gasses that the result-ant gaseous pressures are capable of producing destructive effect on contiguous objects or of destroying life or limb.

FLAMMABLE LIQUID: Any liquid which has a flash point of 70° Fahrenheit or less, as determined by a Tagliabue or equivalent closed-up test device.

FOREIGN VEHICLE: Type of vehicle required to be registered when brought into the state from another jurisdiction other than through a dealer.

FREEWAY: A highway to which drivers have limited or restricted right or easement of access.

GROSS WEIGHT: The weight of a vehicle without load, plus the weight of any load thereon.

HIGHWAY: A way or place of whatever nature, publicly maintained and open to use of the public for purposes of vehicular travel. Highway includes a street.

HOUSE TRAILER: A trailer or semi-trailer which is designed, constructed, and equipped as a dwelling place, living abode, or sleeping place (either permanently or temporarily) and is equipped for use as s conveyance on streets and highways; also, a trailer or a semitrailer whose chassis and exterior shell is designed and constructed for use as a house trailer, but which is used instead permanently or temporarily for the advertising, sales, display, or promotion of merchandise or services, or for any other commercial purpose except the transportation of property for hire or distribution by a private carrier.

HYDROPLANING: Skidding on water. Tires ride on water film.

INTERSECTION: The area embraced within the prolongation or connection of the lateral curblines; or, if none, then the area within lateral boundary lines of the roadways of two highways which join one another at, or approximately at, right angles; or the area within which vehicles traveling upon different highways joining at any other angle may come in conflict.

LANED HIGHWAY: A highway, the roadway of which is divided into two or more lanes clearly marked for vehicular traffic.

LEGAL OWNER: A person holding a security interest in a vehicle, including lessors.

LIMITED ACCESS FACILITY: A street or highway especially designed for through traffic and over, from, or to which owners or occupants of abutting land or other persons have no right or easement, or only a limited right or easement, of access, light, air, or view by reason of the fact that their property abuts such limited access facility or for any other reason, such as parkways from which trucks, buses, and other commercial vehicles are excluded; or freeways open to use by all customary forms of street and highway traffic.

LIMIT LINE: A solid white line not less than 12 or more than 24 inches wide, extending across a roadway or any portion thereof to indicate the point at which traffic is required to stop.

LOCAL AUTHORITIES: All officers and public officials of the several counties and municipalities within a state.

MOTOR VEHICLE: Any vehicle which is self-propelled and every vehicle which is propelled by electric power obtained from overhead trolley wires but not operated upon rails.

MOTORCYCLE: Any motor vehicle, excluding a tractor, having a seat or saddle for the use of the rider and designed to travel with not more than three wheels in contact with the ground.

MOTOR-DRIVEN CYCLES: Any motorcycle or motor scooter with a motor which produces speed not to exceed five-brake horsepower, including any bicycle with motor attached.

NONRESIDENT: A person who is not a resident of the state which he or she is in at the moment.

OFFICIAL TRAFFIC CONTROL SIGNAL: Any device, whether manually, electronically, or mechanically operated, by which traffic is alternately directed to stop and permitted to proceed.

OFFICIAL TRAFFIC CONTROL DEVICES: All signs, signals, markings, and devices placed or erected by authority of a public body or official having jurisdiction, for the purpose of regulating, warning, or guiding traffic.

OPERATOR: Any person who is in actual physical control of a motor vehicle upon the highway, or who is exercising control over or steering a vehicle being towed by a motor vehicle.

OWNER: The person who holds the legal title of a vehicle, or in the event that a vehicle is the subject of an agreement for the conditional sale or lease thereof, the person with the right of purchase upon performance of the conditions stated in the agreement and with an immediate right of possession vested in the conditional vendee or lessee; or in the event a mortgagor of a vehicle is entitled to possession then such conditional vendee or lessee or mortgagor shall be deemed the owner.

PARK or PARKING: The standing of a vehicle, whether occupied or not, otherwise than temporarily for the purpose of, and while actually engaged in, loading or unloading merchandise or passengers as may be permitted by law.

PEDESTRIAN: Any person afoot.

PERSON: Any natural person, firm, copartnership, association, or corporation.

PNEUMATIC TIRE: Any tire in which compressed air is designed to support the load.

POINT SYSTEM: System in which points are added to or subtracted from driver's record for each moving violation.

POLE TRAILER: Any vehicle without motive power designed to be drawn by another vehicle and attached to the towing vehicle by means of a reach, or pole, or by being boomed or otherwise secured to the towing vehicle, and ordinarily used for transporting long or irregularly shaped loads such as poles, pipes, or structural members capable, generally, of sustaining themselves as beams between the supporting connections.

POLICE OFFICER: Any officer authorized to direct or regulate traffic or to make arrests for violations of traffic regulations, including highway patrolmen, sheriffs, and municipal police officers.

PRIMA FACIE LAWS: Laws that are always applicable unless otherwise rebutted or disproved.

PRIVATE ROAD or DRIVEWAY: Any way or place in private ownership and used for vehicular travel by the owner and those having express or implied permission from the owner, but not by other persons.

RADIOACTIVE MATERIALS: Any materials or combination of materials which emit ionizing radiation spontaneously, in which the radioactivity per gram of material, in any form, is greater than 0.002 microcuries.

RAILROAD: A carrier of persons or property upon cars operated on stationary rails.

RAILROAD SIGN or SIGNAL: Any sign, signal, or device erected by authority of a public body or official or by a railroad and intended to give notice of the presence of railroad tracks or the approach of a railroad train.

RAILROAD TRAIN: An engine operated on steam, electricity, or other motor with or without cars coupled thereto, operated upon rails, except streetcars.

REGISTERED OWNER: A person registered by the department as the owner of a vehicle.

RESIDENCE DISTRICT: The territory contiguous to, and including, a highway not comprising a business district when the property on such highway, for a distance of 300 feet or more is, in the main, improved with residences or residences and buildings in use for business (varies slightly in each state).

REVOCATION: Termination of a licensee's privilege to drive a motor vehicle, with a new license obtainable only as permitted by law.

RIGHT-OF-WAY: The right of one vehicle or pedestrian to proceed in a lawful manner in preference to another vehicle or pedestrian approaching under such circumstances of direction, speed, and proximity as to give rise to danger of collision unless one grants precedence to the other.

ROAD TRACTOR: Any motor vehicle designed and used for drawing other vehicles and not so constructed as to carry any load thereon independently, or any part of the weight of a vehicle or load so drawn.

ROADWAY: That portion of a highway improved, designed, or ordinarily used for vehicular travel, exclusive of the berm or shoulder.

SADDLE MOUNT: An arrangement, where by the front wheels of one vehicle rest in a secured position upon another vehicle, with all of the wheels of the towing vehicle upon the ground and only the rear wheels of the towed vehicle rest upon the ground.

SAFETY ZONE: The area or space officially set apart within a roadway for the exclusive use of pedestrians and which is protected or is so marked by adequate signs or authorized pavement markings as to be plainly visible at all times.

SCHOOL BUS: Any motor vehicle that complies with the color and identification requirements and is used to transport children to or from school or in connection with school activities, but not including buses operated by common carriers in urban transportation of school children.

SEMITRAILER: Any vehicle with or without motive power, other than a pole trailer, designed for carrying persons or property and for being drawn by a motor vehicle, and so constructed that some part of its weight and that of its load rests upon, or is carried by, another vehicle.

SIDEWALK: That portion of a street between the curb lines, or the lateral lines of a roadway, and the adjacent property lines, intended for use by pedestrians.

SPECIAL MOBILE EQUIPMENT: Any vehicle not designed or used primarily for the transportation of persons or property, and only incidentally operated or moved over a highway, including, but not limited to: ditch-digging apparatus; well-boring apparatus; and road construction and maintenance machinery, such as asphalt spreaders, bituminous mixers, bucket loaders, tractors, other than truck tractors, levelling graders, finishing machines, motor graders, road rollers, scarifiers, earth-moving carry-alls and scrapers, power shovels and draglines, and self-propelled cranes and earth-moving equipment; and not including house trailers, dump trucks, truck-mounted transit mixers, cranes, shovels, or other vehicles designed for the transportation of persons or property to which machinery has been attached.

STAND or STANDING: The halting of a vehicle, whether occupied or not,

otherwise than temporarily for the purpose of, and while actually engaged in, receiving or discharging passengers as may be permitted by law.

STATE ROAD: Any highway designated as a state maintained road by the Department of Transportation or Department of Public Works.

STOP: Complete cessation of movement.

STOP or STOPPING: When prohibited, any halting, even momentarily, of a vehicle, whether occupied or not, except when necessary to avoid conflict with other traffic or in compliance with the directions of a law enforcement officer or traffic-control sign or signal.

STREET or HIGHWAY: The entire width between the boundary lines of any way or place of whatever nature when any part thereof is open to the use of the public for purposes of vehicular traffic.

SUSPENSION: Temporary withdrawal of a licensee's privilege to drive a motor vehicle.

THROUGH HIGHWAY: Any highway or portion thereof on which vehicular traffic is given the right-of-way, and at the entrances to which vehicular traffic from intersecting highways is required to yield right-of-way to vehicles on such through highway in obedience to either a stop sign or yield sign, or otherwise in obedience to law.

TIRE (TREAD) WIDTH: That width stated on the surface of the tire by the manufacturer of the tire, provided the width stated does not exceed 2 inches more than the width of the tire contacting the surface.

TRAFFIC: Pedestrians, ridden or herded animals, vehicles, streetcars and other conveyances, either singly or together, while using any street or highway for purposes of travel.

TRAFFIC TICKET FIXING: Removing a traffic citation from the files so that the violator will not have to appear in court or pay a fine.

TRAILER: Any vehicle with or without motive power, other than a pole trailer, designed for carrying persons or property and for being drawn by a motor vehicle.

TRAILER COACH: A vehicle, other than a motor vehicle, designed for human habitation and for being drawn by a motor vehicle.

TRUCK: Any motor vehicle designed, used, or maintained primarily for the transportation of property.

TRUCK TRAILER: Any motor vehicle designed and used primarily for drawing other vehicles and not so constructed as to carry a load other than a part of the weight of the vehicle and load so drawn.

VEHICLE: Any device, in, upon, or by which any person or property is, or may be, transported or drawn upon a highway, except devices moved by human power or used exclusively upon stationary rails or tracks.

VIN: Vehicle identification number.

INDEX